GEORG LUKÁCS
SELECTED CORRESPONDENCE 1902–1920

GEORG LUKÁCS

Selected Correspondence 1902–1920

Dialogues with Weber, Simmel, Buber, Mannheim, and Others

Selected, edited, translated, and annotated
by Judith Marcus and Zoltán Tar
With an introduction by Zoltán Tar

COLUMBIA UNIVERSITY PRESS
New York 1986

Columbia University Press
New York and Guildford, Surrey
Published in Hungary by Corvina Kiadó, Budapest
Published in the United States
by Columbia University Press

This book is based in part on the selection
of Éva Fekete and Éva Karádi
Georg Lukács: Briefwechsel 1902–1917
J. B. Metzlersche Verlagsbuchhandlung Stuttgart–Corvina Kiadó,
Budapest, 1982

Printed in Hungary

Library of Congress Cataloging-in-Publication Data

Lukács György, 1885—1971.
Georg Lukács: Selected Correspondence, 1902—1920.

Includes bibliographical references and index.
1. Lukács, György, 1885—1971—Correspondence.
2. Philosophers—Hungary—Correspondence.
I. Marcus, Judith. II. Tar, Zoltán. III. Lukács György, 1885—1971.
Correspondence. German. Selections. IV. Title.
B4815. L84A413 1986. 199.439 85—19027
ISBN 0-231-05968-X

CONTENTS

PREFACE

A fortunate incident stimulated interest in the young Georg Lukács. In 1973 a suitcase containing 1,600 letters to and from Lukács, fragments of manuscripts, and a diary were discovered in a bank safe in Heidelberg, where Lukács lived from 1912 to 1917 when he was attempting to launch an academic career. This treasure trove of source material was deposited by Lukács himself in 1917 before he returned to his native Budapest from his sojourn in Heidelberg.

The letters reveal many aspects of Lukács's life, of his personal problems and disputes, his friendships and feuds, and his ruminations on the genesis of his ideas about aesthetics, ethics, culture, and political action. As Lukács remarked in one of his essays, "The great crisis that drew Europe into the First World War was echoed... in the entire literature" of the continent. It was also evident in the correspondence of Lukács, a perceptive participant and observer of his age, and the correspondence Lukács maintained with many of the noted scholars, poets, artists, social reformers, or just plain well-educated, concerned young people of the time, before and during World War I. A reading of the letters uncovers a well-delineated view of (Central) European cultural and intellectual life of the period and a new appreciation of the extraordinary contribution of these intellectuals. Since the "great crisis" ended in revolutionary convulsions in many Central European states (and in the emergence of the first communist state in Russia)—and many of the correspondents were involved in those events—the letters provide insight into the preoccupations, fears, anxieties, motivations, and assumed roles of a large segment of the intellectual elite in a rapidly changing world; thus, the correspondence might prove relevant to contemporary concerns.

Since space limitations allowed publication of only 161 letters out of 1,600, the selection was not an easy task to perform, and the editors had decided against publishing extracts of letters. Occasional deletions are made only when absolutely necessary either for reasons of privacy or to avoid repetition. The translators have tried to preserve idiosyncrasies in the epistolary style of the correspondents.

The selection of 86 letters to and from Hungarian partners may appear to underplay Lukács's "Hungarian connection" and the role of his Hungarian roots; that was not our aim. One of our principles of selection was to include as completely as possible the correspondence of Max Weber, George Simmel, Martin Buber, and Karl Mannheim, thereby aiding scholarship dealing with these people. The exchange of letters is presented chronologically, as Lukács suggested in discussing his career.

New York City
December 1985

Judith Marcus and
Zoltán Tar

ACKNOWLEDGMENTS

In the course of selecting, translating, and annotating the letters for this book, we have benefited from the help and wisdom of more people than we possibly could thank here. It is our pleasure to give special thanks to Prof. Ferenc Jánossy, stepson and executor of Lukács's literary estate, for his kindness in assisting us at every stage of the project and for sharing with us many insights that helped us better understand Georg Lukács, the man and the thinker.

We are indebted to many scholars, critics, and friends whose related work, criticism, advice, or suggestions helped us in more ways than we could publicly thank them for. We are grateful to Profs. Lee Congdon, Joseph B. Maier, Ivan Sanders, Laurent Stern, Alexander Vucinich, and Harry Zohn in the U.S., and to István Hermann, Éva Gábor, László Sziklai and Erzsébet Vezér in Hungary.

In addition, various institutions have aided our work. Zoltán Tar received generous support from the National Endowment for the Humanities (1981–82), from the Fulbright Exchange Program (1982–83), and from the American Philosophical Society (Summer 1983).

The Introduction was first presented as an expository paper at the Historical Institute of the Hungarian Academy of Sciences, Budapest, at the University of Erlangen–Nürnberg, and at the University of Heidelberg. For invitations and incisive criticism thanks are due to Professors Péter Hanák (Budapest), Reinhard Kreckel (Erlangen), and Wolfgang Schluchter (Heidelberg).

For rendering invaluable help regarding style and other problems of translation, thanks are due to Profs. Robert Lilienfeld and Harry Zohn, and to Mrs. Hope McAloon.

We wish also to thank Dr. György Balázs of Corvina Press, Budapest, and William Bernhardt of Columbia University Press, for constant encouragement and good advice throughout the years this project has engaged us.

Either the originals or copies of the selected letters are housed at the Georg Lukács Archives of the Hungarian Academy of Sciences in Budapest, Hungary, where the expert staff aided us in innumerable ways. The following literary estates have generously provided copies of their holdings at the disposal of the Lukács Archives: Franz Blei estate, Staatsbibliothek, Berlin (letters 90, 135); Martin Buber estate, Hebrew University Library, Jerusalem (65, 72, 74, 86, 92, 149); Artur K. Elek estate, Országos Széchényi Könyvtár, MS. Archiv, Budapest (7, 14, 18); Paul Ernst Archiv, Bonn (43, 67, 80, 84, 85, 87, 97, 120, 132, 133, 134, 136, 155, 157, 159, 160); Lajos Fülep estate, Hungarian Academy of Sciences, MS Archiv, Budapest (47, 59, 117); Karl Jaspers estate (Deutsches Literararchiv, Marbach (141, 142); Gustav Radbruch estate, Universitätsarchiv, Heidelberg (152); Margarete Susman estate in the care of Manfred Schlösser, Berlin (106); Max Weber estate in the care of Dr. Max Weber-Schäfer, Konstanz (139, 140,161), and in the care of Zentrales Staatsarchiv, Merseburg, E. Germany (109, 110, 114, 115, 116, 121, 137, 138, 139, 144, 150). For special permission to use letters no. 161 and 158, thanks are due to Prof. Wolfgang Mommsen, Düsseldorf, and to the Thomas-Mann-Archiv, Zürich, respectively.

Judith Marcus
Zoltán Tar

INTRODUCTION

> There is a beautiful, profound book by the young Hungarian essayist, Georg von Lukács, entitled *Die Seele und die Formen.* In it there is a study of Theodor Storm that is, at the same time, an investigation of the relationship of *Bürgerlichkeit* and *l'art pour l'art*—an investigation that to me, when I read it years ago, immediately seemed to be the best that had ever been written on this paradoxical subject, and that I feel I have a special right to cite, since the author was perhaps thinking of me—and at one place expressly mentioned me.

So wrote Thomas Mann, the greatest German novelist of the 20th century, in his wartime musings that became the book *Reflections of a Nonpolitical Man.* The young Hungarian essayist with the *von* affixed to his name, a sign of an ennobled family, was Georg Lukács, born 100 years ago in 1885, the son of a Hungarian-Jewish banker who later became known worldwide as a Marxist philosopher and literary critic.

Georg Lukács, the Hungarian philosopher and literary critic, has for a long time been regarded by many Western European intellectuals and artists as the most important, the most sophisticated, and the most original thinker in the Marxist camp. His work has been extensively read by German and French intellectual audiences ever since the publication of *History and Class Consciousness* (1923); but only in recent times has he become better known in the English-speaking countries, through the pioneering efforts of Laurent Stern, Morris Watnick, and Irving Howe, and the availability of translations (as of today 15 volumes) often in inexpensive paperback editions. A spectacular outpouring of secondary literature and a flood of dissertations on Lukács and Lukácsian themes have followed.

Even more recent is the interest in the young Lukács, that is, in his pre-Marxist thought. In the last decade, many of his early works have been translated and published, among them the collection, *Soul and Form* (1911) and *The Theory of the Novel* (1920). What remains undisclosed is the man himself, the enigmatic personality of the banker's son turned Bolshevik Commissar of Culture of the 1919 Hungarian Commune, the inspiration of the post-Stalinist renaissance of Marx. Thomas Mann captured some essential features of Lukács's personality in the character Naphta in *The Magic Mountain,* but during his lifetime Lukács did everything in his power to hide behind *das Werk.*

Only in the last years of his life did he mellow, allowing republication of the works of his "bourgeois period", writing lengthy introductions for them, and giving numerous interviews, reminiscing about his youth. His autobiographical sketch, *Gelebtes Denken* (Lived Thought), and the tape-recorded interview series based on it (both available now in English) are valuable sources of information on Lukács the man.

The selection of correspondence herein is aimed at highlighting Lukács's complex personality and extraordinary diversity. He associated with both scholars and artists, and this diversity as well as common concerns and problems is reflected in the correspondence. It is hoped that these letters will also illuminate some central figures of the time. The correspondence in its entirety is so rich that the weeding out was almost painful, but our principle of selection was intended to insure a well-balanced, enlightened, and illustrious edition with such well-known names as Max and Alfred Weber, Georg Simmel, Martin Buber, Ernst Bloch, Emil Lask, Heinrich Rickert, Karl Jaspers, Ernst Troeltsch, Gustav Radbruch, Margarete Susman, Paul Ernst, Karl Mannheim, Karl Polányi, Arnold Hauser, Frederick Antal, Béla Balázs, Leo Popper, and others. The volume is in two parts, representing the stages of Lukács's personal and intellectual development.

Part One, 1902–11, contains letters of Lukács's family, boyhood friends, and partners in Budapest in early artistic and intellectual ventures, such as the founding of the Thalia Theater. Through this selection of letters, the beginnings of his youthful productions and their echo in Hungarian intellectual circles can be reconstructed. The aim is to illuminate Lukács's Hungarian roots.

The correspondence in Part One also reveals the stage of Lukács's life that he called his essayistic period, which culminated in the publication of *Soul and Form.* The book is dedicated to Irma Seidler; their correspondence documents their love affair, which was terminated by her suicide in 1911.

Part Two covers Lukács's sojourn in Heidelberg from 1912 to 1919, and his return to Budapest interrupted by a one-year stint of military service in Budapest and frequent trips in and around Germany. The correspondence of this so-called Heidelberg period, when Lukács was a respected member of the Max Weber Circle along with his friend, Ernst Bloch, is particularly rich in names and intellectual content. It is also the most tension-filled, especially after the outbreak of World War I in August 1914 and the commencement of what Lukács termed "the age of complete sinfulness."

The Story Behind the Correspondence

Born György Bernát Löwinger in 1885 in Budapest, the son of József Löwinger, a self-made man and director of a leading bank, Lukács was, so to speak, *von Haus aus,* predestined to travel beyond the geographical and intellectual boundaries of his native Hungary. His father changed his name to Lukács in 1890 and became ennobled (szegedi Lukács or *von* Lukács) in 1901. The son continued the assimilation process and converted to Protestantism in 1907, a year after he received his doctorate. Lukács *père* provided all the necessary support—financial, emotional, and intellectual —to motivate his son to enter the world of scholarship (see letter to Lukács, August 23, 1909). The father's very generous support enabled Lukács to live as a member of the *freischwebende Intelligenz* (see letters of June 1, 1911; November 17, 1911; and May 25, 1914). Near the end of his life, reflecting on the pre-World War I intelligentsia, Lukács said: "At that time there was a large section of intellectuals, university intellectuals, in particular, who belonged to the rentier stratum by virtue of their private incomes, which gave them financial autonomy. This was the economic basis of Mannheim's free-floating intelligentsia."

Lukács *père* cherished, encouraged and furthered his son's ambition to engage in a prestigious academic career; he presided over a home environment that welcomed the leading intellectuals, artists, and public figures of the time, Hungarians and foreigners alike. He entertained the likes of Max Weber and Thomas Mann during their visits to Budapest; Béla Bartók, the eminent Hungarian composer, lived in the Lukács home for years. Georg's relationship with his mother, Adele Wertheimer, who was born in Budapest but brought up in Vienna, presents an entirely different, more complex picture, which could easily lend itself to psychohistorical treatment. Lukács himself had made references to the antagonistic relationship: "At home, absolute alienation. Above all: mother. Almost no communication." It was Lukács's initial experience of alienation that became the leitmotif of his long and productive life and the search for its *Aufhebung*. On the positive side, it is more important now to consider the effects of the home environment on Lukács's development. Such factors as the bilingual—German and Hungarian—background, and the opportunity to acquire a working knowledge of French and English and to travel extensively contributed to his broadening horizon and experience. Upon Lukács's graduation from the gymnasium, for example, his father presented him with a trip to Norway to visit Henrik Ibsen, at the time his intellectual hero (see letter from Benedek). Soaking up the new trends, such as naturalism, Lukács himself began experimenting with playwriting and later founded—together with like-minded friends and a fatherly financial backing—the Thalia Theater, where avantgarde plays were staged along with the classics and performed for workers at a very low price (see letter of November 26, 1906).

Even before receiving his (first) doctorate in law in 1906 from the University of Kolozsvár (Cluj-Napoca, now in Romania), Lukács traveled to Berlin and attended the lectures of Wilhelm Dilthey and the private seminar of Georg Simmel. As Lukács remarked in his 1918 obituary of Simmel, he was part of a "small group of philosophically inclined young thinkers who were attracted to Simmel, and who, for shorter or longer periods, were all touched by the magic of Simmel's thinking." The older Lukács again credited Simmel with having contributed to his intellectual development: "Simmel posited questions about the sociological aspects of artistic creation, thereby providing me with a perspective which helped me to go beyond Simmel; but proceeding in the direction outlined by him, I studied literary works. The philosophy of my *History of the Development of Modern Drama* is truly a Simmelian philosophy." Lukács reflected later upon how the impact of Dilthey and Simmel was instrumental in the process of clarifying his ideas that by necessity "entailed the reading of historical and sociological works. This was the reason why my first acquaintance with the writings of Marx worthy of the name occurred precisely in this period... Naturally... this was a Marx read through the eyes of Simmel."

Lukács's Road to Heidelberg

Georg von Lukács was still a young, relatively unknown, aspiring scholar when he left the cultural confinement of his native Hungary and entered the German cultural sphere through personal and intellectual contacts (see letters to Ernst, Simmel, Baumgarten, et al).

After the suicide of Irma Seidler, the death of Lukács's closest friend, Leo Popper, and the University's rejection of his *Habilitation** (all in 1911), he spent the winter of 1911–12 in Florence working on a systematic philosophy of art. His friend at that time, the German-Jewish philosopher Ernst Bloch, persuaded him to move to the intellectually more conducive academic environment of Heidelberg. The favorable reception of Lukács's writings, such as the essay, "Metaphysics of Tragedy," published in the prestigious journal *Logos* (1911), and the essay collection *Soul and Form,* praised by Thomas Mann, provided an added incentive.

Lukács's entry into German intellectual circles was helped along by many friends, among them Emil Lederer and his wife Emmy, the sister of Irma Seidler, the playwright Paul Ernst, Ernst Bloch and Baumgarten.

Simmel's endorsement was especially helpful (see letter of May 25, 1912). The decision to leave his "Italian period" behind and to commit himself entirely to the German sphere was not without reservation. As he reflected in 1969: "I always preferred the Italian everyday life to the German one, but the motivation to find understanding was irresistible. When I finally took off for Heidelberg, it was without knowing for how long."

The Heidelberg that Lukács and Bloch first saw in mid-May 1912 was populated by a galaxy of brilliant minds such as the philosophers Wilhelm Windelband, Emil Lask, Karl Jaspers, sociologists Max and Alfred Weber, Ernst Troeltsch, the poet Stefan George and his friend, the Goethe scholar Friedrich Gundolf, among others. Today we have a picture of Lukács

* Those possessing a doctorate who opted for an academic career had to do scholarly work at a university under the supervision of a professor. After sufficient scholarship had been produced *(Habilitationsschrift),* a university senate consisting of full professors had to judge the junior scholar as qualified to give lectures to students in his own right *(Privatdozent).* The process was called *Habilitation,* a qualifying inauguration.

drawn from the reminiscences and impressions of some of the witnesses of the period. Marianne Weber, hostess at the best known gathering of that period, the Weber-*Kreis,* reported:

> "From the opposite pole of the *Weltanschauung* the Webers also met some philosophers from Eastern Europe who were becoming known around that time, particularly the Hungarian Georg von Lukács, with whom the Webers struck up a close friendship... These young philosophers were moved by eschatological hopes of a new emissary of the transcendent God, and they saw the basis of salvation in a socialist social order created by brotherhood."

Another member of the Weber-*Kreis,* Karl Jaspers, later commented on the impression that Lukács (and Bloch) made on the gathering: "Lukács was regarded by some as a kind of 'Holy Man'... The philosopher Lask quipped: 'Do you know who the four apostles are? Mattheus, Marcus, Lukács and Bloch.'"

The Heidelberg experience was a fruitful one for Lukács. As he himself commented: "I found greater understanding than ever before. Of course, I soon had to realize that a Max Weber and an Emil Lask were rather exceptional phenomena within German intellectual life." Even in his old age, Lukács repeatedly spoke of his Heidelberg experience, of its congenial intellectual atmosphere:

> "It was in the winter of 1911–12 in Florence that I first contemplated the writing of an independent systematic aesthetics, but I sat down to it in all seriousness only in Heidelberg, during the years 1912–14. Even today, I remember with deep gratitude the interest—both sympathetic and critical—that Ernst Bloch, Emil Lask and Max Weber showed toward my work."

Although Weber and Lukács stood at opposite poles of the *Weltanschauung,* as Marianne Weber put it, they shared many interests, at times had the same preoccupations, and together developed some new concerns that constituted an intellectual bond between the two men:

(1) Their rejection of the vulgar Marxism of the Second International type and search for an epistemology for the social sciences, along the lines of neo-Kantianism.

(2) A shared interest in problems of the philosophy and sociology of art and literature.

(3) Reception of Dostoevsky, Tolstoy, and the Russian experience.

(4) Mutual interest in problems of ethics as related to politics.

The Lukács–Weber exchange on problems relating to art and literature has to be placed in the context of Lukács's attempt to get his *Habilitation* through at Heidelberg University, a matter that also involved Weber.

Although *Soul and Form,* Lukács's first book, published in Germany, impressed an array of his contemporaries, including Thomas Mann, Ernst Troeltsch, Martin Buber, and Max Weber, it also put off the more conservative, that is, traditionally inclined academic circles in Heidelberg, whose backing Lukács needed if he was to succeed. An important concern for both Weber and Lukács was the positing of the problem of aesthetics in Lukács's planned *Aesthetics* (or *Habilitationsschrift*). Shortly before his death, Lukács recalled the key issue in his relationship to Weber. He told Weber: "According to Kant, the essence of aesthetics is the aesthetic judgment. In my opinion, no such priority of aesthetic judgment exists, only the priority of *Sein.* I put the question to Weber: Works of art exist; how are they possible? And that made a deep impression on him." Indeed, Weber, impressed enough to reflect on the Lukácsian question, refers to it in his "Science as a Vocation" (1917) lecture. As the recently recovered Lukács treatise shows, Weber quoted the opening sentence from Lukács's *Heidelberg Aesthetics.* Lukács's systematic *Aesthetics* was intended to prove to Weber, and through him to his colleagues at the university, that Lukács was, after all, "the systematic type, and beyond his essayistic period."

For Lukács, the years 1913–14 became another turning point that did nothing to further his entry into the club of German mandarins. In August 1913 (see p. 22. below) Lukács met the Russian SR (Socialist-Revolutionary) anarchist refugee Yelena Grabenko at an Italian sea resort and married her in May 1914. In August 1914, World War I broke out and was greeted with enthusiasm in German intellectual circles. Weber exclaimed: "It is a great and wonderful war." But the war brought a change in Lukács's relationship to German intellectuals, among whom was his spiritual home, and to a lesser degree, to the Webers.

Lukács recalled his immediate reaction, his negative evaluation, almost half a century later:

> "My own deeply personal attitude was one of vehement, global and especially at the beginning, scarcely articulate rejection of the war

and especially of enthusiasm for the war. I recall a conversation with Frau Marianne Weber in the late autumn of 1914. She wanted to challenge my attitude by telling me of individual, concrete acts of heroism. My only reply was: "The better, the worse."

Lukács's personal attitude was so shocking to the Webers and their friends that they discussed it repeatedly. Simmel, for example, complained in a letter to the Webers regarding Lukács's lack of understanding and enthusiasm for the war: "The experience has to be on a practical and personal level, so to speak, in an 'intuitive' way. If Lukács is not able to share this experience, we cannot explain and demonstrate it to him." There were a few friends of Lukács who shared his rejection of the war or his lack of enthusiasm for it. Ernst Bloch, for example, left Germany immediately and settled in Switzerland. Lukács himself made every effort to escape being drafted, or as he put it, not to become a "victim of the war Moloch". He enlisted the help of Karl Jaspers, a licensed medical doctor, and received a medical excuse. Beyond this practical reaction, Lukács also responded to the events and feelings about the war in an article entitled, "The German Intellectuals and the War". The article was written for the *Archiv für Sozialwissenschaft und Sozialpolitik* but was never published.

It is safe to say that in Heidelberg circles, after the outbreak of the war, Lukács became somewhat of an "outsider," as he described himself, using the English term. His state of mind at the time was epitomized in his outcry: "Who is to save us from Western civilization?"

In December 1915 Lukács renewed his efforts for *Habilitation*. He based his hopes on rumors that Simmel and Rickert would be appointed in Heidelberg and thus approached Weber to act as mediator with Simmel or Rickert (see letter to Weber, December 30, 1915). We don't have Weber's answer but it must have been positive, judging from Lukács's letter of thanks (see January 17, 1916).

Yet, no doubt under the impact of the war in "the age of complete sinfulness," as Lukács called the war years, he felt that to work on aesthetics would be "barbaric"—to borrow Theodor Adorno's post-Auschwitzian exclamation. Thus Lukács turned to ethics, as he reports to Paul Ernst: "At last I will begin my new book on Dostoevsky. I put aside the aesthetics" (see letter of March 1915).

Lukács then centered his ethical position around the problem of guilt; in turn, the ideas of the Dostoevskyan world began to occupy a certain position in his thinking and reflections. In this connection Lukács's letter of March 1915 is of great significance. First, he tells about his stopping work on the *Aesthetics,* at least temporarily. Second, he reports that he started his book on Dostoevsky, which "will contain much more than just Dostoevsky; it will contain a greater part of my metaphysical ethic and history of philosophy, among other ideas." Finally, Lukács asked for a copy of a book—or its serialized publication in the *Berliner Tageblatt*—by Ropshin (pen name for Boris Savinkov, a Russian SR terrorist) entitled *The Pale Horse.* All of these new themes mentioned in the single letter were harbingers of Lukács's thinking, work, and actions for years to come. As Lukács explained to Paul Ernst in a follow-up letter: "I am not interested in the book as a work of art. It is the ethical problem of terrorism that matters most to me, and the book is an important document in this respect." Indeed, we have another theme that preoccupied German intellectuals both before and after World War I. At the Sunday gatherings of the Weber home, for example, Lukács, Bloch, Jaspers, and others participated in lengthy debates during the war about the problem of justifying the use of force at decisive historical times.

As stated at the beginning of this introduction, among the interests that Weber and Lukács shared, the problem of ethics loomed large. At times the use of force, that is, violence, in order to bring forth a just society was at the heart of the discussions. If we accept Lukács's numerous autobiographical utterances, backed up with his correspondence and life work, we can safely state that in Lukács's case we can speak of the "primacy of ethics". As late as 1968, in his new introduction to the reissue of his *History and Class Consciousness,* Lukács asserted: "My decision to take an active part in the communist movement was influenced profoundly by ethical considerations." Moreover, in one of his rare bits of autobiography, Lukács spoke of his "greatest childhood experience," which was reading the Hungarian translation of the *Iliad* at the age of nine, and specifically, "the fate of Hector, i.e., the fact that the man who suffered defeat was in the right and was the better hero, was determinant for my entire later development." Even if we take such a statement with a grain of salt, we cannot disregard the evidence in Lukács's life work and the fact that his contemporaries, among them Max Weber, were in 1912 already deeply impressed by his "profound artistic essay" entitled "On Poverty of Spirit". In this essay, Lukács went beyond the Kantian, formal ethic and opted for one of a "higher order". The essay discusses means and ends, and the possibility of giving up conventional ethical norms for the sake of an ultimate end is contemplated, thus pointing the way to Lukács's later development.

Reflecting on the "meaning of goodness" (Lukács's preoccupation in "On Poverty of Spirit") and the *Problematik* of means and ends, Weber wrote his wife about a jailed anarchist and his female friend, both of whom he tried to help in the spring of 1914:

> "The facts that the *result* of good actions is so often wholly irrational and that "good" behavior has bad consequences have made him doubt that one *ought* to act well—an evaluation of moral action on the basis of *results* rather than intrinsic value. For the time being he does not see that there is a fallacy here. I shall try to obtain *The Brothers Karamazov* for him and at some later time Lukács's dialogue about the poor in spirit *[sic!]*, which deals with the problem. . . ."

It is obvious that, while Weber could still approve Lukács's ethical position in the "On Poverty of Spirit," he would not draw the same conclusion as Lukács when contemplating the "political realist's" violation of the absolute commandment. Lukács put in a nutshell his ethical statement that took new directions after the war experience and after his immersion in Dostoevsky–Russian–anarchist themes:

> "I discover in [Ropshin] a new form of the old conflict between the first morality [i.e. duty toward the established social order] and the second one [duty toward one's soul]! The order of priorities is always dialectical in the case of politicians and revolutionaries whose souls are not directed toward the self but toward humanity. In that case, the soul has to be sacrificed in order to save the soul; on the basis of a mystical morality one must become a cruel political realist and thus violate the absolute commandment, "Thou shall not kill!" In its inner depth it is and remains an ancient problem expressed maybe most succinctly in Hebbel's *Judith* as she says: "And if God has placed sin between myself and the action I am ordered to do, who am I to be able to escape from it."

Lukács never succeeded in working out his "metaphysical ethic" in the Dostoevsky book; soon he went beyond the "metaphysical ethic" and on August 2, 1915, reported to Paul Ernst that he had "abandoned the Dostoevsky book". It was too long. But a larger essay taken from the book had been finished; it was going to be called "The Aesthetic of the Novel" (which turned into *The Theory of the Novel*).

A large segment of the European intelligentsia prior to World War I was caught up in Dostoevsky fever without regard to differences in politics or ideology and the ultimate conclusions drawn from that experience. Spengler held that Tolstoy and Dostoevsky pointed to the future of humanity. Rainer Maria Rilke exclaimed: "Other countries are bordered by mountains, rivers and oceans, but Russia is bordered by God." Heidelberg and the Weber–*Kreis* were no exception. As Paul Honigsheim reminisced: "I do not remember a single Sunday conversation in which the name of Dostoevsky did not occur." He may have stretched the point a little, but he also quotes Weber as agreeing with Bloch that the wife of every professor keeps a cup of tea ready in her salon every day at five in anticipation of the Messiah whom she expects to come straight to her." Karl Mannheim, eight years Lukács's junior, just starting out under the benevolent guidance of Lukács, also planned to write a book on Dostoevsky and justified the project to Lukács in a letter in 1912: "I wish to write on Dostoevsky. Not only because I feel that I shall best be able to pose my problems and questions through a study of his work, but also because I feel that his life and world are most akin to our own in all of their vicissitudes, lack of fulfillment, and distortions."

Lukács's reception of Dostoevsky was different from that of his intellectual peers in Germany and Heidelberg. Although he and Weber shared an interest in the author, their reception was by no means identical. To state it summarily, Weber's (Western) individualism contrasted sharply with Lukács's belief in collectivism. It was Honigsheim again who remembered their differences:

> "With regard to... Max Weber's position on Lukács, one should not forget one thing: Weber's ability to empathize with, and to interpret, the meaning of human action was... unlimited; he was therefore able to understand Lukács's position, or more exactly, his turning from modern occidental individualism to a notion of collectivism. Weber explained it to me this way: "One thing became evident to Lukács when he looked at the paintings of Cimabue [who painted at the beginning of the Italian Renaissance but who had more affinity for the Middle Ages than to the Renaissance], and this was that culture can exist only in conjunction with collectivist values."

Lukács's reception of Dostoevsky had already taken on a collectivist coloration in 1913 when he first personally encountered Dostoevsky's Russian spirit. Lukács was vacationing in an Italian coastal resort in August 1913 with his friends, Béla Balázs and wife, when he met Yelena Grabenko, a Russian SR anarchist and painter who had to flee Russia and had moved around from Paris to Italy and Heidelberg. Balázs, the poet, described Yelena as

> "a wonderful example of a Dostoevsky figure. Every single one of her stories, experiences, ideas and feelings could have come from some of Dostoevsky's most fantastic passages. ... She was a terrorist. She spent years in prison. She destroyed her nerves, stomach and lungs by working so hard."

Interestingly enough, Yelena must have held the same kind of fascination for Weber, who mediated between Lukács's father and Lukács himself, thus becoming instrumental in the former's agreement to the marriage. Max Weber suggested that Lukács "tell them that she is a relative of his in order to help overcome their objection." Lukács then married Yelena in Heidelberg in May 1914. According to Ernst Bloch, his friend at the time: "Through her Lukács married Dostoevsky, so to speak; he married his Russia, his Dostoevskian Russia." The marriage turned out to be a complete failure but was not formally dissolved until 1919. (Parenthetically, it might be noted that Bloch's first wife was of Russian extraction.)

We may ask what this Dostoevskian and/or Russian experience may have meant for both Lukács and Weber, what the similarities were—besides the difference already noted—and how it influenced either Lukács's career or his relationship to Weber. Weber's interest in Russian matters dates back to the turn of the century and to the abortive 1905 Russian revolution. As reported in Marianne Weber's book:

> "His political interests were again powerfully stirred when the first Russian revolution broke out in 1905. He quickly mastered the Russian language, avidly followed the events of the day in several Russian newspapers... Weber *fully empathized* with the psyche and civilization of the Russian people, and for months he followed the Russian drama with bated breath."

We have to remember Marianne Weber's report of the role of the young "philosophers from Eastern Europe...from the opposite pole of the *Weltanschauung*" who were stimulating Weber's interest in the Eastern European ideas and culture. It is a fact that the "intellectual atmosphere provided by these men [among them Lukács] stimulated Weber's already strong interest in the Russians. For a long time he had been planning a book about Tolstoy that was to contain the result of his innermost experiences." It is alleged that during his prolonged illness Weber once remarked: "If someday I am well again and can hold a seminar, I shall accept only Russians, Poles, and Jews."

In September 1915 Lukács returned to Budapest and served in the Army's "auxiliary service" in a censor's office. Very soon his old friends and new disciples, about two dozen intellectuals, gathered around him and formed the so-called Sunday Circle, modeled after the Weber-*Kreis,* under his undisputed leadership. Other participants of the evening discussions included Béla Balázs, Karl Mannheim, Frederick Antal, and Arnold Hauser, to name but a few of the people who achieved fame later on. The discussions revolved around problems of ethics, aesthetics, Kierkegaard and Dostoevsky. In the spring of 1917, the Free School of Humanities *(Szellemtudományok Iskolája)* grew out of the Circle. It gave a series of public lectures with such well-known speakers as Béla Bartók, Zoltán Kodály, Karl Mannheim, and Karl Polányi.

After Lukács's "escape" from military service in Budapest, he returned to Heidelberg in 1916 and resumed work on his *Aesthetics.* Max Weber followed the renewed efforts closely; and in a truly Weberian manner he discussed the alternatives, means and ends for possible action in the matter of getting Lukács's *Habilitation* accepted. In his letter of August 14, 1916, as an addendum to their conversation on the previous day, he outlined the following three alternatives. First, a *Habilitation* with Alfred Weber in sociology and political economy because of the close relationship between the two men. As it turned out, Alfred Weber became one of the staunchest supporters of Lukács in the long battle for a *Habilitation.* Max Weber's own preference was for the second alternative, both for Lukács's own sake and for the sake of his intellectual development: a *Habilitation* with Rickert in philosophy, although the relationship between the two was at times somewhat strained. After all, wrote Weber, "the most direct road leads to the man whose field really encompasses your interest". The third alternative reiterated the old *Problematik* of "the essayistic nature of Lukács's intellectual work". As Max Weber bluntly told Lukács:

"A very good friend of yours, Lask, was of the opinion: '...he is a born essayist and will not stay with systematic work, therefore should not be habilitated. Of course, the essayist is not less than the systematic scholar, perhaps even the contrary! But he does *not* belong to the university, and it would not do any good for the university, and what is even more important, for himself. On the basis of what you read for us from the brilliant fragment of your *Aesthetics,* I sharply disagreed with this opinion. And because your sudden turn to Dostoevsky seemed to prove Lask's view as correct, I *hated* that work and I still hate it..."

As it turned out, what Weber had begun questioning was Lukács's Dostoevsky project, a fragment of which was published as *The Theory of the Novel.* Although deeply resenting this work, Weber nevertheless mediated between Lukács and the would-be publisher of the study, Max Dessoir, and advised Lukács of necessary changes, especially regarding style. Weber also supported Lukács's efforts to gain recognition through this study and wrote to him on August 23, 1916: "There is nothing else I'd like better than to have you as a colleague of mine here. The question, however, is how to achieve this goal?" Many who received a copy of the monograph reacted enthusiastically, among them Alfred Weber, Ernst Troeltsch, Ernst Bloch and Karl Mannheim. Others—important to Lukács's *Habilitation* quest—like Rickert remained unenthusiastic. It can only be assumed that this circumstance must have contributed to Lukács's change of mind and return to the original project, the *Aesthetics.*

Lukács sounded a very optimistic note on his progress in a letter to Gustav Radbruch in the spring of 1917: "I am working away on my *Aesthetics,* and I do hope to finish the first volume—approximately 900 pages—by the summer." Instead, Lukács went into a deep depression as "never before" experienced in his life and had to admit: "I am absolutely unable to work." The reasons for this were certainly personal, intellectual, and complex, but can only be surmised. Some clues are provided in a letter written to Paul Ernst in September 1917 in which Lukács reported on his wife's move to Munich (complete with her young lover, a German pianist, whom she had been living with, along with Lukács, for some time) and on his plans to return to Budapest to "live only for my work" and to "exclude life entirely". Now Budapest beckoned to him: in the spring of 1917, the informal gathering of young intellectuals, the Sunday Circle, mentioned earlier, developed a Free School of Humanities with a lecture series and stepped-up intellectual activities.

On November 7, 1917, before leaving for Budapest, Lukács deposited in a safe in the Deutsche Bank in Heidelberg a suitcase full of manuscripts, his diary, and some 1,600 letters, which survived the wars to be discovered some fifty-six years later. After 1945, Lukács had either forgotten or did not care enough to recover his suitcase.

Although Lukács returned to Budapest in the fall of 1917, he did not give up his hopes or attempts to have his *Habilitation* accepted at Heidelberg. During 1918, there seemed to have been more activities on his behalf by Alfred Weber and Eberhard Gothein, both on the faculty of the university, than by Max Weber. In May 1918, Lukács asked Gothein about practical details as he assembled the topics of his *Habilitation* presentation. He then submitted his formal application on May 25, 1918, along with a *curriculum vitae* and topics of the colloquium to be presented (see Appendix). The Heidelberg University files show that Rickert, Alfred Weber, and Gothein campaigned heavily on his behalf but met with strong opposition.

Lukács was informed in a letter by Dean Domaszewski, dated December 7, 1918, that his application for *Habilitation* had been rejected. The reason given: he was of "foreign nationality," a Hungarian (and certainly, Hungarian-Jewish, although this remained unstated). Lukács answered this rejection on December 16, 1918, stating that he was withdrawing his request "with pleasure" since he "intended to embark on a political career". Although these external circumstances alone would not account for Lukács's "conversion," the fact remains that in the middle of December, he joined the Hungarian Communist Party, which he had rejected only two weeks earlier in an essay entitled, "Bolshevism as a Moral Problem."

Lukács had already accepted Marxism as a research method for historical sociology but refrained from the practical consequences and rejected Bolshevism as an alternative for himself. Still, hardly two weeks had gone by before Lukács joined the Communist Party and embraced *praxis* and the "ethics of ultimate ends" justifying the means. He remembered fifty years later:

> "I have to admit that I joined the CP after a certain wavering. ...Although the positive role of violence in history was always clear

to me and I never had anything against the Jacobins, when the problem of violence arose and the decision had to be made that I should promote violence by my own activity, it turned out that one's theory does not exactly jibe with practice."

Lukács's is a classic case of the Marxian proposition that

> "...in times when the class struggle nears the decisive hour, the process of dissolution going on within the ruling class... assumes such a violent, glaring character, that a small section of the ruling class cuts itself adrift and joins the revolutionary class... a portion of the bourgeois ideologists, who have raised themselves to the level of comprehending theoretically the historical movement as a whole."

Thus the coincidence of structural-historical (objective) factors with those of psychological (subjective) ones was the necessary and sufficient condition. Lukács stated the predisposition for the latter as follows: "With me everything is the continuation of something. I believe there is no nonorganic element in my development."

THE LETTERS

PART ONE

1902–1911

1. FROM MARCELL BENEDEK

Kisbacon
August 20, 1902

Dear Gyuri,[1]

I just received your letter from Christiana[2] today, with the attached essay on the "Midnight Sun,"[3] because I have been travelling for two whole weeks across Csík county.[4] Now I do not dare to write to Hamburg anymore, and will risk the Nagy János Street address.[5]

I am sorry to say that you wrote your essays in vain, at least for the time being, with the exception of "Berlin in July." My dad is no longer the editor of *Magyarság*,[6] so he cannot publish them there. Anyway, I will keep the last one for myself, and will try to retrieve the others as well, so that in the fall you can try to publish them elsewhere. Now it is my turn to go out in the world in order to conquer it. . . .

In the meantime you may have learned from newspaper reports why my dad left the paper. He had had to endure some vile treatment, and it will take a long time for him to recover from that experience.

I did not do much in the summer but had a nice time anyway. The books you sent me remain largely unread. However, at least Laura Lengyel[7] reads them. I finished the first part of *Kaiser und Galiläer*[8] and read both volumes of Maeterlinck. I will at least finish *Kaiser*. . . and plan to read *Michael Kramer*.[9]

My warmest congratulations upon your meeting with Ibsen—at least, that is how I interpreted your remarks about your having "succeeded" in your endeavor.[10] I beg you to recount your talk with him word for word. I am sure you remember your conversation by heart; please, do it in the original language (because of the fine nuances!) unless it was in English, a language I have not had the chance to master.

Your friend,
Marczi[11]

[1] Hungarian nickname for "Georg".
[2] Today Oslo, capital of Norway.
[3] Lost Ms.
[4] Part of Transylvania, now Romania.
[5] The Lukács residence in Budapest at that time.
[6] *The Hungarians*, well-known daily.

7 Laura Lengyel (1877–1954), essayist and theater critic in Budapest.
8 Reference is to Ibsen's 1873 play, *Emperor and Galilean.*
9 Drama of Gerhart Hauptmann (1852–1946), German dramatist and novelist, one of the leading representatives of naturalism. Awarded the Nobel Prize in 1912.
10 See "Introduction," p. 14.
11 Hungarian nickname for "Marcell".

2. FROM LÁSZLÓ BÁNÓCZI

Budapest
August 5, 1906

Dear Gyuri,

I read the following in the evening edition of *Magyarország*[1]*:* The *Kisfaludy Társaság*[2] for its yearly competition submits, among others, the following topic, "Main Trends of Dramatic Literature in the Last Quarter of the 19th Century." Deadline: October 31, 1907. I am curious what your excuse will be this time. Between now and the deadline there are five quarters which you spend abroad[3] working away on something similar to this theme. There is no escape for you.

Fejér[4] left for Switzerland yesterday. First he intended to go to the Lido but then a letter arrived from Thunersee—from a woman, of course. That made him change plans. We spent three nights together, the last one in *Ős-Budavár.* We were bored to death because our dates, the Margit Steins, did not show up. We stayed for the shows anyway. Needless to say, we saw the "Folies" and did not even have to pay. I was almost touched to see the curtain rise and recognize the room of *Der Kammersänger.*[5] This time they used it for the play, *The Wife on Loan,*[6] and Sándor[7] had a minor part in it; the few minutes he spent on the stage were a delight. I decided immediately that if I went to the Révai-Street Establishment[8] often enough, eventually all of the actors should one time or another join the Thalia.[9]

I don't have to study yet and have time to do some reading. Just bought Brandes's study on Ibsen.[10] It is 80 pages of cheap and idle talk. One rejoices when finding here and there one smart ordinary sentence. Those parts that are not mediocre are badly written. The letters are interesting but the girl must have been more so. I can't figure them out: Why did Ibsen break off with her this way? Was it really the Aline-factor or did the letters simply outlive the sentiment? The last letter may have been the greetings of a thankful soul. But I don't have time to think about it because tomorrow Bandi[11] brings up the Concha.[12]

Servus. My respects to the girls.

Laci[13]

1 *Hungary,* widely read Budapest daily.
2 Kisfaludy Society. Named after Károly Kisfaludy (1788–1830), dramatist prominent in Hungarian literature. The Society was regarded as an arch-conservative club.
3 Lukács spent the years 1906 and 1907 in Berlin.
4 See "Biographical Notes".
5 Short satire by Frank Wedekind (1864–1918), German playwright, author of the plays *Pandora's Box* and *Spring Awakening*. Renowned also for his satires, and erotic and leftist productions at his famous Munich variety theater "The Eleven Executioners".
6 Maurice Vallier's comedy.
7 János Sándor actor, employed for a while at Thalia Theater.
8 Budapest theater group.
9 Reference is to Thalia Society, a theater group (1904–8), founded by Lukács and a few of his friends, László Bánóczi, Sándor Hevesi, and Marcell Benedek, and financially backed by Lukács Sr. Its program was eclectic, ranging from Goethe and Hebbel to Wedekind, Ibsen, and Strindberg. It aimed at "educating" the public and also instituting regular Sunday afternoon matinees for working class audiences.
10 *Henrik Ibsen* (1906) by Georg Brandes (1842–1927), Danish literary historian and aesthete. It contains the letters of Ibsen to a young girl, Emilie Bardach.
11 Bertalan Schwartz, a friend.
12 Reference is to a textbook by Győző (Victor) Concha (1846–1933), leading jurist, legal scholar and professor in administrative law at Budapest University.
13 Nickname for "László" (Ladislaus).

3. FROM GERTRUD BORTSTIEBER

Vágújhely
September 7, 1906

My dear little Gyuri,

After I finished reading Part 2 of your essay,[1] I leaned back in the easy chair and the thought entered my mind that if you continue your line of argumentation, you'll arrive at the same conclusion I did about a year ago when I wrote to somebody that many people don't understand Ibsen because they are looking for certain trends in his dramas. As I continued reading, I was extremely happy to see that at the end of your discussion you really came to this conclusion. I am sure it has also happened to you that you encountered your own ideas in the work of others—and unless you considered the other person an ass, you welcomed the encounter as much as I did when I read your essay.

I was surprised at first by your calling Ibsen a romantic albeit for the sole reason that I have admittedly had quite a superficial idea of what "romanticism" really is; you made me perceive its essence. In my own collection of concepts, the term "romantic" existed only in its vague, everyday usage; were I asked to define it, I could not have answered anything other than that it was a mixture of the fantastic and the sentimental about which one may speak with a condescending smile. All your other ideas I accepted without resistance.

I don't intend to offer any critical comments, partly because I do not feel competent enough and partly because that is not what you want. I think you want me merely to be a "receptive" reader. I accept this role with pleasure; whenever you need a reader, I am at your disposal. I am only sorry that I will hardly have the opportunity to ask for reciprocity.

It is amazing that here I am, writing a letter not expected of me, something I have never done before. I think I wish to demonstrate that modesty finds its reward—and not only in the "Tales of Hoffman" but in real life. How strange that people like me who insist on sincerity demand from their fellow human beings that they be modest. For myself, I am either angry or have to smile at my justified self-assurance as being a mitigating circumstance. Or to express it better: I regard it as a completely acceptable situation only if somebody is self-assured in a self-conscious manner, that is, if one knows that to do otherwise would be wearing a mask. Thus, it would not surprise me, for example, if you were a little shocked that I consider my letter a "reward". But you are glad about it, aren't you, and will forgive me, since you can consider the mitigating circumstances in my case. What a pity that one can have a meeting of minds only by talking or by writing letters. How perfectly marvelous it would be if the exchange of thoughts, for example, could be affected by touching hands! Sadly, at the present stage of human development only a limited range of feelings can be transmitted this way and only among matching individuals. But it is enough of a good thing for today!

Gertrud

P.S. Please convey to Rózsi[2] that I have been wanting to write her for days but then this letter completely exhausted my energies. Tomorrow, I'll write for sure. I also want her to know that Rosa[3] is in Ó-Tátrafüred[4] with her husband, and I'd be happy if the three of them could arrange a meeting. They'll stay until Tuesday.

[1] "Reflections on Ibsen" was subsequently published in the journal of the Hungarian Sociological Society, *Huszadik Század* (Twentieth Century), in August 1906.
[2] Rózsi Hochstätter, close friend both to Gertrud and to Maria Lukács.
[3] Identity could not be established.
[4] Northern-Hungarian resort (now Czechoslovakia, Starý Smokovec), frequented by the Budapest upper classes in the pre-WWI years.

4. FROM LÁSZLÓ BÁNÓCZI

Budapest
November 26, 1906

Dear Gyuri,

The affairs of the Thalia[1] are again at a standstill but the reason this time is, in Hevesi's opinion,[2] that we have to wait until after I am free of my duties. I can hardly wait! Imagine, I enter the room of Kmetty,[3] and especially of Concha and leave as Dr. Jur.

One source of money would be Peter Herzog; his secretary has promised. The other possibility would be a Teleki campaign.[4] Hevesi has decided to leave the National Theater for good at the end of this season. He may leave even sooner if his contract with Révai[5] comes through; he would edit their encyclopaedia for 6,000 Forint. We might find a temporary solution for the theater by renting a hall. Hevesi's new plan is to end the season with *The Taming of the Shrew*. But before we come to that, we would stage *Romeo and Juliet*, [Ibsen's] *Wild Duck*, a play by Hegedűs;[6] and I would very much like to include *Galotti*, *Miss Julie*,[7] *Citta Morta*[8] (for sure), and *Candida*. There was some talk of *Widowers' Houses*[9] for the workers' matinee.

Your new outline[10] does not make clear to me the connection between chapters four and five. For example, I don't know whether it is true that Becque[11] was untouched by naturalism. He sees things as a naturalist. He is the first in French drama to do justice to man; until then, only actions counted. The same is true for Strindberg's historical dramas. The difficulty with analyzing a contemporary artist is that you have to pinpoint the main point of his personality and discuss his work in the appropriate context. Thus, I don't know whether or not the two chapters as planned are somehow mixed up. Maybe—it is difficult to analyze Goncourt's *Germinie Lacerteux* before discussing naturalism. Besides, it is my conviction that you can't avoid bringing in the problem of the novel in these two chapters. I don't recall the dates, but it is not impossible that when talking of naturalism you have to look at the novel as the starting point.

When will you be back? Do you have more than one week for Christmas vacation? I am asking because Mici mentioned that you plan to write the Hebbel-chapter[12] in Budapest.

But let me now return to administrative law.

Servus!
Laci

[1] See letter no. 2, n. 9.
[2] Sándor Hevesi (1873–1939), writer, critic, theater director, producer. From 1901 on stage-manager of the Hungarian National Theater. He was considered to be the "Hungarian Reinhardt".
[3] János Kmetty (1863–1929), legal scholar, professor of administrative law at Budapest University.
[4] Reference is to possible patrons for the theater venture.
[5] Mór János Révai (1860–1926), one of Hungary's leading publishers, established in partnership with his brother the *Great Révai Encyclopaedia of Hungary,* that remained the main reference source.
[6] Gyula Hegedüs. See "Biographical Notes".
[7] Strindberg's drama.
[8] A play by d'Annunzio.
[9] *Candida* and *Widowers' Houses* by G. B. Shaw.
[10] Reference is to *The History of the Development of the Modern Drama.* Lukács finished the first draft of his *Dramabook* during his Berlin stay in 1906–7.
[11] Henry-François Becque (1837–99), French playwright.
[12] See Part 3, "The Heroic Period," chapter 5, entitled "Hebbel and the Foundations of the Modern Tragic Drama," in *Dramabook.*

5. FROM IRMA SEIDLER

Budapest
December 31, 1907

Dear Lukács,

You have sent me a letter that most people would have put away in a drawer only to write another, even more cruel one. I would guess that you were hesitant to write because you were afraid that I'd read those words in a different way—however slightly—from what you intended. As soon as you find out that I can, indeed, take them as you meant them, you'll know that it was perfectly all right to write them. Your letter was written with the utmost urgency and consequently did not interfere with my fair and honest judgment.

I have the feeling that you approve of me because I left one shore and am heading toward another, and because I disentangled myself from a mass of stillborn ideas and from one-time comrades who turned into enemies. I would like to be able to live up to your expectations, and I wish that our acquaintance made our progress smoother; and I would also like to know whether or not your expectations for the future are too high.

Let us talk about all this as soon as we meet again. I send you my warmest greetings,

Irma

6. FROM PÁL LIGETI

Berlin
January 4, 1908

Dear Gyuri,

You may be right about letters being monologues. But I do have quite a few comments and questions to ask after receiving your letter today, so an answer is in order. In other words, while in theory no correspondence exists, we may have one in practice. Please answer this letter as soon as possible if you have anything to say, that is.

Your references as to why you were silent so long are rather vague; so if you can do without revealing too much, please tell me more about why you were first so depressed and then so cheerful.[1] The latter interests me more, although right now the former state of mind has more relevance for me.

Send me your article as soon as it appears.[2] I am very interested in it. I believe it'll contain much of what also preoccupies me. I see something emerging there, an *Umwertung*[3] of our artistic standpoint, which in fact already was an *Umwertung* of traditional standpoints.

Scheffler[4] I find fascinating; he is also very smart although in this book a little too verbal and is also contradictory at times (e.g., *"Materialechtheit—Architektur als nur Nutzbaukunst"*). He even offers some logical constructs from time to time, as when he talks, for example, about the red tones of iron works. I don't see, though, the basic contradiction that you perceive—and if I did that would have painful consequences for me. Namely I'd have to conclude that I'm still not on the right track, although I did believe that I retained some clarity about some basic questions and Scheffler had a great deal to do with my development after all. You are right in what you say about the triumph of socialism. But the "Virchow-Hospital" and the "Müller Public Bathhouse" also represent a victory for socialism.[5] We are confronted daily by new problems and we may be able to solve them with the help of Scheffler's approach. I would have more to say on this, but first I want to hear what you have to say.

I find your rapid conversion to socialism very interesting. Time permitting, I should develop my own viewpoint in this matter now that I have reached the appropriate stage of maturity. Therefore, you'd do me a great favor if you showed me the way to proceed based on what you already know. Maybe I should begin with the most extreme and outrageously polemic works. Marx, I think, represents an outmoded viewpoint. So, will you recommend an extreme book that would make the greatest impact on me?

One more question: you mention your work at the office.[6] Are you talking about a job in the Ministry? And if yes, what are your duties there?

Today I am going to attend a reading by three German authors: Mann, Ostini, and Thoma.[7] Mann greatly interests me ever since I read his *Tristan!* And *Tonio Kröger,* of course! Write soon!

Servus,
P.

[1] At that time, Lukács was in emotional turmoil on account of his romantic involvement with Irma Seidler.
[2] Presumably the essay on Novalis. See *Soul and Form.*
[3] "Transvaluation" (of all values). Allusion is to Nietzsche.
[4] Karl Scheffler (1869–1951), German publicist and art historian. Editor of the journal *Kunst und Künstler* (Art and Artist), between 1906 and 1933. The book in question is his *Moderne Kultur* (1906).

[5] Both buildings in Berlin, the former named after Rudolf Virchow, the famous physician, and the latter after Hermann Müller, politician and Social Democrat.
[6] For a very short period, after finishing his law studies, Lukács held a clerical position at one of the ministries.
[7] Reference is to Thomas Mann, Fritz Ostini (1861–1927), and Ludwig Thoma (1867–1921).

7. TO ERNŐ OSVÁT

Budapest
January 20, 1908

Dear Mr. Osvát,

I am enclosing the article on Novalis[1] as promised. In case you happen to come across the article containing biographical data on Gunnar Heiberg,[2] please let me know. (I have a bad cold and have been housebound for the past week.) May I ask you to tell me if you are interested in an article, not longer than three to five pages, on the latest dramas of Gerhart Hauptmann[3] (dealing with spiritual content, style, the new kind of dramatic literature, etc. etc.). To tell the truth, the matter is not of the utmost importance to me; since I know what I want to say, writing the article would mean just that: writing it down. It just occurred to me that the topic is timely; and in case you don't have anybody else in mind, I could do it for you.

Yours respectfully,
György Lukács

P.S. If you have no use for the article, please send the manuscript back to my address: V. Nagy János Street, 15.

[1] Published in *Nyugat (West)*, March 16, 1908. *Nyugat* was to become the country's most important literary magazine. Endre Ady, Mihály Babits, Anna Lesznai, and most of the era's literary celebrities contributed. It was described by one contemporary as the magazine in which all *isms* which stood in opposition to each other abroad, such as impressionism, symbolism, naturalism, existed side by side. From the beginning, Lukács (as well as his friend, Béla Balázs) had a somewhat strained relationship with *Nyugat*.
[3] Gunnar Heiberg (1857–1929), Norwegian playwright.
[2] See letter no. 1, n. 9. Throughout the second volume of his *Dramabook*, Lukács devotes considerable space to the discussion of Hauptmann's dramatic career.

8. FROM BERNÁT ALEXANDER

Budapest
January 21, 1908

Dear Herr Doctor,

The Sainstbury volume[1] is at your disposal. Do not believe for a moment that I considered Hevesi[2] [as the author] seriously, on the contrary, I suspected you from the beginning, and I am very happy that by proposing the theme for the contest[3] I may have contributed to the birth of this magnificent, grandiose, novel and interesting work.[4] It is almost certain that you, that is, the author of the two-volume work, will receive the prize. By all means, come to the general meeting on Sunday. I gave instructions that the prize be announced right after the secretary's report, and not, as was done before, at the end of the meeting. I do not want you to have to wait long. If you have time, please drop in either Sunday or Monday, after lunch.

Cordially,
Alexander

[1] George Saintsbury (1845–1933), British historian of literature, author of *History of Criticism and Literary Taste in Europe*, 3 vols. (1902). The reference is presumably to one of the volumes.
[2] Sándor Hevesi. See letter no. 4, n. 2.
[3] Annual literary contest of the *Kisfaludy Társaság* (Society). Submission was author-anonymous and the winner received the "Krisztina Lukács" Prize (no relation to Georg). Alexander proposed the theme for that year. See letter no. 2.
[4] Lukács's entry was the first draft of his *Dramabook*.

9. FROM LIPÓT FEJÉR

Budapest
February 8, 1908

Dear Gyuri,

Let me express my heartfelt congratulations on your splendid achievement.[1] Regardless of what beneficial effect this honor may have on your career, it has, more importantly, the principal significance that someone like you who represents modernity here, has received the prize of the *Kisfaludy Társaság*.[2] This only serves to enhance your reputation. Please, convey to your dear family my warmest congratulations!

Until we meet, I send you my greetings in sincere friendship,

Fejér

P.S. If and when critical comments (on your work) appear in print, I would like to have them.

[1] See notes to letter no. 8.
[2] See letter no. 2, n. 2.

10. FROM KÁROLY (KARL) POLÁNYI

Budapest
February [8] 1908

My dear friend, Gyuri,

Putting everything aside, I am just tossing out words to tell somehow what an egotistic pleasure our victory gave me[1] and that I felt as if my own future were lit up by silver lightning.

My happiness was akin to a physical pleasure, my cheeks burned just as they did the last time on October 10th, when my eyes followed the endless red armies[2] marching right into the future.

My good Gyuri, let me take off those awkward, sad glasses and now let me gently stroke your dusty blond head because I love you so.

Yours,
Karli[3]

Rejoice! Rejoice! Rejoice!

[1] Reference is to the Kisfaludy Society contest. See letter no. 8.
[2] Allusion is made to the so-called "Red Thursday," in Budapest, on October 10, 1907, the day of a general strike and mass rally demanding franchise for the working class.
[3] Nickname for "Károly," the Hungarian version of "Karl," obviously fashioned after "Charlie," in accordance with young Polányi's Anglophile sentiments.

11. FROM GYULA HEGEDÜS

Budapest
April 7, 1908

Dear Sir,

Not until now have I been able to ascertain your address, and thus only now can I thank you for your valuable present.[1]

The reading of the Novalis article rekindles in my soul the admiration I felt when at the age of 18 I read Heine's *Die romantische Schule*[2]. Had he not become unfaithful to Germany,[3] Heine could have given an even more adequate expression of that German soul *par excellence* which, after all, truly manifested itself in Romanticism.

You have succeeded in giving us a marvelously apt portrait of the public spirit in Jena of that time. Allow me to make one remark: you shouldn't overestimate the power of comprehension of the general reading public. Although your suggestive allusions allow us a glimpse into the depth and breadth of your frame of mind, they remain inaccessible to the general reader. But our mission is to write for the educated public and not only to a small coterie of experts.

Once again, accept my sincerest thanks.

Yours faithfully,
Gyula Hegedüs

[1] The Novalis essay. See letter no. 7, n. 1.

[2] *The Romantic School* by Heinrich Heine (1797–1856), German-Jewish poet and feature writer. Leading member of the progressive literary movement, *Das junge Deutschland*.

[3] In 1831, Heine exiled himself to Paris. He continued to visit Germany and his reports and poems show a love-hate relationship (e.g., *Germany: A Winter's Tale*).

12. FROM IRMA SEIDLER

Nagybánya
July 3, 1908

My dear Gyuri,

I received your letter and understood it only too well; nevertheless, its content didn't scare me one bit. There is much truth in what you wrote, and much of this truth has been on my mind for some time. But listen to me, Gyuri dearest, do you really believe that a growing relationship between two people (and I do not mean a superficial one but one that amounts to a near symbiosis) can happen any other way than by passing through chaotic stages of never-dreamed-of sufferings and pleasures—and with lots of loving and caring? I was never afraid of this. I consider this matter a beautiful task to be accomplished with courage, honesty, and joy. The tears that have to be shed will be of sweet sorrow. But don't believe for a minute that I want to put in a false poetic light what for you is an important real problem. After all, you gave expression to some of the thoughts and doubts that I have been harboring myself. Some of these things I wanted to discuss with you when we were together but somehow could not bring myself to do it.

As Goethe put it so wonderfully somewhere,[1] the union between two people is like a chemical process in which crises, shocks, and tensions precede the fusion. Those who adore the metaphor of the gentle ivy clinging to the strong oak probably have an easier time of it. But we both know that the strong oak can turn into a python whose deadly embrace is bound to annihilate the pliant soul. And it is my belief—shared by you, I trust—that *our individual lives will be enhanced by our belonging to each other and vice versa;* for this reason the road we travel will be longer, more painful and noble. We have at one occasion come to the conclusion that a great work, a great deed, all great things bring to our minds the sight of a flexed bow. Love is something like that.

I ask you to always be as good, honest as you were in this letter to me and everything will be all right. I should like to tell you so much more but I better not. Many times I feel the need to talk but then can't bring it off; while I am writing this letter, I am constantly aware of the inadequacy of the words that cannot express many things I want to say. Don't let that deter *you* and write about everything at length.

I can't as yet have any positive impressions about this place;[2] after all, I haven't met most of the people here. My room is cozy, the walls painted white. I can't tell you about my work either; everything is still in a preparatory stage. The sky is clear. The nearby forest smells so good; it is good to be here. This letter is being written late at night—and I know, I didn't give you a deserving answer. Please write about everything. You know I am interested. Bye, bye, dear Gyuri,

Irma

[1] In the novel, *Elective Affinities* (1809).
[2] Nagybánya, a small mining town in Hungary, close to Transylvania, was selected as the location of a famous artists' colony because of its beauty. Founded in 1896 by a group of Western-trained painters (Hollósy, Réti, Ferenczy), the Nagybánya School is regarded as responsible for the beginning of modern painting in Hungary: the predominant influence came from French Impressionism.

13. FROM LEO POPPER

St. Gilgen
July 7, 1908

My dear Gyuri,

First of all, I want to know whether your parents received our letter of congratulations. I met Gulácsy[1] in Vienna the other day; we spent an evening together at my place and he offered to mail the letter. Since then, I am tortured by the thought and the recognition looms larger and larger that Pre-Raphaelites, especially of the G.[ulácsian] kind, are not qualified to take on mail service (which in itself is based on forgetfulness). Thus we have to assume that the letter never reached you and this is obviously very awkward for us. Please inform your parents about the matter and tell them that the letter—written by my father and I—mentioned that our forthcoming present, which is a woodcut by Orlik,[2] will be sent to you after the exhibition closes. The gift should be kindly accepted and our *Schlamperei* [sloppiness] added to the long list of our sins begging forgiveness.

As far as my affairs are concerned, nothing worked out as planned. I am not in Ischl with Karli but in St. Gilgen with the whole tribe, marinating in Jew-juice complete with cousins and nieces (little devils)—God help me! If shame of one's own race at its highest degree put weight on one, I would return to Budapest as a 176 lb. *bocher* [young lad].

The sins of my forefathers, which consist of their mere existence, have never been more thoroughly revenged than in the case of their descendant: me. I have to walk up and down the shore with Hansi! Nobody but me is to blame. The house, the garden here appeared to me so beautiful and peaceful that I was convinced I could recuperate best here. Neither the housing nor the air would have been so great in Ischl, not to mention the many temptations that extend their deadly cool arms to me (in a manner of speaking).

My gamble turned out to be only half as clever as I thought. On the one hand, there are the relatives; on the other, there is no Karli! On top of that, I have no patience for work because—*was tut Gott!*[3]—there are many temptations around here too. ...

What do you think of the *Nyugat* having published nothing but our works lately?[4] What is your opinion of Z. Szász's article on Wilde?[5] What an *Oberlehrer der Entgötterer* he is, an untalented dog, and a mean one to boot. But I really liked Margit Kaffka's novelette.[6] If you care to analyze her technique in depth, you'll see that the seemingly overly Romantic tale is necessary to prepare us for the coming *pointe,* namely, the deadly fear of the impotence of the old man who is in love. Isn't it a wonderful piece?

I ran out of paper. More to come, same time next year. Write if you can spare the time and you will make me very, very happy.

With warm embrace,
Leo

P.S. Did you tell Jászi[7] to send the galleys to Ischl?

[1] Lajos Gulácsy (1882–1932), Hungarian painter, who was attracted by the British School of Pre-Raphaelites, Böcklin's exotic art and the Berlin *Sezession.* Known as a loner, his schizophrenia became apparent after 1916 and he spent the last decades of his life in an asylum.

[2] Emil Orlik (1870–1932), born in Prague, lived and worked in Vienna, and went to Japan to study the art of woodcutting.

[3] As God wills!

[4] This is meant ironically. *Nyugat* refused to publish Popper's articles or reviews; Lukács also had a somewhat strained relationship with *Nyugat.* See letter no. 7, n. 1.

[5] Zoltán Szász's article, "Wilde Oszkár," in *Nyugat* (June 16, 1908).

[6] Margit Kaffka (1880–1918), teacher and writer. She was the most acclaimed Hungarian woman novelist of her generation. Married Ervin Bauer, the

brother of Béla Balázs. Lukács thought highly of her. The story in question was "One Day," published in *Nyugat* (July 1908).

7 Oszkár (Oscar) Jászi, editor of *Huszadik Század*. Popper's survey of the spring exhibitions in Budapest, "Tárlatok," was published in *Huszadik Század* (May 1908). Reprinted in the 1983 publication of his essays, *Esszék és Kritikák* (Budapest: Magvető, 1983), pp. 41ff.

14. TO ERNŐ OSVÁT

Budapest
July 10, 1908

Dear Mr. Osvát,

I'm sending along my article[1]—only one day past the deadline. I hope you don't mind too much that it turned out a little longer than planned. I should very much like to ask you to give me at least one whole day to work on the galleys. Because it had to be done in such a hurry the last time, a few printing mistakes remained—and what is worse, some breaks in the immanent rhythm—in the Novalis piece.[2] I wish to avoid such mistakes this time.

Respectfully yours,
György Lukács

1 "Rudolf Kassner," published in Osvát's journal, *Nyugat* (July 16, 1908). See *Soul and Form.*

2 See letter no. 7, n. 1.

15. FROM KÁROLY (KARL) POLÁNYI

Bad Ischl
July 21, 1908

My dear Gyurika,

For days now I have been thinking of you, and of postcards (I fear, namely, that I lost Leo's[1] postcard that I was supposed to mail to you). I keep thinking of you—as an advisor and promoter—because I so want you to spend your summer holidays in St. Gilgen instead of Dresden, *quelle horreur!*

This is not going to be a real letter as I received your Kassner essay[2] only yesterday and will wait until I have more to say.

At first reading, without quite digesting it, it impressed me as a beautiful, worthy, and generous piece of writing. "Standing in mourning, draped in silvery clothing I choke on the smoke of torches. ..."[3] That is what it's like! It is shamelessly many-faceted, deceptive, and hoodwinking, in a witty way too—but I persevered because unexpectedly at the next turn, it throws many a handful of gold coins in my face. ... Such a piece of work is allowed to deceive because at the end it alone pays the price for it.

The writing is dense, audacious, sympathetic, and lively. It resembles honey—not the thin, syrupy one, but the kind that gathers around the remaining clumps of wax or even floats around the corpses of a few bees. The style is something like that.

I should say, it is like a cemetery full of dark soil and blooming flowers bringing forth a special kind of weed that oozes a heavy, sweet, and intoxicating humus-smell, and I feel like lying down on it and inhaling its rich musty smell. Great expression, isn't it: "Something is rotten. ..." [Hamlet]. Beautiful word!

Yours, Karli

[1] Leo Popper, closest friend of Lukács, who at that time stayed in St. Gilgen at a T.B. sanatorium.
[2] "Platonism, Poetry and Form: Rudolf Kassner," in *Soul and Form,* pp. 19ff. See letter no. 14, n. 1.
[3] Paraphrasing a line of a poem *(Sirni, sirni, sirni)* by Endre Ady (1877–1919), the most famous twentieth-century Hungarian poet, and a central figure in Hungary's intellectual life. His poetic vision of a "regenerated Hungary" influenced a whole generation of progressive intellectuals, Lukács included.

16. FROM IRMA SEIDLER

Nagybánya
August 5, 1908

Dearest Gyuri,

Your letter arrived at noon. I have been thinking about it ever since and came to the conclusion that it contains many things which are difficult to write about, or respond to adequately, but I will give it a try.

First, about things in general. I am terribly sorry that I told you about my having been ill and caused you worry. I myself never took it seriously and I was right; since yesterday I have been perfectly well. It cost me a tremendous amount of time, though. And I am not pleased with you! I beg you again, sweetheart, to go to see your doctor[1] (you can afford that much time), and tell him that your schedule doesn't permit a long, drawn-out treatment; he'll take that into consideration. I am convinced that something can be done to help without complicating your life. Gyuri dear, *do as I ask you,* please.

All day I looked forward to a quiet evening and to taking care of my correspondence, and now I am so very tired. I worked hard all day long and then went over to the Ferenczys'[2] around 7 p.m. They are the sweetest people I have ever met; they have such a wonderful life together. I love to be with them. Theirs is not a vulgar existence but a noble and simple life based on inexhaustible inner richness; it is a higher form of existence. I like it there, especially when all of them are together. My life—or is it my way of life—is somewhat overtaxed, and not just by work. All my time is accounted for; by the time I sit down to write to you, exhaustion has already set in. That is why my last letter was written in such a nervous state—and I shouldn't do that to you. But Gyuri, I was very depressed because I wasn't out of the house for eight straight days. You have no idea how happy I am that I feel so strong and alert and can work full steam. As I said, I shouldn't write you such letters but it happens. . . . After having read your letter today I again have to fight a wave of depressing thoughts and moods but I know they will be overcome because they are more presentiments than anything else.

And now, my sweet Gyuri—how I would like to stroke your dear head. Would you believe if I told you that everything you wrote about I already knew? That is, I knew that you harbor *such thoughts and sentiments,* which doesn't have to mean, of course, that things are as you describe them; they are important in themselves be they the truth or not. And it isn't so either that things—whatever they may be—are not prone to changes. My feeling is that one has to let things run their course and that changes will inevitably occur. Emotions are nothing but phases, stages. For one thing, you accord undeserved dominance to certain things; for another, you are capable of perceiving insignificant nuances (and magnify them), but, of course, they matter to you. Still, let's wait and see. The time will come—after we come to know each other *even better* and to understand each other's essential self—when you'll realize how much you are able to give me, just as you are; and then you won't ever feel sorry for me again. Besides, Leo[3] is quite right—and I say this without self-delusion—in that you possess within yourself precisely that certain capability that you think is amiss.[4]

It is there but was subsequently repressed and then it surfaced again in what you call the "sensuous" perception in your literary and artistic sphere of activities. But once this faculty is there and one's life is regarded as deserving tender care and love, then it is possible to *live* (and thus, the poet, the *non*-Platonic element also, will enter this *life-sphere*).[5] Do not brood so much over whether or not one should talk about these things. It hurts much more, you know, if you are aware of them but keep them all bottled up inside.

If it is possible for you to do so, please try—for your own sake—not to analyze everything to death. It reminds me of the gathering of flowers into a bouquet, scattering them and then gathering them anew without, however, being able to achieve (and this I know from my own artistic experience) the spontaneous harmony of the first arrangement that existed before one moved *each* of the flowers from its original position. One should always retain a fixed point in any reordering and search for harmony; otherwise, one may spoil the whole arrangement. I see now that I went a little too far... but don't read more into it than it originally contains.

One more thing. You write that one always has to go alone on the difficult path to the work: *"keiner kann keinem Gefährte hier sein!"* Maybe so—or certainly so. But one can still have somebody who pays attention to what one is doing. And this is a lot, something to cherish. I regard the most valuable aspect of a relationship, of two people being together, to be the fact that *one is not alone.* I think it is easy to endure difficulties, disappointment, or loss if somebody stands by holding one's hand; and it all may become unbearable if one is all alone in one's solitary, distanced existence. But no more of this today. Sometimes, when I think about the past week or two, it seems that your attitude toward me has changed, as if you saw me in a different light; and I don't understand what is going on inside you.

I can see that you are working hard and suffering greatly. I was pleased by what you wrote about your new insights on history because it means a new awareness for you. What is going to happen with "George"?[6] I will reread Kassner in the light of Benedek's remarks.[7] I must say, however, that I never had such an impression from any of your works but then I wasn't looking for it. I would like terribly much if we could talk again in all earnestness and without side issues about your work, so that I would know about everything. Correspondence is a miserable substitute. I can't express what I really think. Everything comes out so insufferably categorical. I know, I truly believe that I came close to understanding you in these matters—just as I believe that we can one day reach each other—but let's stop right here.

I love you dearly.

Irma

My work is not going too well.
Lots of suffering with little result.

[1] Especially in his letters to Leo Popper, Lukács frequently mentions his nervousness, insomnia, and anaemia.
[2] The family of Károly Ferenczy (1862–1917), impressionist painter and leading figure of the Nagybánya School, consisted of his talented children: Valér (1885–1954), painter; Béni (1890–1966), sculptor; and the only daughter, Noémi (1890–1957), originator of modern Hungarian tapestry. See letter no. 12, n. 2.
[3] Leo Popper.
[4] See letter no. 29.
[5] See letter no. 30 and the Kassner essay in *Soul and Form,* pp. 19ff.
[6] Essay in *Soul and Form,* pp. 79ff.
[7] Reference is to Marcell Benedek (see "Biographical Notes"), who wrote in a letter of July 21, 1908, that Lukács seems to be acquiring a typical *Nyugat* style, i.e., impressionistic in tone.

17. FROM IRMA SEIDLER

Nagybánya
September 20, 1908

Dear, sweet Gyuri,

You are good, and a sweetheart. Thanks for the two letters. Don't be cross with me because I didn't answer; I just couldn't. Everything is as you say. Of course I'll stay here and work. I should not have written such things in the first place. It is the woman's duty to safeguard the harmony, quiet, and inner peace between two people. But it is not always easy. It must be apparent to you what art means to me, that it has become a part of me. And because it is such a significant part of me, I feel very strongly about this *"entweder-oder"* position of the *Brand*-type,[1] which is difficult to reconcile with our lives and with life *per se*. But one has to strive to find the order of things. I believe—indeed, I know—that I'll be able to live a life of harmony. But one has to reach that stage first. It will take a long while; and until I arrive at the stage when my own tranquility can *always* calm you, I harbor in myself many immature and vehement elements that make me weak. I do things I shouldn't and then I am in need of your support. I thank you for the two letters. They gave me just what I needed. Maybe I have more in me of the woman and then of that which is unfeminine—the artist and the human being—than you perceived, and the two sides are often in conflict.

Please write. Don't expect more from me today, but maybe tomorrow. I think I will send this to your home address. I very much dislike this complicated arrangement of yours; I can't predict when you should go to the main post office.[2] If you still think that we have to do it this way, tell me; but how can I decide today, Saturday, that I'll write Monday? I might not be able to do it that day, or I may need to write you on Sunday; and I would be compelled to write you when I didn't feel like it, or you'd go to the post office in vain. Should you still wish to keep this arrangement, write me immediately. I was very glad to hear about the Kassner and Bíró matter,[3] and I was also glad to hear that you are on good terms with Mici and Alice.[4] Did Mici mention my letter to her? What did she say exactly? Don't *forget* to answer this question. How are things with the journal?[5] I still have to write Rózsi.[6]

Your letter has told me a lot. This was the first time that you wrote that way. Bye, bye Gyuri! I love you so much.

Irma

[1] Henrik Ibsen's play, *Brand* (1866). The reference is to the "either-or" position.
[2] Obviously, the letters had to be sent *post restante* [will call] in order to keep the relationship secret, especially in Lukács's family.
[3] Both articles were published in 1908. "Rudolf Kassner," in *Nyugat* (July 16) and the review essay, "Bíró Lajos novellái," in *Huszadik Század* (September issue).
[4] Mici is Lukács's sister; Alice is presumably Alice Jászi.
[5] Reference cannot be established.
[6] Rózsi Hochstätter. See letter no. 3, n. 2.

18. TO ERNŐ OSVÁT

Budapest
September [28] 1908

Dear Sir,

Yesterday evening I took my manuscript[1] to the Café[2] and even stayed there for a while; I was told that you had been there and left but might be coming back.

As far as the galleys of the articles[3] are concerned, I could come by at the Bristol Tuesday night, but only if you have the galleys with you *for sure*. If that is the case, either send word with the messenger delivering this letter or call me at home (20–27); in case I am not in, any of the servants will take the message. Of course, all of this is necessary only if you plan to put the articles in the next issue.

It really doesn't matter that much to me except that I'd prefer to have one of the articles in the next issue; two articles in the same issue by Georg Lukács would be a little too much, don't you think?

I remain

Yours faithfully,
György Lukács

[1] "*Der Weg ins Freie:* Arthur Schnitzler's Novel," a review essay.
[2] Café Bristol, a favorite meeting place of the Budapest literati.
[3] Lukács meant both the Schnitzler review essay and his essay on "Stefan George". Both of the pieces were published in the October 1, 1908 issue of the *Nyugat*.

19. FROM IRMA SEIDLER

Nagybánya
October 25, 1908

[No salutation]

I have started to write you many times but was unable to find the exact words that would have truly reflected the state of my mind. By now I am resigned to the fact that this letter too will be inadequate but I have to write about everything, finally. Things have crystallized in my mind to the point that it'd make no sense to analyze their *Werdegang*.[1] The only thing that matters is where they stand.

Gyuri, we have been together for quite a long while, together in the true sense of the word. I went along with you a good part of the way, partaking in your life and development, especially intellectually, and I was in turn greatly enriched by doing so. But we were not together with *every particle* of our being. We were not together at the point wherein my real life lies, that which is terribly human and tangible, and made up of blood and throbbing substance.

We have not been together lately and our letters show more clearly than any personal exchange would where our relationship—not our character—now stands. I have tried in my letters—I have to be absolutely honest with you—to adjust, to accommodate you as wholly as I can, always conscious of a self-willed sacrifice. I have accepted your parameters for the understanding of each other. Now I have decided not to continue this embattled togetherness because I felt too strongly at times that I cannot live with some of your categories; they cannot serve as substitutes for my inner life and therefore have to remain mere intellectual pleasantries.

My decision is not dictated by today's "moods" or those of yesterday, but rather by the many long days and sleepless nights when my conscience debated with my weakness. The ongoing inner conflict stopped me many times from writing and telling you all this, and from letting my conscience win. Or it might have been my desire for the truth that finally forbade me to get intoxicated again and again with the "fullness," with that overwhelming richness, that derived from the intellectual life shared with you and with which I intended to feed my soul. I have a disharmonious disposition which demands a work constantly filled with tension, emotionally and intellectually speaking; only this can insure an orderliness, and prevent inner chaos. I have inside me a tremendous amount of primitive, human, ordinary desires; my artistic approach has *this* character too. But as far as life is concerned, these desires are *dominant*. Just as strong is my love for everything that cannot be corseted in and expressed by any artistic categories. But it is mainly the strong call of an uncomplicated great life that finds its echo in me and its call is stronger than you—or I, for that matter—ever imagined. You and I should not be allowed to belong to each other for life because it would not lead to happiness. We would never be able to jump over that narrow but deep ravine that separates us. I didn't dare to dwell on this before, but you had the courage to analyze it fully many times.

Only when the existential significance of things became pressing could my feelings and thoughts ripen to their present state; I think that your many letters also helped to intensify the process.

You never told me and I never knew for certain (because there were always good reasons to suppose the opposite as well) whether or not you think *in earnest* about binding my life to yours. In spite of your never stating that you want it that way, I am asking you today to give me back my freedom—which you perhaps never took away and which you were always hesitant and afraid to take away. Now I want it returned. You know that I had to suffer a great deal before gathering the courage to tell you this.

That things have developed and matured to this point has not so much to do with my will or wish than with the commanding force of life or truth—and that being the case I know I can count on your understanding. I had to take this road and do what I did.

You, Gyuri, will grow better without me, without the ever-present ties concentrated on one person. You need people for your work, the stimulation that comes from many people and from different directions. People distract me because they transform my artistic energies into unproductive all-around activities. Now you will be able to develop greatly, to branch out and surpass yourself; you will feel more keenly that you are sailing on an open sea. Use the immeasurable advantage of being able to live for years for your development only. Now you have all the chances to achieve your heart's desire and become as great a figure as Walter Pater.[2] The material is there and now so are the conditions, provided—as you wrote—that you can devote the next three to four years to your studies.

I on my part have to bid you farewell; I part with a long, warm press of the hand and with those words which rang out at the end of your wondrously beautiful George article.[3] God be with you, Gyuri. I bid farewell because we cannot go on together any more.

God be with you,
Irma

[1] Process of becoming.

[2] Walter Horatio Pater (1839–94) British writer and aesthete. His declaration that "all art constantly aspires towards the condition of music" has been said

to constitute the "charter of abstract art" (Peter Gay). See Lukács's discussion of Pater's conceptualization in his *Heidelberger Philosophie der Kunst,* p. 101. Pater's main work is *The Renaissance. Studies in Art and Poetry* (1913).

[3] "The New Solitude and its Poetry." *Soul and Form,* p. 90.

20. FROM IRMA SEIDLER

Nagybánya
November 2, 1908

My dear and only Gyuri,

I am packing and coming to Budapest. Before I leave, just these few words to you. I can best explain everything about our relationship in person only. I have to talk to you. I want to make myself understood; I also have to find out if there is still a way to reach each other; if yes, we should try everything possible. If nothing can be done, I will bid good-bye to you with all my love, with all the warmth of my soul that belonged to you, assuring you that my loving gaze will always be following you from afar wherever you go. My only fervent and deeply felt wish is to part without bitterness and recriminations, to go with deep and sweet feelings intact—gently.

I will probably be arriving tomorrow, Tuesday. Come and visit me Wednesday morning. Gyuri, do not be angry with me and do not regard it as a high-handed play if I want to *say* good-bye in person. Accept it for what it is: I want to lay myself open to you, to disclose the *innermost* workings of my life and my self that until now you couldn't fathom. Have patience with me, give me the opportunity to tell you all that and then take your leave from me with caring and blessing as I will from you.

Irma

P.S. Your letters were unbelievably touching and heartrending.

21. TO IRMA SEIDLER

Budapest
November [?] 1908

(Final Draft)

[No salutation]

There is no counting the drafts that preceded this letter of farewell. (You yourself did not want to bid good-bye.—Don't be cross with me now that I feel a need to say good-bye even if it has to remain without echo.) Please forgive me that, although you ceased to care for me, if ever you did, you remain the only meaning of my life. That alone would not compel me to write. You would not hear from me had I enough energy to go on living, to carry on my empty and wretched existence;—but, I ask myself, why should you care how I am coping? I know that it is of no interest to you and I do not wish it otherwise.

And yet, I have to write now—so that you get these lines along with the news of my death.[1] It has to be done because—perhaps—I meant something to you once and because the remembrance of the times we spent together won't let you remain indifferent as to why I threw away my life—a life that everybody thought to be something special[2] and of which undoubtedly great things were expected, even by myself. It may sound to you as though I were frightfully vain and have greatly overestimated my capabilities. If this is the case, try to see it as the overindulgence of a human being who is now weak, quite ill and utterly devastated. Thinking of what I intend to do, I sometimes fear that upon receiving the news—of an act thought to be unmotivated by everyone because nobody could possibly know the real reasons—you might blame yourself because of your great and beautiful kindness. I might overestimate myself and my meaning in your life, but I really do not want you, out of self-recrimination, to start speculating about what might have happened had you done things otherwise or had you tried to save me, etc. In order to avoid this, I'll try to explain to the best of my ability why it is that I cannot tolerate life anymore. I will be brief. It was a little over a year ago that I saw you for the first time, and for a short while it seemed springtime had come. But now my "ice-age" has returned, that is, a time of complete loneliness, of total exclusion from all human community, from everyday life.[3] (May I assume that you still remember the details of what happened before—my alienation from Mici,[4] my estrangement from Laci[5] and others?) But in due time I regained my peace of mind. I worked and my work was coming along so well that I could expect to accomplish great things. In fact, I must add that at the very moment I am writing this, I am more sure than ever of my "talent". In sum: I got used to a state of affairs. To be sure, the hope lurked in my subconscious—and may have helped to keep up my spirits—that maybe one day somebody would come along who would understand and love me, to whom I would mean everything, and thus my life would attain a meaning. Let me repeat: I did not dare to admit this possibility even to myself but entertained the hope nevertheless or, at least, did not think of it as a sheer impossibility. And then we met. And everything I did not even dare to hope for became a reality. Past relationships lost their meaning, seemed to have been mere lies; and only the present one seemed true. (Again, forgive me if I overestimate what I meant to you. I have no way of knowing and do not even want to speculate upon it. But I remain convinced that at one time I meant something to you.) So I became a different person: a good man.[6] I learned to value the lives of others. You have no idea to what extent my relationship to people has changed and how often I was helping people or helped things happen just because you gave me the gift of life; and a life that was repressed now wanted to assert itself in every possible way. But I knew that it is impossible to forget such a problematic youth as I had and remained somewhat sceptical that so much beauty could be real, that all that beauty and richness could be mine and even that it is right for me to aspire to such a life. When I questioned you about this, you answered in the affirmative. Do you remember our first evening in Florence[7] when you said "yes" to my question? Remember how I kept telling you that I was unable to hold on to anything or anybody, and that I could never become the meaning of another person's life? Then you answered my question about the possibility of overcoming all this with another question: whether I still believed this to be the case. How I wanted to believe you! But life defied my expectations. You wanted to redeem me, and I thank you for it with a grateful heart, with eyes tired from tears and with a voice grown weak. You wanted to be my savior but I cannot be saved.[8] Although it was mainly out of honesty and a clear conscience that I did not keep anything from you, it was also for the selfish reason that it might help eliminate certain bothersome traits of mine. And all the while I was hoping that any remaining problems were nothing but the rearguard actions of my receding past. I even seemed to perceive signs of a bright future that would mean that I was redeemed by you, and I hoped to be able to compensate you for my redemption.

You must have realized by now that you wanted to accomplish the impossible, or shall I say that it was life that made you realize the futility of your efforts? Life, after all, embraces those who know how to live and hates the likes of me, who does not. (By the time you read this, you can use the past tense.) I did not wish you to be bound to me until I was sure that I could become the man you deserve, but this was impossible to expect because I will never become such a man.

No human being was ever as close to me as you were, and I do not see that that could happen again. I was proven right in my belief that I will never be the meaning of another person's life. Although the intensity of my love may inflame and consume my poor life, it is clear that it can never be sufficiently encompassing and it is therefore worth nil.[9] It was on that evening in Florence—the 5th of June to be exact—that I posed the question of my life: Should it be my fate to lose out every time I try to establish a person-to-person relationship that goes beyond that of the intellectual one? On October 28—the day of the delivery of your letter[10]—the verdict was returned: "Yes, this is how it is going to be." And I cannot live with this verdict. Everything that you built up has now collapsed. Goodness[11] has left me forever; even its roots are torn out. I have become bad, coldhearted, mean—and a cynic. There followed a period of intellectual ecstasy: books and ideas became my opium. For a few weeks I felt an intellectual richness as never before: the swarm of ideas was almost overwhelming in its greatness, strength, and complexity. But one evening the ecstasy was all but spent. I suddenly realized that my thoughts derived their value from your listening to them and loving them; you were able to identify their source and meaning which at times remained obscure even to me. They seem devoid of purpose now because there is not one who loves and appreciates them. Thus, the ecstasies gave way to depression. My life seemed to have meaning only in those moments when new lines of thought presented themselves and new perspectives opened up and brought with them exultation. But one cannot live permanently on the summit; and because I am no longer capable of going on with everyday drudgery, with performing the drab routine tasks of my craft, those moments of exultation became more and more rare. Even if there were millions of such moments, they wouldn't satisfy me in the long run. I can state quite dispassionately that I am very talented but this fact alone cannot bring satisfaction since you have allowed me a glimpse into paradise. But now life has made me realize that I am not allowed to partake of it.

These are the reasons why I am going to die. I have shown you so much of myself (for which I beg your forgiveness), because I wanted you to understand that although meeting you has firmed my decision to end it all (you remember my telling you about those occasions when I played with the thought of suicide?), you are not at all to blame. It is not your fault, after all, that what was an interlude for you has turned into the overwhelming experience of my life; that upon remembering some slight remark of yours I came close to bursting into tears on a street corner; or even that I became indifferent to whether or not some great scholars came to extol one of my particularly valuable thoughts. All I wanted was your looking at me and smiling while I was explaining my ideas to you. As I said, all that is not your fault; so don't think about me any more and don't be angry because I told you all that I did. Merely writing you (that is, being able to 'talk' to you) has had such a calming effect on me that it has helped, for today, to postpone my death. Needless to say, it won't be enough to change my mind permanently.

I have only myself to blame for everything; or the blame should be placed upon what made me the kind of human being who, while starving for happiness, is incapable of it, and yet is unable to live without it.

God be with you. To have met you may have destroyed me but I am happy for it nevertheless. With an intensity that defies words, I am thankful for what you gave me and wish you the very beautiful and happy life that you deserve. That is what I wished for myself and it's what you let me experience for a few fleeting moments.

[unsigned]

[1] Lukács has seriously considered committing suicide as this letter and passages from his diary show. The letter was never sent.

[2] Not only Lukács's family, especially his father, but also his peers in Hungary regarded the young man as exceptionally talented.

[3] Many of the concepts and phrasings appear in the early works such as *Sou and Form,* especially in the Kierkegaard essay, and in the 1912 "confessional" writing, "Von der Armut am Geiste." In his Hungarian language essay, "On the Aesthetic Culture," (1913), Lukács criticizes the cultural scene as lacking "relationships between people; now there is complete loneliness, the complete

absence of relationships". Thus, cultural criticism and autobiographical elements are fused.

[4] Sister of Lukács.

[5] Nickname for "László". Reference is to László Bánóczi, a lawyer friend of Lukács. See "Biographical Notes".

[6] One of the key concepts in the "profound artistic essay," entitled "Von der Armut am Geiste" (On Poverty of Spirit), referring to Lukács's mystical interpretation of the category "goodness". It is combined there with an elitist-aristocratic notion of "castes". In the scheme of two kinds of lives, there are those who are condemned to an "ordinary," an "everyday life," and then those who are "possessed by goodness".

[7] See Irma Seidler, in "Biographical Notes".

[8] Identical text with the closing passage of "Von der Armut am Geiste".

[9] See n. 6. In the essay, the Kantian categorical imperative is rejected and a "higher," personal ethic embraced.

[10] Reference is to Irma's letter of good-bye, no. 19.

[11] See n. 3 and 6.

22. FROM LEO POPPER

Paris
November 23, 1908

My dear Gyuri,

Today again only a few lines. I am working on the translation of your essay,[1] which takes all of my spare time; thus, I have put aside everything I have been thinking about lately until it is done. All I have to say now is that I find this piece beautiful in regard to its tone (or rather its moods), because it does not have the uninterrupted flow that, for example, the Kassner essay did. It strikes me rather as if you wanted to talk about something else in a very detached way but you were overwhelmed by sentiment and that made you sing. Perhaps the nicest thing about it: one feels a certain generosity in the form of "let's talk about him", which is even more of an accomplishment; the essay shows that you want to embrace the other but instead you keep embracing yourself. Indeed, it is so very human, one wants to cry!

(And I think I can do it!)

The book[2] is an entirely different affair. As is fitting with a book, it is more of a structure than a flower garden (or maybe it is that *too* only cultivated by a botanist; thus, it won't let you get intoxicated). As a concept, it is very impressive and the (still to be written sociological) introduction that you've told me about fits so well into the whole even I—who am not very knowledgeable about the subject matter—can feel the ever-present societal skeleton underneath the (not too thick) flesh. I was taking notes while reading and could send them to you if you're interested.

All in all, I am sure of your success in Germany, as the *Dramabook* is entirely unique as a construct; but I must say I like you much more the way you are now. It is extremely late. I can't hold the pen any longer. Forgive me for not writing more today. You'll be hearing a lot about everything, I promise.

That is all I wanted to let you know today.

Hugs,

Leo

P.S. I opened the envelope just to add one more word: what you wrote to me on my birthday made me feel very good, as very few things in my life have done. I closed my eyes, and sank into a dazed, enriched state as if hiding a shy and trembling thought that doesn't dare move. I felt I should remain immobile forever if I wanted everything to stay the same as it is now; because if I moved I would change and wouldn't be the same person you know. Maybe you'd also see me in my ugliness and poverty and would maybe perceive some of my shortcomings that even I don't know about. That is why I wished for an absolute stillness, a wonderfully frozen state, and didn't write immediately.

But I have thought it over, changed my mind and moved in God's name, come what may. I regained my confidence. It was my love that helped to bring it back. I trust that nothing bad will come of it if I kick up my heels a little bit. The bond between us is strong enough.

I embrace you,
Leo

[1] On Stefan George. See *Soul and Form.*
[2] In fact, the Ms. of *The History of the Development of the Modern Drama,* or *Dramabook*.

23. FROM KÁROLY (KARL) POLÁNYI

Budapest
December 9, 1908

Dear Gyuri,

The Galileo Scientific Club[1] (as it is called now) will hold a debate on Sunday, at 6 p. m., on the premises of T. T.,[2] entitled "What is Scientific Truth?" I hereby extend to you a formal invitation. In case you are interested, you can get the details either from me or at the T. T.

Please come! (1) It is going to be interesting. (2) You will find many friend there and (3) I'd like to have a *very good* audience. (I may add that the above topic will be discussed from the point of view of modern theory of knowledge.)

We welcome additional participants provided they are knowledgeable. In addition, send me the addresses of everyone you wish to invite. Send it to my home address. I will send out the invitations.

You know, you could contribute to the first point of the debate, which is "Criteria of Scientific Truth as Contrasted with Other Truths" (for example, moral, artistic, et al., truth). This will be the first topic on the agenda. Perhaps you have something to say about scientific and artistic truth. That would be very interesting and useful, too.

You will learn the art of debating in public (which you have not done before); and after all, nobody can blame you for being preoccupied with aesthetics because... etc. etc.

Yours,
Karli

P.S. Pikler[3] accepted the position of honorary president.
Armer Mensch[4]

[1] Galileo Circle (1908–18), a group of young radical intellectuals, was one of the centers of intellectual and social revolt among students of Budapest University. Polányi was a founder and first president of the Circle in which the scientifically inclined predominated. It had its own journal, *Szabadgondolat* (Free Thought), in which Lukács published his famous essay, "Bolshevism as a Moral Problem" (December 1918).

[2] *Társadalomtudományi Társaság* (Social Science Society), founded in 1901 as a forum for social, scientific, and cultural debates and lectures. In 1906 it split into a conservative fraction and a progressive reformist fraction, the latter also belonging to either the Galileo Circle or to that around *Huszadik Század* (Twentieth Century), the journal of the sociological society.

[3] Gyula Pikler (1864–1937), legal scholar, professor of law at Budapest University. After the 1906 schism and subsequent takeover by the progressive fraction, president of the T.T. until 1919. Also honorary president of the Galileo Circle.
[4] Poor Fellow.

24. FROM KÁROLY (KARL) POLÁNYI

Budapest

December 18, 1908

My dear Gyuri,

Many thanks for your thoughts and for everything you wrote.

The truth is, I'd like to write the Introduction.[1] They probably want something other than what I have in mind right now—but it doesn't matter, really, if one has to do something other than what one originally was inclined to do.

That it is useful for me, at any rate—is without doubt.

As a matter of fact, Alexander[2] is not going to put a great deal of trust in me although to get to the heart of the matter—there are not too many people around who could do a better job than I.

I know only of the socialist clique. Among them, only Szabó,[3] Rónai[4] or Diner[5] could be considered. Szabó would not do it, however. Diner would not be acceptable to them, and I can do at least as good a job as Rónai.

As for the "philosophical" group, I obviously don't know them well; it is possible that there are excellent Marx experts among them, but I think it unlikely, based on the fact that Alexander extended the invitation to you.

Thus it seems a plausible enough proposition. It is true that I've devoted minimal effort to classical philosophy; I should say, I know only Hegel. But I know Marx and Engels well and I am acquainted with their philosophical critics. What I consider *most* important is the fact that I know the theoretical implications and can evaluate them from the viewpoint of contemporary theory of knowledge, etc.

In other words, there is no reason why I could not do the job well. Of course, should the matter create any difficulties for you, do not force it—and don't cause yourself any inconveniences.

All this is for your information only, if by some accident the matter suddenly becomes a real possibility. We will meet soon anyway and we then can discuss both issues.

I will be at Heini's[6] Saturday night. Do come old chap!

Sunday night at 6 o'clock; a continuation of the debate.[7] It may turn out to be quite interesting but don't dare promise *you* anything great, because I was severely reprimanded in the past.

I'd be happy if you could say something about the connection between artistic truth and how it relates to scientific truth.

The question is: how can one distinguish between what is artistic ideology and what is artistic *truth?*

With warm embraces,
Karli

[1] Reference is to the Introduction to a volume of Marx's writings for the planned series of Philosophical Writers. The plan never materialized.
[2] Bernát Alexander. See "Biographical Notes".
[3] Ervin Szabó (1887–1918), sociologist, director of the Budapest Public Library. Theorist of syndicalism, influenced Lukács's early reception of Marxism. Translated many works of Marx and Engels into Hungarian. His main works are on socialism (1904) and syndicalism (1908).
[4] Zoltán Rónai (1880–1940), sociologist. He was a socialist.
[5] József Diner-Dénes (1857–1937), publicist and art historian. His main Hungarian work is *Darwinism, Marxism, and Modern Natural Sciences* (1906).
[6] Allusion is to Henrik Herz (1885–1944), entrepreneur, who has later become a well-known patron of the arts. He was a close friend of Polányi, Lukács, and Leo Popper.
[7] See letter no. 23.

25. FROM LEO POPPER

Paris
January 6, 1909

My dearest Gyuri,

I will mail your book[1] tomorrow morning with all of my scribblings in it. Forgive me for not sending it a month ago; you know why I couldn't do it, don't you? I am going to write at length about the book, including the notes. Today only this much: I expect the German edition to have considerable success especially with the public. It is even possible that if you add a bit of sociological leaven to the dough, the book may be received—as your friend, Baumgarten[2] predicts—quite favorably by Simmel and his circle.[3] I wouldn't guarantee it, though. In the case of your current article,[4] the answer is a resounding yes. And the conclusion I reached with the greatest pleasure from reading your book was how different you are from the Georg Lukács of yesteryear. It also gave me great pleasure to see that while before your most significant characteristics didn't flow from your pen, or even came out all wrong at times, today they are displayed with ease; one can see this right away when comparing the book with your review essays on Schnitzler or on the Ibsen works. The book in itself is a source of great pleasure, and I wondered at times whether or not you'd be able to write today the *same way* as you did with certain chapters, such as the one on naturalism —what I mean is: without all the stylistic embellishments but armed with pure intellectuality. But more on the book later.

Now my sweet, good Gyuri, something about myself, since I know with a feeling of immense gratitude that it truly interests you.

You know, by and large, what has happened in the meantime, namely that I found a human being to share my fate, who loves me and loves me for what I am and who is the greatest wonder of the world, because she endured the process which led from loving me to getting to know me. This woman endured it all, and has grown in stature during the process; above all, she now loves me deeper than before. And there is a lot more: there are her parents who found their daughter's liking for me sufficient enough to see me as the sole way to redemption; their more than divine disposition is of such a serious, basic, and deep nature that upon learning everything[5]— most recently that we have to wait for at least another *three years*[6] —they stand by me with even more sincere love. I have never seen, heard of, or even read about people like that. I am so in the midst of miracles happening to me that I keep losing myself (which is for the better!). All I feel is an incredibly warm and all-embracing happiness. . . . I'll tell you what this girl is like. There is much more to her external appearance than the enclosed photo shows (which you should send back quickly and should not show to anyone except Karli and Heini.)[6] I may have a better one by next week and I'll send it to you.

January 7th

I continue my letter of yesterday. I mailed the books in the afternoon; they should arrive in Budapest in four to five days. I am now sitting in my room at the fireplace in the evening and my fiancee is on my side, and I can already see. . .

January 8th

. . . that only today, one day later, will this letter be finished and mailed.

[. . .]

When Karli's letter arrived with my doctor's verdict[7] I thought it was the end of me; I gave the letter to her to read and for a minute she was in shock but then said: *"Ja, das ist sehr schlimm, aber ein Unglück ist es nicht!"*[8] Immediately, she informed her parents, adding that she will gladly wait for three years and her only sorrow is to see me suffer. The next day her parents sent me the enclosed note.[9] I believe it tells you more than I ever could.

I think it is time to tell my parents about our relationship since unfortunately (I call it unfortunate because I have to pay for this fact with three years' wait) it doesn't have the character of a temporary adventure anymore. What do you think? Shall I write now? Practically speaking, it will not have much meaning but I'd like to see her get a nice letter from them. But will they do so? My dear boy, this is one miserable situation. Any ugly feelings that I am capable of in my present happy state of mind is related to them.[10] What is worse, I sometimes fear that I may have gotten something in my genes from them. But then, I am hopeful!

I embrace you, my dear boy, or, shall I say, we hug you and love you because Bé (her full name: Engelberta, Beatrice de Waard) too loves you very much as she does Karli. Soon, she will write herself; she wants to let you both know how grateful she is for your love and goodness, which she senses in your letters to me. (I'll write Karli and Heini tomorrow.)

As ever,
Leo

[1] See letter no. 22, n. 2.
[2] Ferenc (Franz) Ferdinand Baumgarten. See "Biographical Notes".
[3] Georg Simmel. See "Biographical Notes".
[4] Essay on Stefan George. See letter no. 19, n. 3., and no. 16, n. 6.
[5] Allusion is made to the seriousness of his T.B.
[6] Karl Polányi and Henrik Herz both of Budapest, mutual friends of Lukács and Popper. See letter no. 24, n. 6.
[7] Reference is to the three years' waiting period. In fact, Leo Popper was dead by October 1911.
[8] "True, it is bad enough, but it is not a tragedy!"
[9] Not extant.

10 The strained relationship between Leo Popper and his parents, the world-famous cellist David Popper and his wife, was a well-known and much talked-about fact in their circles. Contemporary accounts give most of the blame to the parents' behavior.

26. TO SÁRI FERENCZI

Budapest

January [?] 1909

Dear Sári,

I don't know how to justify it or how to make amends for this letter and the responsibility of it almost takes my breath away. Everything seemed so beautiful yesterday; we looked at each other from a distance and still we saw everything so clearly. We looked into each other's eyes with a certain inevitability, although these eyes could only be like stars, bright and unreachable. Why do I make this attempt to get closer to you? Why?

I have the feeling that after yesterday I know you better and can see what lies behind your gestures. You were sitting on the sofa close to me, then leaned forward as if waiting for something, your arms thrown back in a wide circle; you were motionless for a minute but there was more tension in your repose than in any of your actions. At that very minute anything could've happened, and whatever explosive situation might have occurred depended on whoever sat across from you. Those waiting, thrownback arms could have swiftly entwined the other or with the same swiftness of gesture could have shown him the door. Everything depended on the other person's word. But then I left, aware of the fact that I would never bring myself to say that word, knowing that you are ready only to hear me speak and that your arms would go limp. Thus I disappeared, but not before seeing the whole thing, understanding both you and your friend[1] (who is possibly also a friend of mine) and the world you live in. Oh yes, for both of you facts mean nothing, and still both of you are living very much in the real world. Facts have no part in your lives, but life holds for you uncounted possibilities encircling you in a merry dance, knocking on the door of your soul; and you can't help but let these possibilities in—although the soul of your friend is like a great white circle and yours resembles a many-colored excursion. So, you let those possibilities in but only to touch you lightly and then depart to continue the merry dance. He may—just may—move along if the possibility presents itself but you will, I am sure, remain in your tranquility. Possibilities provide him with form and you with content. But what about me?

I've been debating the whole day and still don't know whether, in fact, I'll send this letter.[2] When I left you, there was a cry inside me—a cry for a great communion, for letting the mask of my intellectuality drop if only for a moment; something inside me was crying out for someone to understand me if only for a moment and to declare: I can see who you are and I love you! I wanted desperately to resist the temptation to let go, and so I held on to the mask with both hands so tightly that the plaster-cast cut into my flesh. I was hoping it would adhere so that there would be no hours of weakness any more and no possibility that I would lose my grip on myself. But now I cannot go on like that; the mask has been dropped and is lying around me in a thousand pieces. Now I am alive again and am myself; but then again: I am ashamed of my nakedness like Adam and Eve once were, trying to cover up their nakedness.

But the question remains: why this need to be recognized by somebody who'd be able to love what has been seen? And why the fear at the same time that somebody would glimpse what is behind the mask?

How could it happen that I could wish for absolute communion —I, a person half of whose life was spent with keeping distances and who (do you remember?) could be utterly miserable because there was an occasion of a break through that distance? I don't care for facts, either, be they mine or somebody else's, with the difference, though, that I have no possibilities whatsoever as you do. My life is neither a pure great white circle nor a many-colored affair. It does not have the tranquility of a mountain lake; it consists of hurrying, noise, and racing—but to where? Who knows? There might be something somewhere to which I would attach myself, a mirror that reflects my rays, a deed that brings self-recognition. Is it really possible? I don't know and can't fathom what that could be; I only know that I am on my way towards something and everything else is but a stop on the road. I see beauty around me but it holds no interest for me; I cannot stop and take a rest although I feel a tiredness now and know only too well that I am heading toward the emptiness of a wasteland. Any accomplishments fall from the tree of my life as so much overripe fruit, leaving the barren branches brooding in the autumn wind, not even remembering the previous crop and not believing that it will bear new fruit. My life possesses nothing but these fruits. I have only accomplishments, and I am aware that they alone can make me human; but how can they do that when they cease to be mine the minute they're born? My soul yearns for them but remains untouched by the possibilities. They have no connection with my life and provide neither form nor content for it. The three of us discuss Platonism a lot. But while you and your friend talk about Plato, I am interested only in Socrates. Plato I am unable to imagine; he is present in every word I utter because I knew him before I had heard of him; yet the more I look at him the less I know about him. And Socrates? Oh, yes, he is a great dialectician, a strong man who is sure of himself; his words can humble the most self-assured. He is a man who has fought many battles and met his martyrdom with peace of mind. The soul of Socrates intrigues me greatly and I ask myself—and you too: What was Socrates like when he fell silent? I also ask: Why couldn't he ever keep quiet? Why did his beautiful formulations cut everything in half?[3] Why did this proud deceiver know everything better than anybody else? How was he able to be so composed and excited only by intellectual matters—and then be able to die this way? What is the meaning of the life of Socrates and that of his death? What was the life that was hidden behind his words really like?

Why couldn't Socrates ever keep silent? Why didn't he ever take the hand of one of the youth of Athens whom he loved and why was it that he never embraced any of them? Why didn't he fall silent at the end of the Eros-hymns but continued to talk into the wee hours and then joined another group of discoursing men? Why couldn't he be without words? But his words were the real thing—not like yours, Sári. When you talk, it is like little windows opening on narrow streets with their little white houses glowing in the afternoon sun, leading toward a definitive point, a beautiful meadow possibly, to watch the sunset from. Oh no, the words of Socrates left nothing unsaid; there was no trace of chaos there. But what was hidden behind those words?[4] We will never know for he was never silent. He went from one group to another, always speaking and never revealing anything; and when his feet began to go numb he said that a cock had to be offered to Asclepius.[5]

Why would Socrates regard death as redemption—a man who was full of pride and went through life so sure of himself? Why this longing for death which rejected all possibility of escape? Why was he happy that he would finally die?

Is it possible that that was kept behind his discourses? *Might it have been the ultimate recognition of the ultimate aimlessness of it all—the ultimate recognition of the ultimate hopelessness of his longing?* Were the discourses night after night only a thinly veiled disguise for the crying of desire within? Were the clear and razor-sharp formulations designed *to cut the roots of sentimentality?*[6]

Socrates had said that he knew nothing except that he could recognize who among any two was the lover. He understood also that these two—the lover and the beloved—must remain forever strangers; he knew that Eros lacks beauty and subtlety and richness. Eros longs for beauty precisely because he remains a stranger to it. I think this is the ultimate meaning of whatever Socrates did not say. *Might it be that the wounds of Philoktetes represent the life of Socrates—and that the magic sword which alone could close the wound has been lost?*

The question is, then: What does it mean that one is longing, and what is the object of longing? Can it be that there is an emptiness in the soul that cannot be filled by what is already one's own; it is a search for what is alien to oneself, does not belong to one's life and hopes to make one's own, to find the other to belong to. Longing may also be two hands touching if only for a minute and eyes looking into one another with the belief that yes, we have become one. Longing may just be the explanation Aristophanes found for the existence of Eros: all living creatures were part of a double cut in half by Zeus at one time and now are in search of the lost other half. Aristophanes was sure that at one time we were one, but Socrates understood that our love that is a striving for perfection must forever remain an unrequited one. There are those who belong to the tribe of Aristophanes' myth and they can find their other half in every tree and every bush; but Socrates is proven right at the end: nothing will ever make one out of the two. Socrates alone was able to glimpse this eternal duality; the others won't ever comprehend the truth of it.

The meaning of Socrates' life as I see it is to show how one can rise above one's own goal. It is a demonstration of how to live our lives, aware of the fact that we won't be tied down to our actions and that a great abyss remains between ourselves and the other in our embrace; nothing changes the fact that the other half remains forever a stranger.

Plato faced all this. He faced up to it squarely and then withdrew into his solitude, and his longing turned inward. His soul evolved into a brilliant white circle, producing mysterious flowers. Side by side they contain desire and fulfillment, joined together by force of the form though they will never become one. Socrates, however, did not possess form. His mask remained an unbreakable plaster-case. His longing never turned inward and he forever strove for the unattainable in order to become one with it. Socrates, however, knew perfectly well that nothing would ever make one of two, that Eros is the son of wealth and poverty who longs for beauty but can never be beautiful and thus remains a stranger to beauty. He could not but hold on to his mask, which consisted of words that never betrayed the desires behind them; the desperate cries of his loneliness remained inaudible behind the pathos of his discourse. This is the reason why he looked forward to his death; he may have been happy—we'll never know for sure—in the belief that the great communion will commence in death and his longing will finally be laid to rest.[7] "I owe a cock to Asclepius; do not forget it", was his last admonition because now he knew he would recover from his illness.

My mask lies in a thousand pieces at my feet—and my desires reach out in the night like so many branches, dried out by all that crying. And they lie in waiting. ... Should anything approach them, however, they'd be taken aback out of fear that old wounds would be reopened and cause new hurts and also out of the knowledge that no embrace would make one out of two. Thus, the time has come to take leave, carrying off a piece of the flesh that has touched one; life will be lonelier still and one will show some new wounds.

Plato possessed form but Socrates did not; pure dialectics is, after all, the very opposite of form. Absolute formlessness is a mask behind which anything can be hidden. Socrates was a sentimental man—in a true and deeper sense—and Plato was an artist; and there are no two things more opposite than form-giving and sentimentality. There is no reason to be sorry for me, dear Sári; being extremely proud because of my problematic existence, I could not tolerate pity. Do not take my hands into yours even if you feel that the gesture would assuage my pain momentarily. I do not want to quite lose you but would have to if you tried to hold on to my hands. I am now on my way. Where to? Who knows? And why? Again, who knows? I am going on my way alone and the day may come when I too will offer a cock to Asclepius, and a recovery will be realized.

You are not cross with me, are you, for my letting you look behind the mask? And you won't send me off, will you, because of what you have seen? Will you allow me now to put together the broken pieces of the mask and hold them against my face? They might just adhere to it permanently.

[1] Presumably Vilmos Szilasi (1889–1966), philosopher, who studied in Budapest, Heidelberg, and Berlin. After 1919, he emigrated to Germany and was assistant to Heidegger and Husserl. He fled Germany after the Nazi takeover in 1933 and lived in Switzerland until 1947 when he became professor of philosophy at Freiburg University. Among his works are *Platon* (1910) and *Wissenschaft und Philosophie* (1945).
[2] The addressee's answer proves that the letter has been sent off.
[3] Parts of this letter have been incorporated into several essays. For these passages see *Soul and Form,* pp. 92 and 93.
[4] Cited in *Soul and Form,* p. 92.
[5] Lukács alludes to Socrates' final request to Crito. See Plato: *Phaedo–The Death Scene.*
[6] See p. 14 of *Soul and Form:* "Socrates lives the ultimate questions ..."
[7] The theme was developed further in the essay "Charles-Louis Philippe" published in *Renaissance* in 1910. See also "Longing and Form," in *Soul and Form,* pp. 91ff.

27. TO BÓDOG (FELIX) SOMLÓ

Budapest
February 14, 1909

Esteemed Herr Professor,

Please do not consider it an importunity if I voice my deeply felt pleasure on the occasion of your appointment,[1] and please do not take it as a sign of arrogance if I express my sentiment that, beside being a personal victory, the appointment also means that a battle was won, an ongoing battle, namely, in which many of us around here have been active participants—with or without a battle-cry. Thus, as is the case with every true joy, our pleasure goes beyond a a subjectively felt satisfaction. May I also use this occasion to thank you for your thoughtfulness and the kind and valuable gift.[2] You obviously won't expect my critical evaluation in this case, so now I just want to express my warmest thanks for the book, and for the thought.

Once again, please accept my most sincere congratulations.

Yours respectfully,

György Lukács

1 Reference is to Somló's appointment as Professor Extraordinaire at the University of Kolozsvár (now: Cluj-Napoca, Romania), in Transylvania, which was preceded by fierce opposition on the part of the conservative forces due to Somló's liberal-radical leanings (and possibly his Jewish extraction).
2 The book in question is Somló's German language sociological treatise, *Zur Gründung einer beschreibenden Soziologie* (Berlin, 1909).

28. TO LEO POPPER

Budapest
[mid-April] 1909

My dear son, Leo,

Thank you for your postcard; I am looking forward to your critique.[1] Don't worry about the translation,[2] if that would put a strain on you. What was the matter with you? Tell me what was wrong and how you are now. *Don't forget!* Write about what you're working on and everything, your everyday life and health. Only this much today: is it true that you want to settle in Holland? If yes, where, and for how long? Do you want me to visit you there? Answer me honestly! I would understand if you preferred not to have extra company right now. You must know that once I am there, we'd spend a lot of time together—that is, with you and Bé—and I don't know how you'd feel about that. I can be heroic and not go; however, as soon as we're together, it is different. You know well that nothing you say will offend me.

I am sending along this fairy tale.[3] Hardly anybody has seen it and *I will not have it published ever!* (It is bad artistically, and in my opinion it is not abstract enough; it doesn't have the necessary light touch nor the translucence. Please comment!) The main reason for sending it is that it was written during the work on the Beer-Hofmann essay. I had already completed the lyrical part, that is, most of Part One, and the beginnings of Part Two, then suddenly this. It made it possible to finish the B. [eer]-H.[ofmann] on which I had already given up. This, however, does not represent the new phase mentioned to you. The most abstract part of that is now being done for the book.[4] If only I have enough time, it [the new phase] will happen. At any rate, my feeling now is that you have understood me and that only you saw everything correctly; and for this reason I am anxious to hear what you think. Don't mention the fairy tale to anybody if my name comes up (e. g., Karli[5] and the others don't know about it and won't ever). Send it back together with the B.[eer]-H.[ofmann].

Have no more time; more the next time because there is not much to tell right now. Write soon!

Hugs.
Yours,
Gyuri

[1] Of the just finished essay, "The Moment and Form: Richard Beer-Hofmann," *Soul and Form*, pp. 107ff.
[2] The Stefan George essay.
[3] "Midász király legendája" (The Legend of King Midas), which Lukács wrote in one single day according to the Ms, dated November 18, 1908. It tells the story of Midas, who offends a fairy and is cursed by the "golden touch." Unbelieving Midas travels merrily through many lands until he meets a girl on the seashore; she offers herself to the king, who first refuses. As she is about to leave for good, Midas embraces her and she turns into a gold statue. Midas breaks it into thousand pieces and scatters them into the sea.

Midas keeps wandering in hopeless longing and loneliness until the day he meets another (the dark-haired) girl. They exchange thoughts as well as fervent kisses but he doesn't dare to embrace her. One day, Midas tells of his curse; although he professes not to be afraid any longer, he refuses to touch her. They stay together but grow apart gradually. One day a shepherd comes along, playing a tune on his pipe. She listens and as he embraces her she protests but only weakly. Finally, she leaves with the shepherd. One day wanderers find Midas dead, clutching a white lily in his right hand. "Although withered, the flower did not turn into gold," ends the tale.
[4] Reference is to the *Dramabook*.
[5] Karl Polányi.

29. FROM LEO POPPER

Paris
April 19, 1909

My dear Gyuri,

About a month ago I wrote in my diary: *"Wie König Midas nie einen lebendigen Griff ins Menschenleben tun kann ohne statt des Lebens etwas Goldenes heranzuziehen, so ist es auch in der Kunst. Was wirr war wird ordentlich, was offen war wird geschlossen, was vielstoffig war wird einstoffig unter ihren Händen, und wenn man will ist das auch eine Tragik."*[1] Strange, isn't it? I wish I could reconstruct the line (from your essay) that started me off. I may have been influenced by the line in your B.[eer]-H.[ofmann] essay about "the tragedy of the subtle egoist who creates everything in his own likeness".[2] You may have been too! If so, it is interesting indeed how our trains of thought run along parallel lines toward a *piazza del Duomo*.[3]

The fairy tale therefore could tell me nothing new. The most surprising thing is that you *wrote a fairy tale*. The tale itself only emphasized certain passages of the Beer-Hofmann essay,[4] which I once underlined myself (with a thick, angry-red pencil too!). The fact that you found it necessary to retell a story out of the past may mean two things: (1) that the Midas-obsession has by now become so much, so neurotic and so painfully difficult to bear in its insistence on uniqueness that it wanted to show its true self by shedding the borrowed garment of abstraction or poetry; (2) that the breakthrough serves as a great healing process that eliminated a significant portion of the disease itself. Midas holds a flower in his hands; Midas is alive as is *the other person* (only the dark-haired girl disappears). Midas did not touch the girl out of fear, and the girl in turn listened to the tune of the shepherd (who was of a different ilk from Midas). Midas then tried his hand on a flower, and it turned out that he should've touched the girl as well.

In such cases the flower is the fairy tale. Midas "as such" cannot write fairy tales, not even a Midas tale, not even a bad one. Only a Midas who regained his health can tell the tale which then itself, *a suo tono,* becomes healthy and more and more beautiful.

My dear boy, don't fret: not everything that shines is gold, and not everything that is gold is solid.[5]

There is such a thing as gold-plated flesh: you only have to pierce it (something Midas is afraid to do and most other people perhaps wouldn't think of doing), and the blood would flow. I punctured your Ms on several pages and can guarantee that it flowed freely. You should try the same.

Following that, you should try to write another tale; even if you had to bathe in *aqua fortis* of 100 centigrade, it would pass. What kind of bath am I thinking of? Try not to write a word about "loneliness" for about six months. For one thing, it is dangerous: the theme may become *fashionable* among the *shmucks* and in a year's time we may encounter the phenomenon of the "Margaret-Islandization of humanity".[6] But above all, do it for your own sake. Go about it courageously or fearfully, but do it; read certain passages, the ending of the George essay[7] and a couple of more like it (you will find them, *now you will be able to*) and after that no more Lukács for you, neither reading nor writing. Because you don't know how to do it, you misunderstand him and would borrow the worst possible things from him.

I know, my dear boy, how you must feel, what your feelings are... But it is not as you think: I am aware that you cannot tell a sick man to be healthy. But you can tell it to someone who is convalescing and get results. And so I am convinced that this letter will be useful; its content is, after all, superfluous. I couldn't wish you any better than writing this kind of superfluous letter. I can see that you are on your way. Thus, I try my best to spur you on so that I can claim my laurels the day you achieve success, just as the heroes of histo[rical] mat[erialism] do. It all depends, of course, on your ability to overlook the trick employed here, and I urge you fervently to do so.

I realize more and more that one need not have to worry about you anymore. My diagnosis is: "growing sensitivity toward everything human and human relationships". Since this is a new condition, both the symptoms and subjective feelings are at variance with it; outwardly, it looks as if you have collected experiences in order to write poetic treatises. Upon closer examination, the opposite turns out to be true. Internally, your writings, as reflecting your state of mind, have such a sense of resignation and sadness in them that one is tempted to think the former is the case. (In my opinion, you are mistaken in your belief that nobody'd notice.) The situation as I see it is that you will still undergo a change with respect to your lyricism. Such magnificent thoughts as those on truth, limits of reality, etc.[8] will turn out simpler and smoother because they will be felt in an uncomplicated and truly lyrical vein. The problem is merely that your melancholy and your heavy-handed style are arbitrarily coupled; they obscure what they flank, namely, the beauty, vitality, and inherent truth of a really powerful reality that lies between the subjective state of mind and the symptoms. With regard to your insight into the *Problematik* of the inner life *(Seele)*, your B.[eer]-H.[ofmann] essay is one of your most profound and most sensitive works. (One can only harbor some doubts in principle about the passages on death, in the sense that *"ewig bleibt uns nur Verlorenes"*;[9] you forgot about that!) You have progressed enormously even since your George essay. Only the style is not yet in place: it tends toward the analytic with the result that the poetic passages have a curiously unfeeling quality instead of a discreetly felt one. And as I said before, the basic mood is all wrong; it is a dead end both in regard to form and content. No reason for a melancholy loneliness if there is so much understanding present; your theory that no road leads from the world of understanding to life is but—if you will pardon the expression—superficial.

While I am at it, something else. My dear boy, you are extremely light-headed because your Midas-theory is engendered by a rash induction. What was it that your Midas touched before that gave him such a bad experience? In my opinion, this Midas only *thought* of touching once in his life but since he didn't *dare,* he now thinks (with a bit of self-tormented sophism) that he is Midas.

And why didn't he dare to touch the girl? Because of the curse? Not at all. He was afraid that it would turn out to be a lie. Because he didn't love the girl enough to touch her. Was he to blame for that? Oh, no, she was not good enough for his love.[10] (M.[idas] has a friend who knows about such things for sure: he wanted very badly to be in love but he just *could not bring himself to it.*) Midas did not touch the girl, because she was already tinted with gold—under the skin. M.[idas] could not see this clearly, only he sensed a strangeness; he was afraid he'd be committing a *lie* if he'd touched her. It would not have been a catastrophe. But nothing good either. The real thing will come *for sure* when the *real girl* comes along; then there won't be any fear of life, or of things turning into gold. She will bring real understanding and M.[idas] will be able to pass through the gate into the world of the real and brightly lit life.[11]

My dear Gyuri, I can't tell you how happy I am about the coming summer and how thankful that you want to spend it with me. It will be beautiful, you'll see. We will work together, take walks, I will play music for you; we'll feel good and feel each other's presence. I think it will be Switzerland but I am not sure yet. Do you mind?

I feel strange nowadays. It looks as if I might be cured. I am being treated with the Marmoret-serum and I get better every day. This gives me great pleasure to notice (in my capacity as a little guinea pig). But let's wait and see.

For the time being, I have to be very careful and not do too much. *That* explains why the translation is not done yet. But it'll be done when you need it; just let me know.

The time allotted me for work (2 to 3 hours a day) I spend on my own work. I am now writing an article in German on Bruegel and the problem of matter.[12] I also do a litttle painting. Don't be angry that the translation takes a back seat.

And now, dear boy, I wish you well, and let me know as soon as you can what you think of my letter. I am very anxious to know, and it is as important to me as my own affairs. I embrace you with love,

Leo

P.S. Bé sends her many warm greetings and she is also looking forward to the summer. (Please try to write a little bit more legibly; I always have to transcribe your letters first in order to be able to read them.)

[1] "Just as Midas the king has never been able to extend his grasp of human life without coming up with a piece of gold instead of life, it is the same in the artist's case. What before was in disarray, becomes well-ordered, what was open will close up and multi-dimensional matter becomes one-dimensional in the artist's hands. If you want, this also can be called a tragedy."

[2] Quoted from the Beer-Hofmann essay, in *Soul and Form,* p. 112.

[3] Meaning the center of things.

[4] The title of the essay itself ("The Moment and Form") indicates the extent of "borrowing". Midas confesses to the girl: "I only possess moments but not life. . . . Life always slips away from my hands," etc.

[5] Ironical reference to the "compactness" of the Midas tale (10 pp.).

[6] Hungarian wordplay, not easy to reconstruct. "Margaret-Island" in the Danube at Budapest was the playground of the *nouveau riche,* complete with Grand Hotel, spas, and gambling casino.

[7] See *Soul and Form,* p. 89.

[8] Ibid., pp. 110–13.

[9] "Only what is lost will remain ours forever."

[10] Reference is to Irma Seidler.

[11] Lukács writes in *Soul and Form:* "From the world of understanding you cannot do more than look across into the world of real life; the gate that separates the two is closed forever..." (p. 113).

[12] The essay, "Pieter Bruegel der Ältere, 1520[?]–1569" was published in *Kunst und Künstler* (Berlin) in 1910, pp. 599–606. Reprinted in Hungarian in the posthumous essay collection, *Esszék és kritikák* (Budapest: Magvető, 1983), pp. 73ff. *Allteig,* a concept of "universal matter," is discussed briefly in the essay. It was basic to Popper's intended theory of the homogeneity of matter in the work of art [painting]. Popper wrote: "Jede Malerei gab seit jeher statt der Mannigfaltigkeit der Stoffe... ein besonderes Material von einheitlichem, spezifischem Gewicht... dem unfreiwillig die mystische Rolle zufiel, zu einen, was Gott getrennt hatte, ... der als ein, 'Allteig' alle Stoffe ausdrücken dürfte. ... Das eigentliche Material der Malerei, die Farbe, schafft eine Einheit, die alle letzten Unterschiede ertränkt." Lukács discusses Popper's concept in his *Heidelberger Philosophie der Kunst,* p. 131. See letter no. 58.

30. TO LEO POPPER

Budapest
April 25, 1909

My dearest Leo,

I should be working (on the problem of fate in Goethe, Kleist, etc.)[1] but your kind letter stopped me in my tracks; I got quite excited about it. It has been so long since I have been the subject of a discussion with someone; I mean that it was really about me. What you had to say hit home even if you're not right in everything. The living flower held by Midas[2] was meant at that time as bitter irony; Midas died at the end of my fairy tale. And today, I still find this to be the real truth of the tale—but more about that later. Now only one question: Why do you want to put down the other one?[3] I believe it is unjustified, therefore you've erred here and consequently you are not entirely right in what you think of me, although it would certainly be desirable if you were proven right. So much for the human side of the problem. As for the writing: everything you say is correct, even more cruelly so. My George–B.[eer]-H.[ofmann] period[4] is over and done with. What will come next? I don't know. The book is in progress;[5] what is new is that it is being written in the style of part one of the first draft, which discusses naturalism. Its tone is objective, powerful and nonlyrical, scientific, presenting many points of view. If I remember correctly, you liked that part particularly and even wrote once that you doubted I would be capable of writing like that today.[6] I am. My writing can be even more powerful; and my riches more plentiful. I am a scholar now without the lyricism of those times. Since the fairy tale and the Beer-Hofmann, I have produced only one lyrical piece, a letter, about what Socrates was like when he was silent. It was written to a girl[7] (to whom I was never close in the profound sense and to whom I was driven because of my hysterical state of mind). As to whether or not there'll again be a lyrical period: I believe so. I have certain plans in which the framework requires a lyrical element but, unlike in the past, it is in a rather indirect, distant, and essayistic vein. Thus you are right in assuming that my own development turned upward, toward health and strength. And what about life? In that respect I can't believe you, and I am not saying this in any hysterical or melancholic mood; I simply don't believe you. What is more, it doesn't even make me sad. I ceased to be Midas in that I have no fears anymore, but I don't think I will ever want to touch "life".

I am not afraid anymore and someone has much to do with it, someone who loves me—I think—with whom I have spent a few beautiful days and have exchanged letters full of hope, and with whom I expect to spend pleasant days together in the future. She wrote to me once: "You walk faster than the others and don't ever stop to pick up the joy of the moment that is offered to you because you fear that you'd want to drop it so fast that it would fall back on the others behind you.

I ask you with great urgency: don't try to show so much forbearance toward others. I can see opening your eyes in sober appraisal whenever fragrance, rapture, or life tightly closes the eyes of the other (if for a second only); and so, the ecstasies of life pass you by. It is a heavy burden, isn't it, to take on the suffering of others? I myself become angry for feeling empathy. It is different in your case. You only need your own tears for your development; and the sufferings of others are a hindrance because they make you stop in your tracks, and you cannot help stopping because you feel sorry for others. Do not show forbearance toward women, and don't ever be sorry for them because it may appear as if you'd devalue them. We are not here to be a hindrance but to be steps leading you upward and forward."[8]

The writer of these lines is a very estimable person; I felt better just reading them; and they gave me courage, but they did not make a believer out of me. No, I don't believe that there are direct paths leading from understanding to life. (Please note, understanding is not meant as one of the many forms of life but—as is the case with me—as a fundamental principle.) The others, the ordinary men, still cling to the belief that understanding may bridge the gap separating one person from another. Fate recoils from understanding, but fate is synonymous with life. Do you remember what I wrote in my Kassner essay?[9] I have an even deeper insight into the problem now: the Platonist is the one who is bereft of fate, to whom nothing ever happens and whose chosen form is the essay, prose, because fate never appears in it in any form. (The Platonist may, at most, reflect upon it.) It is true: you'll find plenty of reflection but you'd do well to remember the simple but wise simile of *Minna von Barnhelm*:[10] one is most voluble about what one does not possess. I think I am a man without fate. I can state this without pain, today when I have people like you, Baumgarten,[11] and someone else, who all love me. I also have to realize that my love cannot be a part of your life and yours cannot partake in mine—I don't have one. I believe this to be the truth—now and forever more. I believe that this constitutes the fundamental *Problematik* of the critic's life, and also that in this respect I represent the purest type of critic. This proud statement contains a tinge of sadness, a lot of self-esteem—and by now, great strength. This is not merely a theory. Listen to me: there were women in my life you don't know about, cannot even guess at, and that is what I learned from the experience.

Midas was afraid, remember this, because already once in the past somebody turned into a gold statue in his embrace. It is true not only in regard to eroticism; it is generally true. Keep in mind that I told you all this in all calmness and melancholy. What is the meaning of our friendship? What can I offer you? George begins one of his poems: *"für heute lass uns bloss von Sternendingen reden!"*[12]

Can't you see that even you, the person who is closest to me in all the whole world, has talked to me only about *Sternendingen,* that our friendship is a *Sternenfreundschaft?*[13] I say this without a trace of bitterness. Tell me: if you are faced with a big problem, a real life-threatening situation, do you ever think of discussing it with me, and would you expect help from me? I am not jealous of Karli or Heini[14]—but don't they come first when it is about "life" and not understanding, when it is a question of reality and not ideas? Would you dare—and here absolute honesty is a must—answer this with a categorical "not true"? You could not, could you? And that is the story of my life, always and everywhere. It is very difficult to explain but whenever there is a touch of real life—even if it is emanating from me—a gradual withdrawal follows; everything slips out of my hands. Your present happiness is the first time things seem to be different, but I still fear that my hands would reach out again only to touch the *Sternendinge.*

In one respect you are absolutely right: the tone is bad, the viewpoint *ditto;* it is bad because it is sentimental, and sentiment should have been kept out. I am convinced, though, that the source of my (intellectual) riches is my being what I am. One pays for everything; I pay by "sacrificing" life. It would be unseemly to shed tears on this account; it would not be aristocratic.

In sum, the healing process is there but in a different sense from what you thought. Now to more practical things: Osvát[15] refused to publish your article. Met an acquaintance, though, who would like to have it for the art journal *Ház*[16] (it is the house organ of *KÉVE*[17]), complete with reproductions. What do you think?

Switzerland is all right with me; it doesn't matter where we meet. I would have loved to see the architecture of Holland with you, but that is now unimportant. I am so glad that we'll be together. Don't worry about the B.[eer]-H.[ofmann]; whenever it's done, it is done. Your main business is your health, take care of yourself, don't work too hard—either for yourself or for me.

One more thing: around here everybody regards me—Karli included—as a man of strength, without serious problems. Don't write to them about me. They don't really know me and I don't really want them to. And nothing about the other person either. They might guess her name—without really comprehending what is going on—and I don't want that. Or is it possible that I am mistaken, and that I misjudge how they perceive me? I'd be interested to know.

God bless you! I really tried to write legibly but I am afraid I didn't quite succeed. Please forgive me for that. Kiss the hands of Bé. I embrace you warmly,

Yours,
Gyuri

[1] *Dramabook,* Book 2, chapter 3, "The German Classical Drama," pp. 219–306 of the Hungarian edition.
[2] See letters no. 28 and 29.
[3] "The dark-haired girl," Irma Seidler.
[4] 1908–9.
[5] The *Dramabook*.
[6] See letter no. 25.
[7] Sári Ferenczi. See letter no. 26.
[8] Letter of Hilda Bauer, sister of Béla Balázs, was written on April 7, 1909. Deposited at the Lukács Archives.
[9] "Platonism, Poetry, and Form," in *Soul and Form.*
[10] Comedy of Gotthold Ephraim Lessing (1722–87), written in 1767. Minna, endowed with much common sense, makes the remark about her beloved, Major Tellheim: "Er spricht von keiner; denn ihm fehlt keine" (He does not speak of virtues because he possesses all of them).
[11] Ferenc (Franz) Ferdinand Baumgarten. See "Biographical Notes".
[12] "Today let us talk only of unearthly things." Stefan George's poem is from the volume *Der siebente Ring*.
[13] "Unearthly friendship."
[14] Karl Polányi and Henrik Herz, mutual friends.
[15] Ernő Osvát, editor in chief of *Nyugat*. The article in question, "Párizsi levél" (Letter from Paris), was written in February 1909, in Hungarian. Popper's radical anti-impressionism was unacceptable for *Nyugat*. First published in Budapest in 1983.
[16] *Home.*
[17] Hungarian artists' club, founded in 1907.

31. TO LEO POPPER

Budapest
May 22, 1909

My dearest Leo,

I have an awful lot to do. I'll be going to the theater tonight (Reinhardt[1] is here with *As You Like It*) and wanted to do some more work before I go; but your letter made me so happy that I sat down to answer it right away (partly too, to make you feel ashamed of your long silence). I know, I know that there are right now other, more important things to take care of. Unfortunately, I am making very slow progress with my book.[2] At present, I am rewriting the part on Hebbel. (The chapter on the French drama is done.) The work gives me a lot of trouble. [. . .]

As things stand now, I will spend my summer vacation with you. The reason I won't be coming sooner is that I have promised myself not to leave [Buda]Pest until the book is finished. I may renege on my promise but not that soon, for technical reasons. I always need a lot of books and it makes no sense to carry along a library for the rewriting of certain parts that may take no longer than 3-4 days. I will need many books for the last chapters too but in that case it is in proportion to the work to be done. Of course, this is not all for the summer: I'll take my doctorate in the fall[3] and have to read Old German literature for that. And since I now have a feeling that I could find a new tone for the essay, I'd like to do some of the writing. You can imagine what an enormous apparatus I'd have to travel with and everything has its limits.

By the way, for the last couple of days I have been thinking about the publication of my essays. For example, there are the essays on Novalis, Kassner, George, Beer-Hofmann, and a few could be written in the summer and fall, namely, a great Storm essay and a short one on the correspondence of the Brownings.[4] The whole thing could be entitled, "A lélek és a formák. Kísérletek" [The Soul and the Forms. Experiments]. What do you think? Isn't "kísérletek" [experiments] a beautifully appropriate word, instead of the dull and abstract "essay"? It would have an "Introduction"—e. g., a letter to you—on the form of the "attempt" and the justification of its lyrical nature from a scientific-psychological and formal point of view. Do you think it's worth the effort? The idea is dear to me; I am afraid, though, that it would make a *belles-lettres*-like impression and I would not want that. Please write and tell me what you think, in all honesty.

I am in a hurry and have to stop. Kiss Bé's hand many, many times; what she wrote moved me deeply. Those guys[5] are reading your article. They liked it but thought it untimely, and asked for something different. I don't have any idea whether they pay or not. Write a few lines about it.

With warm embrace,

Yours,
Gyuri

[1] Max (Goldmann) Reinhardt (1873–1943), German-Jewish theater director, at the helm of the *Kammerspiele* and *Deutsches Theater* in Berlin. Started the Salzburger Festspiele in 1920, then moved to Vienna in 1924. In 1933, emigrated to the United States.

[2] *Dramabook*.

[3] Lukács received his *second* doctorate in October from the Philosophical Faculty of Budapest University (main fields of interest: aesthetics, German and English languages and literature).

[4] For the essays, see *Soul and Form*. The "short essay" on the Brownings was never written.

[5] See letter no. 30, n. 16 and 17.

32. FROM FERENC (FRANZ) FERDINAND BAUMGARTEN

Berlin
May 27, 1909

My dear friend,

I did not want to come with empty hands and so I remained silent. I preferred not to write at all for an unusually long time and then, for an even longer time, not to write you in any detail.

At last, I went over chapter one.[1] My delayed answer will perhaps be more understandable if I remind you that I moved four times in the last four weeks[2] and that the nightmares and the thousand problems of the final move, the search for and the furnishing of an apartment and the start-up of a regular household, are still with me.

The translator often misunderstood the text, which is to a certain degree your fault because you aspire to write concisely and still exhaustively on all possible configurations of a *Problematik*, resulting at times in ambiguities and abstruseness. I have noted on the first page all the places where I have made extensive changes. You have to double check, though, to decide whether I interpreted the text correctly and to make sure that in my eagerness to simplify the language in other instances I did not go beyond your original intention.

Your translator has insufficient sensitivity for the possibilities of the German language, especially with regard to syntax. Most conspicuous are the many Hungarianisms (e. g., excessive use of *pronomina possessiva*). Shall I keep the text here and send it to Simmel later together with chapter two or shall I send it back to you? I'd gladly go over chapter two also. Now that I am more relaxed, the editing should go faster, and it should be even easier once I get to the part on Meyer.[3]

I am very pleased with chapter one: it is to the point, it shows a keen eye for what is essential and is so innovative in its comprehensiveness that it can rightly forgo anything that may be original but merely decorative. One can see that you have a complete mastery of the material and proceeded from there to penetrate the material and to reconcile seemingly accidental details. I am eagerly awaiting the continuation.

You should not torture yourself with ostensibly objective self-criticism. Already your comparing yourself with Dilthey[4] reveals your inclination toward self-recriminations. You want to compare your first work with D.[ilthey]'s most mature and most unique work even within his own *œuvre!* But Dilthey, as you well know, is not simply an exceptionally high measuring rod, he is an entirely unique phenomenon in Germany! Yes, my friend, you may look forward to your future in Germany with great expectations. You may be only 160 cm (or is it more?) tall, but the way I see you is standing up there on the pedestal of your book, and ascending. *Ergo:* have hope and confidence, also a bit of stubbornness and courage like that of our friend, Ulrich von Hutten:

So Gott will, soll's nicht werden gwendt,
und sollt' ich brauchen Füss' und Händ,
Ich hab's gewagt![5]

I would like to persuade you to give the Hungarian text as it is *immediately* to the publisher. Necessary changes could more easily be made in the galleys. I am dying to see our book in print—I say ours, because of the deep interest I took in the fate of the book—*silicet ut prostes sosiorum pumice mundus,* and then go and tell the world how much is in it.

I am still laboring on Meyer,[6] and it will be good if I ever finish it. have put more of myself into it than anything I have done so far.

Otherwise, I have become an old person overnight, emotionally speaking. Or it might just be that I became 10 years younger because I was like that 10 years earlier—namely, withdrawn, reclusive, and resigned. I think it is called the *Gelehrtenstimmung*. I haven't met a a single soul as yet (didn't even look up Frl. Heine[7] and most likely won't go to see Simmel either), and my wish is to stay that way, *regardant le monde à travers les vitres*. The only break in my routine is my daily horseback ride on the beautifully soft paths of the *Tiergarten,*[8] under the young trees. The *Pension* I live at has an excellent location next to the *Tiergarten* and the food is very good. I also like the company of all the extremely well-mannered and extremely dumb people living here.

Write to Simmel, please![9] You may mention to him *en passant* that the George essay has been returned to you and you don't know what to do next. He will no doubt show you good will and offer his help.

Please send chapter two soon. Continue writing on your book and to me. Good bye!

Yours faithfully,
Franz Baumgarten

P.S. Excuse my handwriting but I am very tired.

1 "The Drama," first chapter of Book One of the *Dramabook* (50 pp. long).
2 Baumgarten's eccentric personality and life-style were well known.
3 Conrad Ferdinand Meyer (1825–98), Swiss poet and writer, represented the so-called "poetic realism". Among his many historical novels: *Huttens letzte Tage* (1871), *Jürg Jenatsch* (1874), and *Gustav Adolfs Page* (1882).
4 Wilhelm Dilthey (1833–1911), German philosopher, historian of culture and philosophy. Most influential were his *Weltanschauungslehre,* the theory of *Geisteswissenschaften,* and methodological problems of the theory of history. Author of *Das Erlebnis und die Dichtung*.
5 Ulrich von Hutten (1488–1523), *Rechtsritter,* poet and humanist. After 1520, a comrade in arms of Luther and Zwingli; as an act of defiance against Rome, he switched from Latin to the vernacular. His most famous poem: "*Ich hab's gewagt mit Sinnen*" (1521). Trans.:
"If God will so, it can't be made undone
If I should break all my bones
At least: I've dared!"
6 Baumgarten's main work, *Das Werk Conrad Ferdinand Meyers: Renaissance Empfindung und Stilkunst* (Munich: Beck, 1917).
7 Anselma Heine (1855–1930), German writer.
8 Berliner Zoo.
9 See Simmel's reaction to the manuscript: letter no. 37.

33. FROM LEO POPPER

Wengen
June 7, 1909

My dear good Gyuri,

This time, I really couldn't answer sooner because when your letter arrived I was about to leave for Wengen and had to finish a maquette, which I worked feverishly on, as is only possible with the pressure of an impending trip. I was working on the head of a marvelous mulatto girl, a little "animal" from Martinique, who taught me more about art than a dozen Jean-Paul Laurenses and Matisses and fifteen *ante rem* treatises on Van Gogh. Finally we were on our way; we arrived here and slept, and now my first activity is writing this letter.

And the first thing I will write about is inviting you up here. Do come, if possible in June, before you finish; you won't find such a quiet and peaceful place to work as this anywhere. We won't disturb you; we'll also work and your work is important enough for us not to try to distract you. Nobody is here but us and the *Jungfrau,* the *Chalet Edelweiss,* and the *Heimweh-Fluch;* thus, everything here makes you turn inward and encourages you to concentrate on yourself. The centripetality of this health resort is what we both need. My dear boy, come, because (1) This is the best time of the year, before the crowd arrives. (2) It's a great time for long walks. (3) It is cool. (4) It is cheap (5 francs until mid-June and 6 thereafter). (5) We might not come to Berlin after all but go to Paris for further treatment. (6) The other thousand good reasons I will tell you in person. The route: via Lauterbrunnen-Interlaken-Wengen. Do come, my boy, and do your work here. Both of us await you with love.

It is a very smart idea to have the essays published. I think the Gauguin belongs to it and the old Ibsen article too.[1] Of course, you won't include the G.[auguin], I know you too well; you are afraid that your readers will spot the lyricism and the fact that for you literature is only an excuse for self-portrayal. I still urge you to include it. In a country[2] in which only the (academic) idiots know their material, it means something that a literary scholar (of the stature of a Beöthy),[3] and a solid intellectual also, discusses the inner life and writes about *isolation,* in spite of the fact that the academic elite would gladly engage him in discourse. In this country of ours it is a wonderfully novel thing that there is somebody who knows *and* feels; and if this somebody is courageous enough to demonstrate that what he feels is more important to him than what he knows, then this person should be sovereign enough to demonstrate that he is not afraid to feel when he *doesn't* know. Maybe, just maybe, they would declare that since this person doesn't deserve all that God-given knowledge, they should take it away from him and *voilà,* you'd suddenly be standing on the road with the stigma of a poet and wouldn't have anywhere to go but to the Parnassus (although we have *two* feet, don't we?)!

That you thought of addressing the introductory essay to me touched me greatly; it is such a compliment that one can't do anything else but quietly pocket it (and in no way object to it). I am very curious about it and also a little afraid that in stating and justifying the lyrical nature of the essay (motto: the essay is *nebbech*[4] lyrical), you won't quite succeed in covering your tracks, i. e., the *pro domo.*[5] The lyricism of your essays must have already become obvious to all those people who read and couldn't understand them. Why should the only clear thing that they comprehend be that the author himself lies at the base of the mystery?

Of course you are fundamentally right: the essay is a lyrical form because just as the poet symbolizes concrete experience, the essayist chooses the poet as his symbol. But you shouldn't give people reason to raise the question of whether a Kassner[6] can serve as a symbol for Gy[örgy] L.[ukács]? It may be that the Introduction will be about something else, and so forgive the rash hypothesis. I like the word "experiments". Essay, in fact, seems to suggest the ultimate. One should imagine your essays somewhere between *esto* and *esse.*

God be with you, my boy. I reread your letter and now I see with resignation that one shouldn't expect you to carry along your whole library. I still trust you and my luck. Come, whenever you feel like. Bé says the same.

Yours,
Leo

[1] "Gauguin," a five-page essay on the predicament of modern man (and artist) appeared only in Hungarian, in *Huszadik Század* (1907); for "Gondolatok Ibsen Henrikről" (Reflections on Ibsen), see letter no. 3, n.l.

[2] Hungary.

[3] Zsolt Beöthy (1848–1922), started out as a novelist and literary critic, became an influential Hungarian literary historian of the positivist school and professor of literature at the University of Budapest. He was a member of the Hungarian Academy of Sciences, and at one time the President of the *Kis-*

faludy Társaság. From the 1890s he was known as a staunch opponent of progressive aspirations.

4 Yiddish word, here means "alas".

5 Here means "personality".

6 Rudolf Kassner. See Lukács's essay in *Soul and Form*, pp. 19ff.

34. FROM FERENC (FRANZ) FERDINÁND BAUMGARTEN

Berlin
June 9, 1909

Dear Friend,

Chapter two[1] has not arrived yet.

If I were you, I'd ask Simmel,[2] not George himself, to send the George essay[3] to a journal. In view of George's sacred and unbreachable reserve—which Simmel is aware of and deeply respects—Simmel's approaching George on your behalf would require a much greater effort than his recommending the essay to a journal, which would not involve any personal obligation. It is even possible that George has already heard about the essay from Gundolf,[4] whom he lives with most of the time.

I like your review in *Nyugat*[5] very much; it is somewhat ironic that it appeared in that ridiculous Ady issue side by side with the article by Hatvany,[6] who has become a *commis voyageur* and *agent provocateur* of literature.

My Meyer book[7] is far from finished; it is not really a substantial work. It is significant only for me because it is my first more or less peaceful work in the last eight years—everything else was the product of hysterical ebullitions. I am 28 years old and not even the crown prince of the smallest country, only a Serbian[8] crown prince who has stepped down.

I have often thought of suggesting to you that you prepare a collection of your essays. Diederichs[9] should welcome them with open arms. We will have to do something about it next winter. Perhaps we can involve Paul Ernst,[10] whom you will soon meet, or maybe ask Frau Andreas.[11]

My reply is supposed to appear in the July issue of the *Budapesti Szemle.*[12] Since I do not subscribe to it, I need to find out from you whether or not it was printed. Can you drop me a few lines about it?

Write soon!

Cordially,
Ferenc Baumgarten

[1] Second chapter of the *Dramabook*.
[2] See "Biographical Notes".
[3] "The New Solitude and Its Poetry: Stefan George," in *Soul and Form*, pp. 79ff. Stefan George (1868–1933), German poet and essayist, was an exponent of a lyricism aimed at self-contemplation. Famous for his aristocratic stance. Lived a withdrawn life, but was the "prophetic leader," the high priest of his *Kreis* (George Circle), composed of intimates such as Friedrich Gundolf, Karl Wolfskehl, and Ludwig Klages. Founder of the periodical *Blätter für die Kunst* (1892–1919). Among his works: *The Seventh Ring, Hymns*. References in several studies on Lukács incorrectly claim a personal relationship between him and George.
[4] Friedrich Gundolf, originally Gundelfinger (1880–1931), professor of literature at Heidelberg University, one of the closest friends and disciples of George. Allusion is made to the homosexual orientation of the George-Circle.
[5] *The West*. See letter no. 7, n. 1.
[6] Lajos Hatvany (1880–1961), son of Sándor Hatvany-Deutsch, sugar baron, one of the leading Hungarian-Jewish ennobled families. Sponsor and promoter of cosmopolitan ideas in Hungarian literature and cultural life, cofounder of *Nyugat*. The article in question is entitled "Departure".
[7] See "Biographical Notes".
[8] Allusion to the "Balkans" as a "cultural" region, and to the thwarted ambition of Baumgarten to be one of the "leading" intellectuals.
[9] Eugen Diederich's publishing house in Jena.
[10] See "Biographical Notes".
[11] Lou Andreas-Salomé (1861–1937), German writer of Russian extraction, first a revolutionary, later supporter of the "erotic movement". Friend and lover to many of the most famous men of the time: Nietzsche, Rainer Maria Rilke, Richard Beer-Hofmann, and Freud. Among her works: *Die Erotik* (1910).
[12] "Correction by Franz Baumgarten," was published in the *Budapesti Szemle* (Review) August 9, 1909, pp. 316–17.

35. TO LEO POPPER

Budapest
[mid-June] 1909

My dear Leo,

This is a delayed and superficial answer to your warmhearted letter. I have too much to do, I don't feel well, and I can hardly wait to leave; but it can't be done before the 30th. My work has progressed fast and well until now and even though I had done more work in each case than planned, I kept all my deadlines. Now I am working on the Maeterlinck chapter[1] and have found a neat theory that will help ultimately to link this "ballad-drama" to Wagner and to demonstrate in a thorough fashion—both artistically and sociologically—Wagner's great impact upon Maeterlinck, Wilde, d'Annunzio, et al. But I have headaches and everything goes slowly and poorly. I don't think that this piece and the comedy[2] will be done before September, and I don't want to leave until it is done. It is already a compromise for me to take the last one along to be finished later.

I am glad that you liked my essay plan.[3] I will not include Ibsen,[4] because it is not good, nor the "Gauguin"[5] because it is not weighty enough. I have a few more reviews like that, for example, on Schnitzler, Strindberg (re: Twentieth century), on Lajos Bíró[6] and Dániel Jób.[7] They are all quite good, but I don't want to publish a sort of *Collected Essays*. I'd rather have a few *great* pieces that are profound enough in themselves yet belong together and form a whole. Thus, I won't publish the new essays I plan to write this summer separately, but I'll wait to publish them all later in a volume.[8] You know, they don't understand around here yet that my "Gauguin" is an essay; even if an Ignotus[9] or a Béla Balázs[10] (to mention only the best) writes 30 pages, it is still considered mere journalism, or diary fragments. In our country, they still see a connection between the essay form and length; and since I have to fight for so many things, the "Gauguin" is not worth fighting for. The volume will be rich enough without it. Let's leave something for a volume of so-called "Posthumous Writings".

Well, God be with you, my boy. I am so nervous that I can't write any more, and it is so near to the time when we can talk that... but you know.

Please take care that I'll have a room around the first or the second, if possible with an electric light, because I work in the evenings; but if not, that is all right too. I'll write about the details of my trip when and if I know them myself. On my way I'll stop in Zurich for one day to visit Elza Stern[11] (now Mrs. Elek Bolgár).

So long, my regards to Bé. I embrace you warmly.

Yours,
Gyuri

[1] See part 5 ("After Naturalism") of chapter 12, entitled "Maeterlinck and the Decorative Style" in vol. 2 of the *Dramabook*.
[2] Chapter 13, "Comedy and Tragicomedy," in ibid.
[3] *Soul and Form.*
[4] See letter no. 3, n. 1.
[5] See letter no. 33, n. 1.
[6] "The Novelettes of Lajos Bíró," a review essay published in *Huszadik Század* (September 1908).
[7] "The Novelettes of Dániel Jób," review essay in *Huszadik Század* (January 1909).

[8] *Soul and Form.*
[9] Ignotus (Hugo Veigelsberg) (1869–1949), influential Hungarian literary critic cofounder and one-time editor of *Nyugat*. Promoter of the cause of modern literature, wrote in an impressionistic style. After World War I he emigrated, first to Vienna, then to Berlin, and finally to the United States. He resettled in Hungary in 1948.
[10] See "Biographical Notes".
[11] Friend of the family. Known as Elsa Stephani on the staff of the German-language daily, *Pester Lloyd*. Elek Bolgár was a sociologist.

36. TO LEO POPPER

Budapest
[mid-July] 1909

My dear son, Leo,

I am very scared, that is why I didn't answer your letter before now; but I cannot put it off any longer and have to own up to the truth. My great mistake was not to tell you way back that I won't spend the whole summer with you, that I planned to leave Wengen in early August. Now, the whole thing is turned around and I am so ashamed. In one word, my dear boy: I won't be coming before the end of July or the first week of August. Please forgive me and listen to what I have to say (I don't have to point out to you not to say a word about this to anybody!). You might have guessed by now. You may indeed know it already. And so listen: for the past 3–4 months, I have been having a blessedly beautiful correspondence with Hilda Bauer—no sense in keeping the name from you—the sister of Herbert Bauer.[1] I saw her in February and then again in April two to three times when she was in Budapest. Now, the whole family goes to Ammerland at the *Starnberger See*. And I *have to* go there for at least one month. I will explain it to you so that you won't overestimate what it means to me. I have to go there in order to gain clarity about our relationship. I live in Budapest, Hilda in Szeged; she teaches there and is tied to the place. Whenever she comes to Budapest it is for a few days only and there are others around us, etc.; this way, we cannot judge how things stand between us. We both look forward to those few days with great expectation and consequently they have a certain degree of hysterical tension; it is even worse if we can only snatch a few hours by ourselves. I can detect lately an increasing degree of hysterical tension even in our letters, especially in mine—but hers have something of it too—and I am afraid. I fear namely that a lie might enter into our relationship. Don't misunderstand me: what I am afraid of is that we may read more into our relationship than is actually there. And since this is what I dread, I decided to spend a whole month with her in order to find out where we stand. As for myself, I should not wish for a truly great and deep commitment; but if it turns out to be that way, "mély alázattal hajtom le a fejem", as Ady says,[2] and "görgessen a perc, az ő dolga bizony, merre, mivégre!" Anything that would make me stop on my way and settle with somebody better be a truly great and holy affair. And I cannot help thinking that all this letter-writing and the accompanying circumstances lend a hysterical, somewhat unreal depth and height to the relationship. Since *I don't want that to happen,* I'll go there, will be with her every day for a month or so, experience everyday life with her, and then it will all come out. It may take an even shorter time, and in that case I will come to you sooner.

You can see, can't you, why I want to deal with it this way and now? First of all, I don't want to go through another month of correspondence. Second, Cecile[3] will be there in August, and I want to avoid any gossip. It would be bad enough even if there were something going on, but at this point it would be worse. Not to speak of myself (or rather, of my parents for whom it really would be an unpleasant thing), but I cannot expose Hilda to any unpleasantness. Hardly anybody knows about the relationship and everybody thinks—including Cecile—that I will join the family in Ammerland because of Herbert to whom I am nowadays quite close, although people tend to overestimate the degree of our friendship, especially since I wrote the reviews.[4] But once she (Cecile, that is) is there, there is danger: you know she has a very sharp eye and a great talent for gossip.

There are other, lesser reasons. I am doing some essayistic work for which I can make good use of the University Library there [in Munich] while it is still open. It is the kind of work for which Herbert Bauer can be useful. (Those are the *admitted reasons* for going to Ammerland.) I *beg you to tell this only and nothing else* to your parents and to Bé as well.

I thought I would have the opportunity to respond to your letter in person, but now I can't even write because I have no energy left. I've worked too much, have headaches, feel tired and irritable. Only one thing: I liked the sculptures[5]—and I am not disturbed

by Maillol's influence. We shall discuss all this in detail. There is one thing though that I don't like: the theory of ecstasy. Do you understand why? One has to arrange one's work so that one keeps working away in a continuous process—not for the sake of the work but for one's own sake. One should be able to live the kind of life in which great ecstasy comes upon the completion of one's task; or at least, the completion should bring with it a new but still potent rapture. You have to come to a completion—this is my main philosophy of life. I think you yourself sense the importance of this. But how is this compatible with what you wrote about sculpting. We have to talk about that. I wish the time were already here! You feel, don't you, that not to come see you right away means a great sacrifice for me? But honesty toward myself and also toward her demands this sacrifice. Believe me, my son, you are more and more important to me and more than anybody else; and I know you'll understand what I *had* to do and won't be cross with me. Will you welcome me in August as if nothing happened, as if I had come directly to you? Will you please?
[. . .]

With remorseful love,

Yours,
Gyuri

[1] Alias Béla Balázs. Hilda Bauer (1887–1953), teacher, close friend of Lukács and others from the progressive circle. After the marriage of Irma Seidler, she and Lukács had a short-lived love affair.

[2] Endre Ady. The line is from the poem, *A percek aratója* (The Reaper of the Minutes), written in 1907.
Trans.: I bow my head in deep humility (and let the minutes trundle me along) wherever and to what purpose [they decide].

[3] Cecilia Polacsek, née Wohl, daughter of the chief rabbi of Vilna, married Mihály Polacsek. Her literary salon in Budapest was a favorite meeting place. "Mama Cecil" as she was called by young and old, introduced Lukács to Irma Seidler on December 18, 1907. Her children, Otto, Adolph, Laura, Karl, and Michael, went under the Magyarized name, Polányi.

[4] In 1909, Lukács's reviews of a drama by Balázs appeared both in the *Nyugat* and in *Huszadik Század*.

[5] Leo Popper's works, of which he sent a photo to Lukács.

37. FROM GEORG SIMMEL

Berlin
July 22, 1909

Dear Herr Doctor,

Thank you very much for sending me your study[1] and for the accompanying friendly letter, but I must confess, I am somewhat perplexed. When I told you that I was interested in your problems and I'd be glad to read your work, what I had in mind was to do it for my own enlightenment and to profit from it for my own work. To read the study in a *critical* sense and to pass judgment on it, I certainly would not promise, because that is beyond me. For many years, I have been working exclusively on investigating problems that I would like to see brought to a conclusion. And so, to tell you the truth, I have become a poor and uncritical reader. I have forgotten how to ask objective questions about whether or not a book is good or bad. I am only interested in whether or not the book serves my purpose, which obviously does not include a critical evaluation of it. In consequence, you won't find any book reviews written by me in the last decade, in spite of my many literary activities. It is entirely out of the question for me to read your manuscript and pronounce judgment upon it. Even if I wanted to, the size of your study would make it impossible in the foreseeable future. In view of the task I've set for myself, years may pass before I can study a work on the philosophy of art of such magnitude as yours. Nonetheless, I don't want to hide the fact that I feel very sympathetic towards the first pages in terms of its *methodology*. The attempt to derive what is most inward and sublime from the most external and commonplace conditions seems to me fruitful and extremely interesting. As for the content, however, the ambiguity of the psychological aspect asserts itself, which at times makes it plausible to arrive at opposite conclusions from the same presuppositions. Under these conditions, I feel it's only right to tell you quite bluntly that I cannot fulfill your request. This is not because of lack of interest or good will but simply because of my obligations to my own work.

As to your George article,[2] unfortunately I can't give you any decent suggestions. *Nord und Süd*[3] was the only possibility. I just happen to know that *Die Neue Rundschau*[4] will bring out a lengthy article on George in the near future; other journals are not appropriate, to the best of my knowledge. At any rate, you could try the *Süddeutsche Monatshefte,*[5] where I have no connections; but I don't believe that they would consider such a lengthy piece. On the whole, the length might prove the biggest obstacle to its publication as a journal article. And then again, if it were even longer, it might be an advantage because it could then be published as a brochure. You might consider expanding it. You could work out the individual points in more detail in regard to the philosophy of art, so that it could be offered as a slim volume to Diederichs in Jena or Piper in Munich.

Thank you again for your kindness. With warm wishes, I remain as ever,

Yours,
Simmel

P.S. Where shall I send your Ms?

[1] Lukács sent the translation of the first two chapters of his *Dramabook* to Simmel.
[2] See letters of Baumgarten, no. 32, n. 9., and no. 34, n. 3.
[3] *North and South,* a cultural and literary magazine in Berlin.
[4] *The New Review,* German literary magazine, founded by Samuel Fischer, head of the S. Fischer publishing house. Both the magazine and the publishing house are still extant. Thomas Mann frequently published there.
[5] *Southern German Monthly,* under the editorship of Paul Nikolaus Cossmann, archconservative publicist and German nationalist.

38. TO LEO POPPER

Ammerland
[July 25] 1909

My dear son, Leo:

Your letter remained unanswered until today—and I am sure you'll understand why. I can finally write because I have something to tell: it is final, I'll be in Wengen the first days of August. I had suspected as much. I wrote to you, remember, that all that letter-writing brought with it a kind of hysterical tension and the illusion of a mutual understanding. What shall I say: it turned out as I had thought. Or rather, it is a much more complicated thing than that: I love this girl very much but... A part of myself that is kindly inclined toward her, the poor thing, keeps suggesting to her: "It is not good for him to be with you and the best thing would have been if the two of you had never met". And then there is another voice inside me that keeps telling me: "This is not for you, all this togetherness; leave her." You are probably right in that it is not the Midas-mood this time. The reason: most of the time I don't have the feeling of being driven by metaphysical necessity or my innermost feelings; I think rather that it emanates from the relationship itself that we now have that I wish to leave her. As I said: most of the time... but that is another story. I am a much stronger person than I was last year and don't give everything that concerns me such a sentimental interpretation. What has happened here, I believe, has to do solely with the kind of relationship that has developed between us and is not the result of that self-deception of Midas you wrote about in your letter.[1] This time, it has nothing to do with her. I still regard her as one of the most remarkable human beings that I have ever come across, but ... the only way to express the situation is with that vulgar saying: "We don't suit each other." Were she a married woman, there could be a solution to the problem. Perhaps—and this she recognized clearly—we would stay together for six months, a year, or less, and would then part with a beautiful memory. But in this case, things are not so simple. They might lead to big problems one day. Hilda herself possesses great clarity about these things. However, she loves me much more than I love her; or rather, she is a girl and for this reason her reasoning doesn't influence her feelings to such extent as they do mine. (That is, it is a very complex situation because I do love her and still... But if you don't understand by now, I won't be able to explain it further.) I am incapable of a lie. I cannot commit myself to stay with somebody for a while when I know I would leave her one day (especially if I suspected that she might sustain inner hurts) but I am still unable to part with her in a simple, heroic way. What it all means is that there are serious problems here, mainly on her account.

Your letter was infinitely moving.[2] I thank you for it. It has done me much good in more ways than one. So long now. Will you write me till then? My regards to Bé and your family. I am looking forward to seeing you soon,

Gyuri

[1] See letter no. 29.

[2] Popper wrote to Lukács on July 8 that he was so impressed by Lukács's taking an active step and being "anti-Midas" that he was unable to harbor resentment. Rather, he urged Lukács not to come and mind his (Leo's) feelings; what alone matters is his own happiness. Hence Lukács's thanks.

39. FROM JÓZSEF VON LUKÁCS

Bad Ischl
August 23, 1909

My dear son, Gyuri,

I have received your kind and exhaustive letter of the 17th and above all I wish to express my happiness that you were so frank, honest, and friendly with me. I appreciate it all the more because I want you to know that you don't have a better and more faithful friend on earth than I.

I should write a lengthy reply, but I am incapable of doing so because I fear that I could not write the way I think; therefore, I'll limit myself to what is essential. This exchange of letters will perhaps have the lasting advantage that you'll bare your soul with greater confidence in the future—unlike in the past which was to the disadvantage of both of us.

Regarding Leo's[1] case, we disagree—again. But this does not mean that I do not have an *absolute* and *unshakeable* confidence in you. All I want is to save you from certain disappointments which you can't seem to be able to avoid and which have caused you grief in the past and will, unfortunately, do so in the future.

You are just like me. I too always had to have someone around who is a braggart. First it was Klein,[2] later Kornfeld,[3] and now it is somebody else. They certainly did not possess more energy than me, only more willpower, and the way they displayed it fascinated me and kept me in their bondage. They made me unduly appreciative and impressed so that I was unable to appreciate my own capabilities adequately.

I am afraid you have the same lack of confidence and I want to shield you from its harmful consequences.

Earlier, long ago I admit, you felt insignificant, as if you were a nobody, in front of Laci Bánóczi;[4] and if I disagreed with your glorified opinion of him, your mildest objection was, "Dear Papa, you don't know about these things". I can't say how sorry I am that I was right. I am not sure, but I suspect that apart from myself, you too made great sacrifices[5] that would not have been necessary had you been fully frank with me. Now you put Leo on a pedestal and place him high above yourself. May God see that you're not disappointed as you were with Laci and that the "bluffing" is not even greater than it was in Laci's case.

What I wish for you and consequently for myself is that you

learn to maintain the same merciless, almost cruel, objectivity towards your friends as you are able to do in your home environment.

You yourself freely admit that I am very liberal and have let you develop as you choose. I do this consciously because I have an immense trust in you and because I love you dearly. I will make every sacrifice necessary so that you can become a great man, recognized and famous. My greatest happiness will come when I am known as the father of György Lukács. Precisely because this is the case, I would like to protect you and save you from further disappointments; I would like to see you select your company and your friends by the same principle of well-justified pride in yourself, and aristocratic selection that you deserve on account of your whole personality, your past, present, and future.

I am afraid that I am unable to express adequately what I really have in mind, and so I ask you that we continue this when we are together again. On that occasion, please do not demand only that I trust you infinitely but try to reciprocate with honesty and frankness. It will do both of us good if I am more fully aware of what is going on inside you, of those internal conflicts which affect your heart, emotions, intellectual endeavors, and your future plans.

Until then, I embrace and kiss you warmly, with affection and in friendship,

Your father

[1] Leo Popper. See "Biographical Notes" and his correspondence with Lukács. Allusion to Popper's engagement to Beatrice de Waard from Holland.

[2] Unidentified.

[3] József Kornfeld, at that time General Director of the Hungarian Credit Bank.

[4] László Bánóczi. See "Biographical Notes" and his letters to Lukács.

[5] Reference is to the generous financial backing for the Thalia experiment that Lukács's father provided, and to the investment of time and energy of Lukács himself. Contemporaries mention—without specifying the issues—Bánóczi's irresponsible behavior.

40. FROM OSZKÁR (OSCAR) JÁSZI

Budapest
August 26, 1909

Dear Gyurka,[1]

Back from my trip among the minority population, in the Slovak countryside, I am at last answering your kind letter.

I truly regret that you are apprehensive about my suggestion to shorten your article[2] and even suspect some hidden reasons behind my request. Well, my friend, we have no one else in mind to entrust the field to because there is simply nobody in Hungarian aesthetics who represents a viewpoint that comes close to ours. Under these circumstances, your cooperation is especially valuable to us and would remain so even if another aesthetician with a more congenial point of view suddenly appeared on the scene, because we welcome all kinds of differing views as long as they are earnest and based on as thorough a knowledge as yours.

It follows that my request had no hidden motives. It was simply the outcry of an editor[3] who has no extra space for literary delicacies at a time when the business of sociology and social policy is in such bad shape. As for the Hatvany article[4] you mention, the analogy is not correct: first, because the article was only ten pages, and second, at that time I did not face a surplus of contributions. (By the way, I was severely reprimanded in that case too because of giving too much space to aesthetic concerns.)

Since this is the case, I ask you again for help. Perhaps you could divide the article in two; it would make it easier to place it. Of course, the suggested length of 6 to 8 pages was not meant in absolute terms. It won't be a disaster if it turns out to be 10 to 12 pages.

Regardless of what you decide, rest assured, and I expect you to be assured, that not one iota of undermining or intrigue or whatsoever entered the picture in this case.

Warmest regards from your devoted friend,

Oszkár Jászi

[1] Variation of a nickname for "György".
[2] "On the New Hungarian Poetry," which was published in two consecutive issues of the journal *Huszadik Század* (Twentieth Century).
[3] Jászi was founder and after 1906 editor of *Huszadik Század,* the journal of the Hungarian Sociological Society.
[4] Allusion to an article by Lajos Hatvany on Endre Ady, the 20th-century Hungarian poet, published in the February 1908 issue of the journal.

41. TO LEO POPPER Budapest
October 26, 1909

My sweet good Leo,

My telegram contained a lie[1]—and since you are bound to find it out anyway, I better tell you the truth. Your telegram arrived before your letter did but... but I was afraid there was something seriously wrong with you—an impression reinforced by your post-card—and so I read the letter. I tell you, a great weight has been lifted from my shoulders! I hope you won't be angry at me for all this.

I shall send a detailed answer in a few days after I have reread "Sterne."[2] First of all, let me tell you that your letter made me very happy; you did me a good turn. Through this criticism of yours, all of your and any future approval of me and my work has gained an additional weight. I cannot tell you what a great feeling of security a critique such as this, *coming from the inside,* gives me. It is even more important if the critique is a negative one. I don't want to talk much more about it, but you should be aware of the fact that you were the only one to have ever understood me, and in this respect (but not *only* in this respect, of course) you have become even more important to me. Your word has significance; it gives me pause and makes me reflect and can be the source of either joy or sorrow. As you know, everything that is part of life is valuable, and the sorrow is just as important as the joy, maybe even more useful—for me, at least. I write all this so that you can measure the extent of my gratefulness; I can only say that I am very, very thankful to you my dear boy for all that your letter told me.

Now to the article: I'll go over the "erotic" part. I was afraid that it would turn out just as you said but Béla Balázs[3] (who liked this piece the best) dispelled my doubts. I will take a closer look now. As to the other point you made: more discussion is needed. I feel, namely, that exactly the opposite is true—meaning that your judgment was absolutely correct.[4]

Well, "Sterne" may be a bad article but the approach is good—and regardless of everything—it is mine. I know that we'll have a lot of discussion about this and thus only a few words now. I very much doubt that in this case the problem presents itself as the question between "closed and open art forms"[5] for the simple reason (although the difference appears the same, formally speaking) that everything that is *only a metaphor* in art (after all, all art is closed) is in the case of *literature a fundamental difference of forms;* the difference between the form of drama and the (primitive epos) epic. Because of its spatial nature, art at one point or another has to be finite; the possibility of its continuation is but a metaphor. In the case of the epic form to which I referred, it is not a metaphor but partly an historical and partly a formal truth. Let's go from here to my main argument: the objection you raised here (re: metaphysics) can be applied to all of my writings as well—especially to the first chapter of my book.[6] What is, after all, my aesthetics based on? On the assumption that all genuine and profound need for expression finds its own typical way—its scheme, if you will—which is the form. (By now, I've arrived at the innermost roots of the problem: the content of our self cannot be communicated; a scheme of the art work alone is capable of communicating a reflection of the contents to the receiver. The conscious application of this insight is the artistic form; just think of the Oedipus example I have in the first chapter of my book.)[7]

I concede only this much: that it was premature of me to try to work out a theory of the epic form, and that it is too artificial and inconsequently presented in my "Sterne." It may be so—it is indeed probable. But I regard my approach as basically correct, and I think—at least for now—that I am on the right track. I think it is necessary for my development and the idea happens to be mine (which doesn't mean that it would not be a deep and great feeling to work it out together with you). Besides, although I had sensed the problem of "organicity" and "unity", I have become fully conscious of it through your theory of the *Allteig* (universal substance).[8]

In a word, if you send the article, send the detailed critique along. [. . .] After you have read all the essays for the planned collection, tell me whether or not I should go ahead with the publishing. Only if it appears to make a unified, strong, rich, and good volume will I consider its publication; because it is not that important, nor am I in any big hurry to have something published.

One more thing: I was very vehement in my counterargumentation. If you wonder why, it is because I wanted to make my stand loud and clear. I know that I'll have to reflect on it for a while. Will keep you informed.

Another thing: I have been greatly helped by your letter; I am thankful and glad to have read it. With warm embrace, yours,

Gyuri

[1] Reference is to Leo Popper's letter of October 25, 1909, containing a sharp criticism of Lukács's "Sterne" essay, followed by a telegram of Popper asking Lukács to destroy the letter unread. Presumably, Lukács sent a telegram to Popper stating that since the letter came first, he had already read the letter.
[2] See "Richness, Chaos, and Form: A Dialogue Concerning Lawrence Sterne," in *Soul and Form*, pp. 124ff.
[3] See "Biographical Notes".
[4] Popper wrote, among others: "I don't like this article... not well executed, formally speaking. ...It is excellent in terms of psychology... but there is an arbitrariness in connecting it up with eroticism," etc., etc.
[5] Popper's "A Dialogue on Art," written in German in 1906, begins as follows: "As you know, there are two different art forms: closed and open, the former being the realization and the second the promise... the finite and the infinite." Lukács incorporated some of it in his Sterne essay. See *Soul and Form*, p. 144. First published in Hungarian in *Esszék és Kritikák*, pp. 5ff.
[6] *Dramabook*.
[7] In the German edition of the *Dramabook*, entitled *Entwicklungsgeschichte des modernen Dramas* (Darmstadt-Neuwied: Luchterhand, 1981), see p. 29. Lukács states, among other things: "Die Totalität und den Reichtum des Lebens kann das Drama nur rein formal ausdrücken."
[8] See letter no. 29, n. 12.

42. TO LEO POPPER

Budapest
October 27, 1909

My sweet good son,

Since yesterday I have done nothing but think about your letter. (Your second letter has also arrived in the meantime.) Well, I again reread the Sterne essay and now I am going to tell you what I have to say: I sensed too that something was wrong with the "eroticism" if it was meant to be the same as I had understood it to be at the very beginning of the project when we discussed it. As you know, the essay wasn't finished in Lucerne, and I continued to work on it in [Buda]Pest—making numerous minor changes along the way with regard to the conception of the whole. Your objection is correct as far as it goes; but what is there is not the same as what was intended (it is a different question whether it has come off...). I feel stronger than ever that this essay is a satire, complementing Beer-Hofmann and George,[1] do you understand? My remark should be taken symbolically; remember, you wrote upon receiving the

B.[eer]-H.[ofmann] essay that I should stop writing about estrangement among human beings.[2] Do you also remember that I told you half-jokingly in Lucerne that I am now writing about *inadequacy*. What I mean by that: I write in a detached way, i.e., not in lyrical vein. The point of the whole thing is that last remark, that all that talk was a *highly unnecessary preparation*.[3] In turn, the disclosure by both men of the innermost content of their thoughts is but a preparation for that last remark. I think I didn't quite bring it off; I also believe that the changes that are needed are opposite from what you suggested. I have to *underscore* what you immediately perceived, namely, that the girl becomes a mere tool in the second half of the conversation, or, to be more exact, that both men are carried away in their conversations; and at the end they'll fall from their idealistic clouds down to the realm of the erotic. You are right in that the remark, that the girl "has sensed . . . the element of courtship"[4], is all wrong. What should be there instead is, that the girl "has sensed that even a conversation had an element of courtship (of the erotic)" (and she'd be right, because subconsciously it had). Do you understand now why this essay of mine has a depth which all of my writings lack? Because of its form [a satire], it is the critique of all of my writing and of my entire way of life, that is, the critique of the fact that a life has only one use—it exists only for the purpose of intellectuality and thus has become superfluous here. You will understand this better when you read my "Introduction", which will tell how his longing takes the essayist toward his real goal—life.[5] His situation is depicted in this essay—or at least it was supposed to be. I didn't want to put all this into words—partly because I wasn't conscious of it myself. Now the whole thing has become so clear that I am going to change the sequence of the book and place this essay at the *very end* because it satirizes the whole volume. In this case, however, I am not sure about the final sequence of the book. Please give me your opinion on that.

Let's go on to the main problem: you can't imagine the degree of its importance for me. Still, I repeat what I wrote yesterday: you are wrong. As I argued, the infinity of the epic is not a metaphor but *concrete historical reality* and—listen to this—therein lies the quest for the infinity of the Romantic School. We are not talking here about the difference between *closed* and *open* art but only about the diverse connections within literature, only between the works of literature. (As Vincent remarks: "And our inability to accept life without any connection is what creates the connections between [the] various parts [of literary works]—not their airy, playful lightness."[6] And a few lines further on, I supply the concrete historical example in the form of the poetic writing of the early Middle Ages, the *Ritterepos.*) And I want to remind you of the first chapter of the [drama]book, where I write that reality, i.e., life, in the drama is derived from the completeness of connections. I make reference to this difference in my book (p. 15) where it says: In the drama, "the totality and richness of reality finds its expression only in its forms";[7] this means that the empirical completeness (= the immediate symbol of infinity!) can only be suggested in the drama by way of symbols. (I have come to this conclusion and stated it in my *Szerda* article.)[8] "Both forms", I wrote, "contain the totality of reality... this universe is depicted in its universality in the epic. There is no limit as to its expressive means..." In the case of the epic, unity derives from content, while in that of the drama, it derives from the form. "The former gives us a mirror of the world, the latter only its symbol; while the former describes reality, the latter stylizes it."

I admit that the formulation is both immature and uncertain—the essential contrast is the same, though. At that time I looked at the question from the perspective of the drama only and didn't consider its implications for the epic. I didn't ask: Is epic truly a form? That is the question raised here and for which the pro and con arguments are marshalled. Since here *infinity* is to be taken *literally* (it gives *the mirror of the world*) it is possible that the metaphysical grounding is wrong in its *concrete results;* as *method,* however, it is correct.

But we are not only talking about the epic now but also—and mainly—about Romanticism, which I first criticized in my Ibsen article.[9] "Romanticism is one great flight but a frivolous flight cannot go on forever; there was no goal set because the Romantics strove toward the infinite." Similar ideas lie at the base of my Novalis (essay); the problem will be at the center of my F.[riedrich] Schlegel book.[10] Romanticism is poetry, in Schlegel's words, "progressive Universalpoesie." He states: "Die romantische Dichtart ist noch im Werden; ja das ist ihr eigentliches Wesen, dass sie ewig nur werden, nie vollendet sein kann... Sie allein ist unendlich, weil sie allein frei ist, und das als ihr erstes Gesetz anerkennt, dass die Willkür des Dichters kein Gesetz über sich leide."[11] You probably remember the passage in my Novalis about how 'the Romantics' art of living was poetry in action; they transformed the deepest and most inward laws of poetic art into imperatives for life."[12] Well, my life to a large extent is a critique of the Romantics (the Kierkegaard essay deals with the "art of living"—in its tragic manifestation), and my "Sterne" also takes a step in that direction; this time, however, a critique of the epic form and that of Romanticism cannot be separated. Oh no, it is not by accident that the word *Roman* (novel) and "romantic" are etymologically related! The *Roman* is the typical form of the Romantic era—in life as well as in art (remember again my mentioning *Wilhelm Meister* in the "Novalis").

And yet, Romanticism is more than mere "yearning for the infinite"; it is also Romantic irony. F. Schlegel writes (in the same place my earlier citation comes from): "Und doch kann auch sie am meisten zwischen dem Dargestellten und dem Darzustellenden, frei von allem realen and idealen Interesse auf den Flügeln der poetischen Reflexion schweben, diese Reflexion immer wieder potenzieren und wie in einer endlosen Reihe von Spiegeln vervielfachen."[13] And think back to the discussion we had in Lucerne about humor and about rising above one's situation. As I see it humor is romantic, the form of Romanticism is the novel, thus the question: What is its relation to the forms? (In ethical terms—remember Joachim's last statement[14]—its relation to the categorical imperative?) What I offer is the *critique* of this infinite form and this critique has great importance for me. And this critique is truly and completely mine; I also regard the other parts as truly mine; as you can comprehend now, it was not by accident that I cited (my) old articles (as they all came from notebooks more than three years old). I wanted you to realize that the problem touched upon here is an *organic part of my life*. I don't deny that it is a great happiness to meet you at whatever point, and it would be a base ungratefulness of me to forget even for a minute how much I owe you for having become conscious of certain things (not to mention how much I learned more directly). But the way I have developed is really my own. You can see how your letter affected me; it made me reflect and realize that you are about to leave the road we traveled together—and that fact has been giving me great confidence.

I do not know much about the fine arts and consequently cannot judge whether any parallelism exists between fine arts and literature, that is, what the difference between epic and drama, and then between Classicism and Romanticism could mean for the fine arts. And because in the final analysis I regard my way as a groping for causality, I cannot accept the fact that I offered a makeshift metaphysics. I state only what I know for sure (even if it sometimes is expressed obscurely because I still don't know everything about it). For example, you don't find a word about how individual elements of the two great opposites relate to each other because I myself don't know yet.

Doubtless you see now why I talk too much. It is that I consider the matter important, and I *have to* make you see that I am right and that there was at most a meeting of minds in this matter; and also because every word you utter is of importance to me... but you know all that...

I have to tell you one more thing: nothing has moved me so much as your second letter... I am so grateful that it moved me to tears; if that would be possible, it brought you even closer to me. For this reason I am afraid of one thing: since I think I now perceive the center of things differently, does it mean that a distance has come between us? Will I be somewhat diminished in your eyes? Give me your assurance, please (although I feel the bond is strong enough, but I can be certain only of my feelings toward you and not of yours toward me; thus, I am a little scared). I embrace you with great love. Yours,

Gyuri

P.S. Give my regards to Bé.

[1] Two essays from *Soul and Form*.
[2] See letter no. 29.
[3] In *Soul and Form*, p. 151.
[4] Ibid., p. 150.
[5] Ibid., p. 12.
[6] Ibid., p. 144.
[7] In the German edition, *Entwicklungsgeschichte...*, p. 29.
[8] *Wednesday*, Budapest paper. Excerpt from the *Dramabook*. "A dráma formája" (November 14, 1906).
[9] See letter no. 3., n. 1.
[10] Lukács soon dropped the plan.
[11] Schlegel developed his concept of Romanticism "as progressive universal poetry" in his work, *Athenäum Fragments*. He stated that "romantic poetry is still in the making; indeed, the fact that it is forever becoming and can never be completed constitutes its very essence. It is infinite because it is free and it holds as an absolute law that the caprice of the poet is supreme. ..."
[12] In *Soul and Form*, p. 49.
[13] "[Irony] is best able to hover between what is portrayed and what has to be presented, to float on the wings of poetic reflection free from all real and ideal interest, raising this reflection again and again to a higher power, and multiplying it as in one endless series of mirrors."
[14] "Ethics or—since we're speaking of art—form... is an ideal outside the self," in *Soul and Form*, p. 149.

43. TO PAUL ERNST

Budapest
Nagy János utca 15.
March 10, 1910

Dear Herr Doctor,

Mrs. Plehn[1] was kind enough to show me your letter to her which contained your comments on my very short "Brunhild" essay.[2] That gave me the courage to approach you with this letter.

In the meantime, *Die Zukunft*[3] had decided against its publication—and so I sent it to the *Neue Freie Presse*[4]—without much hope, really, that it will ever be printed. But who am I to complain? After what your *Brunhild* had to endure (total silence!), what gives me the right to complain that they don't want to bring out my work? As it is, the essay achieved its essential and most significant aim in that I now have the confirmation that I understood what you had in mind. This should be more than enough for me. To be sure, the "worthy cause" requires that something be done about it (however little my essay may contribute); but I just cannot see that happening any time soon.

It is the same case, in more general terms, with my chances in Germany right now. (I am Hungarian, from Budapest, and plan to spend the next few years in Germany. As of now, an essay collection of mine[5] is being published in Hungarian; and my large-scale work, *The History of the Development of the Modern Drama,*[6] honored by a prize and accepted by the Hungarian Academy for publication, will come out in the fall.) I came to Germany with all that behind me—a good part of these writings have been translated with the rest to follow. To be sure, there have been no concrete results as yet. One of my essays dealing with Stefan George[7] was very much appreciated by Professor Simmel[8], but to have it published is a different matter. By the way, Professor Simmel told me during our conversation about aesthetic matters—in the course of which I quoted you extensively in relation to my views on the problems of drama—that he will soon write to you about me and my work. I don't know whether or not he has done so.

Be that as it may, may I ask your forgiveness for my bothering you with all these insignificant details? All this was, however, intended to prepare the way for an even greater importunity—for which, dear Herr Doctor, you alone are to blame because of your letter. Namely, I have the following favor to ask you. I plan to go to Berlin at the beginning of April and since I have the greatest desire to meet you, I would love to stop in Weimar and pay you a visit if it wouldn't inconvenience you. Please let met know if a visit around April 1–10 would suit you.

Most respectfully yours,
Dr. Georg von Lukács

[1] Maria Plehn, wife of a Berlin physician and hospital director, Dr. med. Albert Plehn. A close friend of Ernst's second wife, Lilli.
[2] Reference is to a review of Ernst's drama that later was expanded into the essay, "The Metaphysics of Tragedy," first published in German in *Logos* (1911). See the essay collection, *Soul and Form,* pp. 152ff.
[3] *The Future,* a Berlin weekly (1892–1922), edited by Maximilian Harden. Ernst published there frequently.
[4] *New Free Press,* a renowned Viennese liberal newspaper (1864–1918) with its famous "Feuilleton."
[5] *A lélek és a formák* (Soul and Form).
[6] See letter no. 8. See also no. 69, n. 4.
[7] See Letter no. 34, n. 3.
[8] Georg Simmel. See "Biographical Notes".

44. TO IRMA SEIDLER (RÉTHY)

Budapest
March 23, 1910

My dear Madame,

I beg your forgiveness for this intrusion into your life, but since I have already made a mistake for which there are no amends, I'll try to set it right by committing another one. You wrote me in your last letter[1] that your "gaze will follow" my "steps from afar". Thus, I feel encouraged to send you my most important work with this letter.[2] I also realize that your statement has been dictated by a refined politeness and should not be taken as empowering the other to anything. I am writing for the following reason: this book, as you may recall, represents the scholarly summary of my life so far, the concluding chapter of my so-called youth to which I bid farewell by sending off this book. On this occasion I feel it my duty to give thanks with a handshake to everyone who helped me along. My introduction was such a thank you;[3] and to you, dear Madame, I owe an especially great and varied debt and the time has come to pay my dues. And so I send you this book accompanied by a few explanatory lines, because I fear that you might be offended by certain things, especially if you'd heard it from others instead of me. In that case, my motives might be even more misunderstood than this way. I owe it to myself, dear Madame, to write you today just as I owed it to myself to dedicate the work to you.

You probably don't need and hardly expect thanks, nor my gratefulness or love, so this letter is written because I need the assurance that I was finally able to tell you how it was. What I couldn't tell there (in the book) I tell you now: those few months when I had the good luck to have known you and been close to you were so significant for me, it was so intense and gave me so much that I can say with every certainty that without this experience I would never have become what I am today—at least, I'd be a poorer and lesser man. At that time I believed that it meant the same thing for you too; today I know better. I see clearly that I was not more than an accidental constellation, a rather pleasant preoccupation in the final interlude of the play.

You came up to Budapest, not yet healthy enough to work; and there were other things missing in your life—which you obviously now have—and you were bent on making the best of a rather unpleasant transitional period in your life. There was I, in a crowd of insufferably smart or insufferably stupid people, and you found me to be cleverer, more entertaining, refined, and—certainly—more cultured; and I didn't bore you with my talk until—until talks turned to more meaningful things. The fact that those talks with you became the ultimate content of my "life" and from which I derived undreamed-of pleasure and riches is my luck, good or bad. This fact doesn't put you under any obligation; I am obliged, though, to thank you with deepest gratitude and love for everything you have done for me, what you meant to me and what you made of me.

There is another thing, dear Madame, for which I have to express my thanks and I do it today. Until I was lucky enough to get to know you I was convinced (although retaining a degree of hope for the opposite and not daring to draw the final conclusion) that my mode of existence would inevitably exclude me from all human community and make it impossible to ever become the meaning of someone's life. In one of your weaker moments you declared that I was mistaken; since I had never been so close to anybody before, I succumbed to believing you. The facts showed me otherwise; now I not only know but hold on to the belief that what I first thought was true, and it is all right with me. (I don't mean that it should be so but only that once it has to be so I better be aware of it.) For this, I again have to thank you and I am doing it here and now. I think you'll misunderstand me—as is inevitable. Today I am glad that you can't ever comprehend my state of mind. Why should understanding be so important anyway? I obviously cannot explain the whole thing to you in a few words (so that you won't see irony where there is none and value judgment which is not meant!). There are people who understand and cannot live; and then there are the others who can live but cannot understand. The first kind can never reach the other even though he understands; the second kind can never grasp the essence but it doesn't matter. The feeling of love or hate, the liking of somebody or the possibility of learning to like somebody exists, but the concept of understanding does not.

You, dear Madame, won't understand what I meant; and because I fervently wish you to be happy, I am glad that you won't. I told you all this because I felt it imperative to let you know about it. It may convey to you the extent of my unchanged sympathy, my gratitude and my respect for what is the essence of your strength. I also want to emphasize that I don't expect any degree of appreciation of my innermost feelings. I wrote this for my own sake; you are not in need of anything coming from me. With a special intensity of feeling, I wish you every happiness and good tidings.

Your respectful friend,
Dr. György Lukács

[1] See letter no. 20.
[2] The Hungarian edition of the essay collection, *A lélek és a formák. Kisérletek* (Soul and Form. Experiments). with the dedication "To Those From Whom Received" (Budapest: Franklin Társulat, 1910).
[3] To Leo Popper.

45. FROM IRMA SEIDLER (RÉTHY)

Budapest
March 24, 1910

Dear Gyuri,

My heartfelt thanks for the book. There was never the slightest danger of misunderstanding on my part—even without your accompanying comments.

My sincere regards,
Irma Seidler R.[éthy]

46. FROM ERNST BLOCH

Ludwigshafen
April 22, 1910

Dear Doctor Lukács,

You will no doubt be surprised to receive a letter from this remote spot and such a belated answer at that. Your manuscript[1] made quite an extraordinary impression on me, above all for the way you made aestheticism appear at once as the aesthetic problem of solipsism; and Beer-Hofmann—as all these reflections on the history of literature—apparently serves as an excuse for the metaphysics to be gained from it. I should like to ask you to let me have all of your works on the aesthetically encapsuled subject and his outbreaks and deliverances through artistic or theoretical objectivity. This is a *Problematik* wherein all great ideas have to converge. I hope to repay you with the first two chapters of my book in progress (the title of which, by the way, has changed in the meantime), which is devoted exclusively to the very curious problem of objectivity, and encompasses all the possible configurations of posing the problem.

I'll stay here until the beginning of May and then go to Berlin for the whole summer. It would be a great pleasure to meet you there. You must be busy right now with your Schlegel book.[2] Your outline was so inspiring that I have started toying with the idea—albeit in a rather dilettantish way—to put somewhat of a damper on the destructive splendor of this most famous of all literary epochs.[3] Otherwise, I am still stuck with my metaphysical treatise, first of all dealing with the problem of consciousness, then with nature as an enclave of history, and with the historical function of time.

My warmest regards and hope to see you again soon.

Most respectfully yours,
Ernst Bloch

[1] "The Moment and Form: Richard Beer-Hofmann," an essay from *Soul and Form.*

[2] Lukács made mention of his plans for a book on Schlegel in his letters to Leo Popper. See letter no. 42.

[3] German Romanticism.

47. TO LAJOS FÜLEP

Berlin
May 24, 1910

Dear Sir,

Your letter has arrived and I immediately forwarded it to Sándor Hevesi.[1] It is with great regret that I tell you that nothing can come of our meeting and discussion because I will stay in Berlin for at least another year. At the earliest, we may meet in Florence this coming September. Will you be there? If yes, please let me know somehow.

As far as the project is concerned,[2] I don't have to tell you that it meets with my approval. Its appeal to me is even greater now after the project my friend and I planned—the publication of a German-language magazine—had to be postponed for a few years due to internal and external circumstances. This is my situation in short: I am at present preoccupied with a difficult and concentrated problem and have no idea where my research will lead me or when I'll come to writing it down. Therefore I would be an extremely unreliable partner in such a venture. The situation might change any time; I might abandon it or get deeper into it. In any case, I felt my duty to tell you openly how things stand with me at present. I am not your typical Hungarian writer who promises six articles every day and may one day deliver three. If you have read anything by me you must know that such a journal is straight from the heart. Should I be doing any writing in the near future, you have my promise that your journal will get it. I am hopeful but can't guarantee anything. This is also an answer to your other question concerning my co-editorship: if I am not in [Buda]Pest, I can't possibly commit myself. By next spring, the situation might be different. I just don't know. Should I be in [Buda]Pest again, we can talk about it. The same applies to the problem of finances. I have no idea whom we could approach (there are a few people I can count on), but it also requires that I be there.

I deeply regret and feel uncomfortable with my answer, which must sound to you as a categorical "no"; this is, however, not the case. Should we have the opportunity to talk it over, you'll see that my answer is not a negative one. I was also thinking about whether or not the venture would prove more successful if it were not in Hungarian. A German-language journal, for example, with contributions by four or five truly talented people, would prove to be a surer bet, both intellectually and financially. My answer is not a vague promise; by the time the journal is realized, I might contribute more.

As far as my publications are concerned, I wish I could send you a copy of my book[3] but I don't have one left. If you want to read it, the Vedres[4] family would surely lend you theirs. I am expecting the reprints of my latest treatise any day[5] and will send you one as soon as I get them in. Have you seen the journal, *Renaissance?*[6] It is not quite good yet but it has more decency and respect for scholarship than the *Nyugat*. For the present and for my meager accomplishment, it is my chosen outlet. Would you care to send them some of your papers (until the real journal comes along, that is)? Judging from the attitude of its staff, your contribution would respectfully be accepted.

Sincere regards,
Yours,
György Lukács

1 See letter no. 4, n. 2.
2 Plan of founding a "house journal" on philosophy and culture, which later became *A Szellem* (Spirit).
3 *A lélek és a formák* (Soul and Form).
4 Márk Vedres (1870–1961), leading Hungarian sculptor, member of the activist avant-garde group *Nyolcak* (The Eight). Through his wife, Mária Polacsek, he was related to the Polányis, Irma Seidler, and Ervin Szabó.
5 Reference is made to the essay, "*Megjegyzések az irodalomtörténet elméletéhez*" (Notes on the Theory of the History of Literature), published in the *Alexander-Emlékkönyv* (Alexander-*Festschrift* on the occasion of his sixtieth birthday), Budapest: Franklin, 1910, pp. 388–421.
6 *Renaissance*, the cultural revue, was launched in 1910. For a short while, Lukács and his friend, Béla Balázs, took over the editorship but abandoned the journal by October 1910. It folded at the end of the same year.

48. TO LEO POPPER

Berlin
May 28, 1910

My dear son, Leo,

How times are changing! I don't write letters anymore either! Although I think of writing daily and have had many things in mind, nothing comes of it, which is not a bad sign in itself. It is not a loss for you because you never needed it (you understand what I mean by that), and it is especially good for me. It means that the sentimental period is over, and the subjective indications are all there that one day I'll become what you call a "critic of the form". And that reminds me of a couple of things I have to tell you before I forget: (1) It was not Mici[1] who corrected your article; although I asked Márkus[2] to do it, it was finally done by some jackass at the paper. (2) Do you have any of your Hungarian-language articles with you? Would you give them to the *Renaissance?* If yes, I'll submit them and they almost surely will print them; they pay 5 Krone per page. Both Balázs and myself write for them in hopes that the journal may develop into an anti-*Nyugat* organ. If you have the articles, mail them *to me* and I'll forward them. By the way, I had my most recent article sent to you.[3]

And now to more important things. Well, my sentimental period is slowly passing. What remains is some *désir du désir,* which is harmless because it won't last forever. And after that? Then I'll be ready for what comes. It is just possible that I feel that way because my work progresses at a slower pace than it could or should. It goes better though than before, and there are hours when I see my new book taking shape.[4] What I see most clearly is, unfortunately, that it will take many years. But then this process of maturity will most likely result in a better work. Nothing much as yet can be said about it, especially not in a letter. In the beginning (at the very beginning!) I thought to myself: F.[riedrich] Schlegel, meaning that I would force myself into the direction of historicism, concreteness in perception and realization; enter: romantic irony; part of the Sch.[legel] project split off and became the present book. A peculiar monograph, indeed, the peculiar inadequacy of the beginnings and the consequences, namely, what the starting point was and yet how independently things developed from that. (In other words, the concrete and the historical aspect is still there; concreteness and historicism, however, are mere background, the ironical background of the real process; the problem itself, the symbolic nature of it, is alone important—and the trick is in what way accidents contributed to its intensification. The less significant the external circumstances and the more intensified the problem, the deeper is the trick itself. The book was conceived as a strongly philological-historical one.) Now the problem itself is in the forefront; or rather, a part of the problem. It is difficult if not impossible for me to articulate it yet. You may grasp what it's all about if I tell you that it amounts to a *prolegomenon to a metaphysics of form,* i. e., the meaning of form in a cosmic sense—the position it [the form] occupies in the *Weltbild* both in its capacity as an ordering of things and its capacity as what has been ordered as things. It is a prolegomenon because neither today nor in the next few years can I possibly arrive at the correct question—maybe at the positing of the question, certainly not at the solution of the problem. Had I attained that end, I'd have arrived at an aesthetics of literature. I couldn't say I wish I'd gone that far. What would become of me if I'd written it prematurely? "Fame and rest?" It wouldn't suit me, don't you think? I'd surely become second-rate and shallow; only hard work can bring results for me.

Well, back to the book! As I said, a prolegomenon, because it would offer but a critique of the concept of form of the Platonic-rational-metaphysical world view that has reached its peak in the aesthetics of German Romanticism (Schiller, Schlegel, Schelling, Solger, Hegel, Schopenhauer). It would tell of the tragedy of this world view that ultimately aims at the concept of form but has to lead inevitably to the dissolution of form. I cannot explain it any better. There are times when I could explain things with a certain degree of clarity but I am not at the stage where I can write it down.

Ergo, I believe it will be written—but when and in what form is another question which I don't even dare to ask of myself! Only this much is certain: I want very much to write this book and have some reason to be hopeful—which takes me back to the other project. We'll see. Objectively, there are favorable developments: certain projects of mine are at least *pending*. First, I had a talk with Singer[5] who thinks it possible that Fischer will publish the essays[6] (albeit without honorarium and/or asking for subsidy). By the way, Otto[7] (whom I like better every day!) is translating the Kierkegaard essay. Then they all will be mailed to Heimann, the editor at Fischer's;[8] but don't tell this to anyone, please, with the exception of Bé or Thiele;[9]—I mean not to Karli and Heini, in case you are about to write them. I don't want to appear anything but a successful man in Budapest.

Another thing: Imre Lessner, my brother-in-law (the brother of Richard) has more or less succeeded in placing Heimann at the *Österreichische Rundschau,*[10] that is, they liked it but wanted me to add certain informative passages on Heimann. I did it. Now, I am waiting for the decision. Since I gathered from their letter that there is an interest in my stuff, I sent them some more, for example, the George and Beer-Hofmann essays, and the Brunhilda piece.[11]

That is all. As I wrote down the word "all", it suddenly dawned on me how much I wrote about myself and nothing about the really important matter, i. e., about you. I was frightened when Otto told me that you are not well. First I got scared but then considered the circumstances and calmed down. That doctor, after all—who, according to Otto, is the worrying type—recommended only peace and rest; and now all the external and internal circumstances promise this to be the case (at least in my judgment).

Be strict with yourself and with others and don't even try to work on anything until you are completely well. This past winter brought with it many important possibilities that bade well for the future. It doesn't make any difference whether you start right now or in three to four months. Everything may be completely all right by fall or winter, but it will be so only if you don't exert yourself and do only what is absolutely necessary. I take my "prohibition" so seriously that I ask you not even write letters (unless inevitable, like to your parents). Don't even write to me! Bé will be kind enough, won't she, to send me a postcard once in a while about how you are doing?

There would be many more things to discuss but I don't want you to have to think about that, right now. The time will come for talks. You will either write or we'll meet in the summer and will discuss everything we left out the last time in Berlin. There are certain things one cannot ask and can only wait for their natural outcome. And that will happen, right?

After I started writing this letter, I received an invitation to Weimar from Paul Ernst. I'll be going there next week.

With warm embrace,

Yours,
Gyuri

1 Sister of Lukács. The article in question was Popper's review essay on Lukács's *A lélek és a formák* (Soul and Form) in a Hungarian newspaper, *Magyar Hírlap* (April 27, 1910).

2 Miksa Márkus, editor of *Magyar Hírlap* (Hungarian News).

3 *Esztétikai kultúra* (Aesthetic Culture), in *Renaissance* (May 1910). It has not been translated into any other language; the essay is important for the understanding of Lukács's intellectual development.

4 The planned Schlegel book.

5 Sándor Singer, editor of *Pester Lloyd*, German-language Budapest daily with a progressive-liberal orientation.

6 *Soul and Form.*

7 Otto Mandl, mutual friend, translated several Lukács essays into German.

8 Moritz Heimann (1868–1925), writer, essayist, critic. For many years editor-

in-chief at S. Fischer Verlag, Frankfurt am Main. Also served as editor of *Die Neue Rundschau,* published by S. Fischer. His writings appeared in a posthumous collection, *Prosaische Schriften,* 5 vols.

[9] Thiele de Waard, mother-in-law-to-be to Popper.

[10] *Austrian Review,* Viennese literary magazine (1904–19). Lukács reviewed Heimann's play, *Joachim von Brandt.* The review was never published in German.

[11] Review of Paul Ernst's play. See letter no. 43, n. 2.

49. TO LEO POPPER

Berlin
[June 8] 1910

My dear son, Leo,

You both took my request not to bother with writing too seriously. But it is all right. I learned from Otto[1] that you are doing fine. This letter is not to provoke an answer but only to tell you about a couple of pieces of good news which, I am sure, you'll be glad to hear.

First of all, I have been to Weimar. It turned out to be altogether a very pleasant and fruitful visit.[2] We became quite close, intellectually speaking (so much so that he accepted my criticism of his play); and other things also might be within reach. In all likelihood I'll again go to Weimar in the first half of the summer; I will stay with the P. Ernsts. This is very important. I discussed Bruegel with him *("Allteig"[3])* and he was very interested and liked your idea.

Most importantly, my "spring moods" seem to be over and done with. Now I can "exist" relatively well and even though I haven't done too much work as yet, I have been steadily working the last four or five days. I can't keep it up but it is good to know that it is still possible. Moreover, I don't think that it is a frivolous preoccupation but rather the reappearance of the old consciousness of mental energy. When I will have something to show for it, I just don't know. That is not the main thing right now. If I could go on like this for years, it would be all right with me. This tells you almost everything. Strangely enough, one writes long letters only when one feels miserable, at least that is how things are with me. I sat down in the belief that this would be a long letter and look what happened...

Let's talk about secondary, more up-to-date things. Enclosed is Baumgarten's article.[4] The poor guy was in a very bad frame of mind when he wrote it; it is neither very deep nor good. But I find its tone moving; others may feel differently about it. Béla Balázs[5] was enthusiastic about your article.[6] (I don't know of any other opinions of it, except for Ignotus[7] who said that he didn't understand it at all.) Balázs thinks that it is very deep, very much to the point, and very well written.

One more thing I wanted to ask you about long ago—as an answer to your first letter. The matter is that I'd like to dedicate the German essay collection[8] *openly* to Irma. But I fear this is impossible, isn't it? I need you to persuade me not to do it, otherwise I'll go ahead. There is no problem on my account: after all, it is absolutely true as you once remarked to me, namely, that she is still the source of everything I write. (It is amusing what I have found out recently: even my form problems grow out of my experience with her but in such a way that she is distanced from it, etc., etc.) In other words, there is no danger in it for me. The question remains how she will take it. Well, think about it and either write me about it (it is not urgent) or we'll talk it over in the summer when we get together. If it can't be done openly, well, then we will have to find another way to thank her. It is a matter of honor to repay one's debt.

By the way, what happened to your Hungarian articles? Don't you want to send anything to *Renaissance* (or rather to me for forwarding)? Or aren't they done yet? How did you like my "Aesthetic Culture"?[9] All these questions do not mean that you have to sit down and write an answer; do it only if you are quite well and feel like it.

I sent the Kierkegaard[10] essay to your mother-in-law (see my letter to her). Regards to Bé and to your father-in-law.

Your,
Gyuri

P.S. One more thing: I met a Dutch lawyer (Dr. Fakker) who knows the de Waards[11] while at the Philosophy of Law Conference that I attended because of the Somlós.[12]

[1] Otto Mandl, a close friend of Popper.
[2] Allusion to the beginnings of a longstanding friendship between Lukács and the German playwright, Paul Ernst.
[3] A concept of Leo Popper's used in the discussion of the technical aspects of painting. See letters nos. 29. n. 12. and 41.
[4] In reality a review essay by Franz Baumgarten, on Lukács's *Soul and Form*, in *Pester Lloyd* (May 9, 1910).
[5] See "Biographical Notes".
[6] See letter no. 48, n. 1.

[7] See letter no. 35, n. 9.
[8] *Die Seele und die Formen,* published in 1911, was in fact dedicated "To the Memory of Irma Seidler".
[9] See letter no. 48, n. 3.
[10] See letter no. 48, n. 3.
[11] Reference is to the Dutch family, intended to be in-laws of Leo Popper.
[12] Bódog Somló and wife, sister of László Bánóczi. See "Biographical Notes".

50. TO LEO POPPER

Berlin
June 15, 1910

My dear son, Leo,

I again feel with the old vehemence and intensity that you're my only reader, the only one who counts. Had you not been tired, you'd have noticed—and so told me—that while this article[1] was being written in Berlin, there were many visitors (the Somlós, et al.[2]) and that the author had been running around with them during the day and was writing at night—or vice versa. This should never happen. And you wouldn't tolerate any counterargument such as that the Kassner essay was written under the same circumstances because (1) the Kassner essay turned out well; (2) it is a hazardous undertaking in any case and, once it succeeded, one shouldn't tempt fate again; (3) the situation is not the same when the "meeting" is not with an Irma, etc., etc. In other words, you could have justifiably said all these things along with your other criticism.

In my opinion, the original sin of the article consists of its being a continuation of the "Kernstok" essay;[3] and yet, it is not quite the same case. I felt compelled to rethink certain aspects of the problem, and as is so often the case, the reformulation turned out to be less powerful. I am thinking of a German version in the form of combining *the two,* most likely retaining the tone of the Kernstok piece. What do you think? Because it is so different in mood and theme, I wouldn't include it in the essay volume.[4] This article represents *praktische Vernunft* [practical reason] while the other was *reine Vernunft* [pure reason]. (In the Sterne essay, the ethical problem finds its expression in aesthetic form.) I may write it up as an article!

Once more, I am very grateful for your admonitions; they were necessary and to the point. I did the galleys with some trepidation and never reread the piece (not even now). I received many enthusiastic letters about the article, especially from Balázs,[5] and so was reassured a little bit. It undoubtedly contains something good—stylistically speaking. It is an attempt to overcome my "indecisive" style; it strives to develop an apodictic form, i. e., that doubt should exist only during the thought process—*ante rem*—but the finished work should have an apodictic character. Don't you think that this is a correct path to follow and that in this sense the article is a sort of a beginning—a beginning even in regard to content (even if the Sterne and Kernstok came before it)? It is the prolegomenon to what is in the making (in a very hazy and rudimentary form): for the metaphysical justification of the concept of form. The way I feel about it is that form is a biological need (not in the "natural science" sense of the word, of course, but in a deeper sense, as a necessary element of life in its *totality*).

And as a parallel process, the great settling of accounts is in the works, in the book on Romanticism. It is a settling of accounts with rationalism which projected form into the world by stating: form= world=*Ding an sich,* thus, a settling of accounts with aesthetic sensualism. I could write this article because it was easier to deal with; as to the other, I can't write it as yet. In the case of this article content was still important to me. You could counter by saying that one should not publish what is not yet clear. You may be right. I only wanted to point out to you that if a mistake was made, it has nothing to do with R[enaissance].

Something else, you must have noticed (and this is where we disagree): that the end of the article, the positive part, brings something *new*. Anyway, it is done; and I'll probably write it up in German.

Please send the review of the *Death-Aesthetics*[6] and something else (to make it not appear as a review among friends), maybe the article on Hungarian folk art;[7] it is a beautiful and really good piece of writing.

As for the case of Irma, I certainly wouldn't have dedicated the book openly *to her* without first asking permission. A dedication without permission would be conceivable only in a very disguised form. The problem first came to the fore (a conclusion that emerged from a subsequent self-analysis) when the form of the German dedication was contemplated because the double meaning of the Hungarian text couldn't be duplicated. I have been trying to think of a dedication ever since. How do you like this one? "In die Hände sei dieses Buch gelegt, die es mir gaben." [This book is given to the hands that gave it to me]. I also thought of another one: "In memoriam: December 18, 1907" (the date of our first meeting) but it sounds strange, I think. And it is rather obvious, although no one knows, of course, but it is impossible because of her. Similarly, the old version is an impossibility too: "In Ihre Hände lege ich dieses Buch. Denn mehr als mir darin zu sagen vergönnt war, gaben Sie mir: alles was ich erwarb und geworden. Und wenn Sie auch diesen Dank nicht wollen und nicht dulden—leise fällt er dennoch auf Ihr Haupt, wie welkende Blätter im Herbst."[8] This too reveals too much. In any case, please let me know what you think about them.

I would write to her as a last resort—or I may do it on impulse.

No news from Fischer. Heimann is reading the translated essays. We'll see. I don't have high hopes but one never knows.

And now about you. I find it *absolutely necessary* that you don't travel and experiment before you're quite well. You'd better write your parents openly about the situation—or tell them something else. Since we are talking here about a couple of weeks at most, you should not endanger your recovery with the hardship of traveling. This is the main thing; everything else is of secondary importance.

[. . .]

Regards to Bé, Thiele and your father-in-law.

Hugs,
Yours,
Gyuri

1 "Esztétikai kultúra" (Aesthetic Culture). See letter no. 48, n. 3.
2 Bódog Somló. See "Biographical Notes".
3 Lukács gave a talk at the Galileo Circle on the search of the new generation of artists for "a new path," which has been published in *Nyugat* (January 1910).
4 *Soul and Form.*
5 Béla Balázs.
6 "Halálesztétika", a study of Béla Balázs, originally written in German and read at Georg Simmel's seminar in Berlin; Simmel was impressed by it. Published in Hungarian in 1908.
7 *"Die Fackel",* June 2, 1911.
8 "This book is given into your hands. After all, you gave me more than I could give credit for: you gave me everything I know and everything I have become. Even though you don't want and reject these words of thanks, they quietly settle on your head as fading leaves of the autumn." By the time *Die Seele und die Formen* was published (1911), Irma Seidler was dead. Thus, the dedication openly acknowledged her "contribution"; it reads, "Dem Andenken Irma Seidlers" (To the Memory of Irma Seidler).

51. FROM MRS. JÓZSEF VON LUKÁCS

Budapest
June 23, 1910

Dear Gyuri,

My heartfelt thanks for your friendly letter. We're all happy about the review in the *Renaissance*.[1] Did you receive the *Hét*[2] we sent you? Dad must have informed you of the Eisler journal.[3] Nothing new here, at least nothing that would be of interest to you. Everybody is doing fine. Kati & Co. are visiting the Lederers[4] and will stay until the end of the month. We just received the wedding announcement from the Alexanders[5]; the wedding is taking place next Saturday. Dad is planning to go to Bad Gastein, but I won't be going because the spa somehow doesn't agree with me. The Lessners[6] are going to Salzburg (to the Mozartiana) at the end of July. I am very happy that at last Mici will get away from the kids and can take in some music and things.

Karli[7] was here for a short visit last Sunday. His Baron, whom he had been tutoring in his spare time, has finally passed his exams; Karli deserves a Nobel Prize for this achievement. He promised to come again to visit along with Cecil.[8] The Poppers also paid a visit last Sunday and mentioned that they will go to St. Gilgen, with poor Leo[9] following them. Ervin has started to talk, utters whole sentences; in his movements he resembles you greatly—even his hair grows in the same abundance as yours in your "beautiful period". He even has your characteristic high forehead! Edit is the sweetest baby possible, always cheerful and satisfied.[10]

Let us hear from you once in a while, my little son. I embrace you warmly.

Mom

[1] Reference is to a review of Lukács's *Soul and Form* by Ernő Ligeti.
[2] *The Week*, Hungarian weekly.
[3] Reference is to a German-language newspaper, published in Budapest, the *Neues Pester Journal*, and Michael Joseph Eisler's review on "Hungarian Literature Today" (June 15, 1910).
[4] Emil and Emmy Seidler-Lederer of Heidelberg.
[5] Bernát Alexander's daughter Magda, married Géza Révész, the renowned psychologist. See also letter no. 53, n. 13.
[6] Richard Lessner. Married to Lukács's sister, Mici.
[7] Karl Polányi.
[8] Karl's mother, Cecil (Polacsek) Polányi. See letter no. 36, n. 3.
[9] Allusion is made to Leo's illness.
[10] Ervin and Edit Lessner, Mici's two children from her first marriage.

52. FROM KÁROLY (KARL) MANNHEIM

Balatonfüred
July 3, 1910

Dear Sir,

I am returning with thanks the essay[1] that you kindly lent me. I want to take this occasion to express my gratitude for your kind hospitality and especially for the many useful hints that you left with me.

I hope I can convince you that your guidance is invaluable to me at this stage of my development—precisely because it has come from you. After all, who but the person who has traveled along the same path would be in a better position to know how easy it is to lose ourselves in a maze of countless detours.

Nothing shows the importance of your advice more than the fact that as of this summer my studies have acquired a definitive direction.

I know only too well that in the end one has to find one's own way; but I also believe that one human being can help the other, that there is the possibility of learning from one another, and that, when that happens, we receive a precious gift which comes with great responsibility.

I hope, Sir, that you accept my sincerest gratitude. Asking for your continued good will, I remain

Your respectful follower,
Karl Mannheim

[1] Presumably one of the essays from the essay collection, *A lélek és a formák* (Soul and Form), published individually in the progressive literary magazine *Nyugat*, and in book form in 1910.

53. FROM BERNÁT ALEXANDER

St. Ulrich-in-Gröden
August 23, 1910

Dear Doctor,

Your long letter is truly appreciated; I could even read most of it (except the name of Leopold Drejler or Drexel or whatever,[1] so please print the name the next time as I am curious about his book[2]). I begin to hope that we may reach a complete understanding. I still have serious reservations about historical materialism; it is very true that the arts and literary criticism are social functions, as is aesthetic sensibility, either in its capacity as a receptive or a productive factor. It is obvious that to explore this relationship—in its concrete manifestations—is partly an empirical investigation. That Hegel overlooked this is one of the weakest points in his conceptualizations which, after all, were directed by his vast, *de facto,* empirical knowledge. Even his dialectical scheme is an empirical abstraction. But better leave the discussion of all this to our next meeting.

As to more practical things: Beöthy[3] has been communicating via postcard lately so that any serious discussion is impossible. It seems that he even suspects me of having gone over to the enemy.[4] But he surely is not a conservative in the negative sense of the word; it is only that he is more attached to one or two theoretical schemes while I have to admit to having an aversion to them since I respect reality too much and see it as much richer and deeper than any hastily concocted theoretical scheme. A theoretical scheme is like a bicycle, comfortable, but it doesn't take one upward and it makes one give up walking altogether. The scheme is always present at the end, but the later one arrives at it the better. Even then, one better regard it as temporary.

You'll have your problems with Beöthy and even more so with Petz[5]—no doubt about that. Petz is quite a solid philologist but I am afraid he is a *Schulmeister* [schoolmaster] when it comes to literary criticism. In regard to König's *Musset,*[6] I haven't read it yet. On the basis of that study, he will never get his *Habilitation.* There are a lot of bad feelings about it: an anonymous reviewer cut it down in the *I.K.*[7] and called the piece a worthless stylistic exercise. I told König that he'll never get his *Habilitation* with it; but now he is in no hurry and is working on a study of Balzac. Ignotus[8] had some words of praise for the work in *Nyugat* but they were spoken in a thankless way. First he's condescending; then he went on to state that König doesn't know a thing about Musset. In the end it comes to the same conclusion as the *I. K.* criticism except that there it was stated in a more direct, vulgar and hateful way.

I don't know the whole story behind how the *Renaissance* magazine started.[9] It is true that several *Nyugat* writers contribute to it but there are other problems. Nobody knows where the financial backing comes from, whether it's from Kristóff or from Bánffy or from somewhere else. The magazine is not that flush anyway. The name of the editor, Z.,[10] doesn't help. Méray-Horváth,[11] the sociologist, is a strange creature with whom I would not like to be in the same camp. He is the true type of the scientific sociologist. You surely read B. Lázár's article on Dürer?[12] Such editorial laxity goes beyond what is permissible even during the hot summer. I was asked to contribute and there were rumors that I promised to... but I declined, citing other commitments.

Fülep was in Switzerland on vacation and is now in Freibourg and plans to be back in Budapest in mid-September. He was quite exhausted.

Magda[13] left Wolkenstein—so near to us—yesterday. She is now a very happy woman.

We are going to stay here one more week and then proceed to Lovrano, provided the cholera doesn't scare us away. My family sends their warm regards.

Yours truly,
Bernát Alexander

[1] Correctly, Leopold Ziegler. See "Biographical Notes".
[2] Lukács presumably recommended the then just published book, entitled *Das Weltbild Eduard von Hartmanns* (1901).
[3] Zsolt Beöthy. See letter no. 33, n. 3.
[4] Allusion to the liberal and/or radical factions at the University in particular and among the Budapest intelligentsia in general.
[5] Gedeon Petz, influential faculty member of Budapest University.
[6] György (Georg) König published his study of Alfred de Musset (1810–57), French Romantic poet and playwright, in 1910.
[7] *Irodalomtörténeti Közlöny* (Announcements in Literary History). The review in question appeared in issue no. 2, 1910.
[8] See letter no. 35, n.9.
[9] See letter no. 47, n. 6. It turned out that one of the financial backers of the journal was the Archduke Franz Ferdinand (Habsburg).
[10] Árpád Zigány, a Budapest journalist.
[11] Károly Méray-Horvátht (1859–1938), sociologist, writer.
[12] Béla Lázár, "Albrech Dürer," in *Renaissance* (1910), pp. 663–66.
[13] Allusion is to his daughter, Magda Alexander, sister of Franz Alexander, the noted psychoanalyst. Herself a well-respected art historian, she married Géza Révész, the psychologist, and emigrated with him in 1919. They settled in Holland.

54. TO LEO POPPER Florence
[early October] 1910

Dear Leo,

Writing is nowadays almost a physical impossibility for me. I did not want to send just a postcard, and it took this long for a letter to materialize (if you can call this a letter). It is, actually, because I have very little to say about myself. Everything is all right. Florence is beautiful—very beautiful. It is good to be here. What it offers is very hard to articulate—and it is quite problematic too. But it is something good. I'll stay on for a while and perhaps return again in the spring. The Florence I visited the first time is now split into two cities. There is the real one where I am staying and where I wish you'd be too; you are the only thing missing. And there is (or was) a strange fairy-tale-like city where there has been singing in the streets.... (I could never understand why they had to do this silliness when they are so filled with marvelous palaces and don't need that kind of romanticism, but it was beautiful anyway.) In other words, there exists that old Florence, Irma's[1] Florence, and I was afraid first that it would prove stronger than the real one and would stand between us. But things are so far removed now that this didn't happen. Fülep[2] is here too; he is intelligent, well-educated, and cultured. He is on the right track but the question is whether or not he will have enough perseverence.

It is true that Herbert[3] will be in charge of the *belles-lettres* and review section of *Renaissance*. I will contribute and so might Karli and Herbert himself (on economics), also Hevesi,[4] sometimes Fülep and Margit Kaffka,[5] Anna Lesznai,[6] Laci Bánóczi,[7] and others. Please submit your pieces. It pays well (five *Krone* per page). Herbert will translate the German texts, and the Hungarian ones will be printed as they are. Please do it.

I remind you of your promised letter: be detailed, tell of everything, especially of Turban's[8] opinion, etc., etc. Don't wait as long as I did. As you can see, I don't have much to say, and I cannot express how much I need to know what is happening to you. It is vital for me. Please write (I'll be here approx. till the tenth of the month). My address is: Pensione Consigli, Via Robbia 54. If you think it won't reach me here anymore, send it to Budapest (Városligeti Fasor 20a). Write soon!

One more thing: can you do the Novalis piece?[9] This is just a question, not a request. I only ask because if you can't do it, I should take care of it.

Write, my boy.

I embrace you,
Gyuri

[1] Lukács refers to his first visit in 1908 in the company of Irma Seidler and Béla Balázs.
[2] See "Biographical Notes".
[3] Herbert Bauer, later Béla Balázs.
[4] See letter no. 4, n. 2.
[5] See letter no. 13, n. 6.
[6] Anna Lesznai (originally Amália Moskovicz) (1885–1966), painter, writer and poet, industrial artist. Respected contributor to *Nyugat,* member of the progressive avant-garde artist group, *Nyolcak* (The Eight). Married (1913–20) to Oszkár Jászi, the political scientist. She was a regular member of the Sunday Circle and although never joined the CP, she was persuaded by Lukács to participate in the cultural activities during the 1919 Commune. Fled Hungary in the winter of 1919 and settled in Vienna with her new husband, Tibor Gergely, the well-known illustrator. She emigrated the second time, in 1939, to the United States and settled in New York City. Her book, *Kezdetben volt a kert* (In the Beginning Was the Garden), published in Budapest (Szépirodalmi Kiadó, 1966), gave the best account of Lukács's "conversion to communism," that "took place in the interval between two Sundays: Saul became Paul."
[7] See "Biographical Notes".
[8] Allusion is made to Leo Popper's attending physician.
[9] See essay collection, *Soul and Form.*

55. FROM LEO POPPER

Davos
October 7, 1910

My dear Gyuri,

Many thanks for your good and warm letter. I am grateful that at least in an indirect way I can be with you in Florence. I understand everything you said about "earthquakes" and the singing streets, although I am somewhat puzzled that those great palaces looked on passively as this great Dionysian feast went on. Didn't you overlook, dear boy, that they were singing too? Silently I envy you very much. Florence could have given me a lot, too, at this stage of the great "misunderstanding"[1] and maybe everything would have become clear to me. I realize that it can't be; and so in lieu of other material, I search for the (theory of) misunderstanding in my temperature curve. My theory has arrived: changes come in a cluster every three days, etc., etc. Somehow it doesn't seem to work, though, because either a "normal" day intrudes into the "fever-cluster" or *vice versa,* although I'd be ready to die provided it happened within the cluster of three days (or to become healthy, on the same basis).

All my joking about it is in vain, however; it doesn't even improve my mood. You should know, my boy, that I am dissatisfied with myself and for good reasons. My fever curve showed a steady decrease; I gained three pounds in the first week, thus all the signs were positive and Turban was happy.[2] But my temperature has gone up and I gained only 300 grams the second week so here I am, facing darkness again, not knowing what is going on and what's going to happen. Everything, even my continued stay here, depends on the examination next week. It'll then be decided whether Bé can come and we can set up a "household" here, etc., etc. For the time being I am lying in a nice, clean and comfortable bed and read like crazy—for example, Thomas Mann, [Knut] Hamsun, Chesterton, and [Henry] James and will also write if I can think of something; otherwise I wait for my fate to be decided one way or another.

My mood is good or bad depending on what Bé or the others write, and on the face that Gertrud, the stern chambermaid, makes. I keep watching myself like Christian[3] and get from it as little as he does. Christian is poorly done, don't you think? The character is drawn with a degree of meanness. He is exposed albeit in a very sophisticated way; all he does is to employ the few tricks he has up his sleeve. The reason people think the figure is well done is that the type is presented in a primitive and impressionable way. I think it is a shortcoming. The book's main problem lies in the fact that it is ultimately an *Ich-Novel,* written in the third person, and not an epic. Thomas[4] is the only figure who lives, moves around, is capable of introspection, is shown in his development and is tragic in his suffering; the others are just standing there, repeating the same phrases time and again. It is true that if a complex intellect surveys the puppet theater of life and sheds a few tears over it, some beautiful philosophical insights come out of it. Or consider the simple trick of little Tony[5]—that throughout her life, she reacts to every new situation with the phrase she heard as a child from a medical student. When that little trick, I repeat, reveals itself in a sudden flash as a scheme of universal experience, with one stroke it makes ridiculous all that "experience," the conceptualizations, and everything else we held in such holy regard as intellectual acquisitions. Am I right? I think that implies a deeper poetic introspection than T.[homas] M.[ann] himself realizes; it can be applied in a broad sense with considerable success as we contemplate all the aspects of our own lives. You understand what I mean, don't you? Please tell me how you see this; it is important to me.

I am glad about the *Renaissance* affair; on account of Bauer,[6] you yourself, and also because I will have a place to go. As of now, I sent only my Bruegel article and I was told that they like it in Budapest. I hope *Renaissance* likes it too and it gets printed.

[. . . .]

Of course I will translate the Novalis essay! But not right now, though; you don't need it anyway yet. Tell me when you do need it. Please don't tell anybody about my not feeling well, first, because it is not good for "business", and also because my parents would learn about it and it would sadden them; lastly, I don't want it myself. (I know you wouldn't have said anything!) Please write as often as you want; I am always happy to get your letters. It is not blackmail but right now I need them badly. I think of you with love, with a special kind of love, reserved for you. Perhaps one day I can tell you what kind of love it is; I can't do it now—I only feel the weight of it. Have a good time, my boy, and let me know what it is like [to have a good time].

Hugs from your
Leo

[P.S.]
Did you get the pictures?

[1]Allusion to Popper's intended theory of "double misunderstanding" (at the level of artistic intention and that of reception).
[2] Physician at the Davos T. B. sanatorium.
[3] Christian Buddenbrook, one of the main protagonists in Thomas Mann's first novel, *Die Buddenbrooks*.
[4] Thomas Buddenbrook, the other brother.
[5] Tony Buddenbrook, their sister.
[6] Alias Béla Balázs.

56. TO LEO POPPER

Budapest
[October 25] 1910

My dear son Leo:

I couldn't imagine anything worse than spending a few weeks in Budapest. I wanted to write you every day, not just a postcard but a real letter, and look what happened. I am awfully sorry and it pains me, but that won't change the situation.

Well, my dear boy, don't think me overly optimistic (to begin *in medias res*) if I am convinced that in an objective sense you don't have any reason for feeling disconsolate, as you felt the last time. To be sure, it would have been better to stay in Davos; I myself didn't like it a bit when I first heard the news and the reasons for your leaving. And yet, I still remember how much better we both felt physically in Lucerne than in Wengen (I can best judge the effects on my own disposition). At that time I promised myself never to visit the high mountains except, maybe, to pay you a visit in Davos. I happen to believe that many *absolutely healthy* people couldn't tolerate the high altitude for too long.

The fact that you felt differently in the past proves nothing. One experiences things differently in childhood. No matter what the doctors say, I am convinced that the period between 20 and 25 is a decisive aging period for us. In the summer of 1906 I had a very fine time physically in Csorba, while last year in Wengen it was just bearable. Thus, I don't see anything wrong with your leaving Davos and expecting a lot from Bozen. Please keep me informed how you are doing.

I already have my train schedule for Berlin. (I'll probably leave on Monday and go there via Vienna–Weimar. Send the mail here until then, it will be forwarded to me; keep in mind that if it is a postcard, they will read it!) I am anxious to hear how Bé is doing. She must be busy because she only sent me a postcard so far. I heard from Karli that she intends to take her exams in piano. Wouldn't it better to take them in Budapest? There it would be just a formality and a smooth procedure.[1] (I may sound silly to suggest things I don't know anything about.) I would like to be informed, though. Arrangements might be made in case she planned to give piano lessons, and I could ask my parents to help. Besides, I would welcome any information on how things stand.

I don't think that anything will come from your articles. Herbert and I left the *Renaissance*.[2] We cannot yet get a good journal going, at least not around here [Budapest]. Send your "Dialogue"[3] to me in Berlin. Something can perhaps be arranged, maybe in Fülep's philosophy journal.[4] I think I mentioned it to you (and I also wrote then that it is a "secret" operation). The only problem is that you'd have to translate it; Herbert hasn't time for anything right now. He wants to finish two dramas this winter, and is now working on part three of the dialogue.

I saw Karli a couple of times. I am glad to see that he is on the right track. He is interested in law, and I am convinced he'll make an excellent lawyer and a famous criminal lawyer at that. Such a totally independent existence (internally and externally) is the only way that will lead him to a political career.[5]

The trouble with Irma is something else. I saw her fresco sketch at Karl P.[olacsek]'s[6] the other day; it has beauty but it is still not very good. One has the feeling looking at it that Nagybánya and Réthy[7] never existed, and this is a bad sign with regard to her marriage. (You know under what influences she labors.) The fact that she will spend the winter in Budapest while her husband stays in Nagybánya is only a symptom. I call it a symptom because one can deduce from it what I have already seen in her fresco sketches. It is good that by the time she arrives in Budapest I'll be gone. I can look at this only with human sympathy. Now, I could act as a well-meaning friend of hers if it wouldn't be too dangerous (for her). But it won't ever come to that and I can't even say I'm very sorry.

I am ashamed to say how good I feel nowadays. I think now of life only as something written and put in quotation marks; Philippe[8] was most likely my last *Soul and Form* essay. Now will come "science," slowly but surely. Perhaps there will arrive real metaphysics as compensation for the poetic lyricism that couldn't be. But this too, slowly. I have the patience to wait it out. What I was trying to tell you in Berlin in the spring I experience today in a different way, complete with different emphases, with more peace of mind and in a more somber mood.

Objectively, there is nothing new. I don't even feel like making inquiries about my book at Müller's and about the fate of the essay at *Logos*.[9] I don't intend to spoil my good mood with such matters. (Inwardly, I am certain they won't be published.)

One more thing: I reread your articles the other day. Bruegel made a very good impression on me and I like "Aeroplan."[10] Its tone is good, sure, and sovereign.

God be with you! Don't be cross for this belated and superficial letter

with your
Gyuri

[1] Allusion to the influence of family and family friends, and business acquaintances of Lukács Sr.; Lukács often refers to the usefulness of "connections."

[2] Béla Balázs and Lukács had high hopes of "capturing" the magazine and giving it a new direction.

[3] See letter no. 41, n. 5.

[4] Reference is to *A Szellem* (Spirit), sometimes called the Hungarian *Logos*. The public announcement of February 1911 described it as a journal of metaphysics, ethics, and aesthetics. Only two issues came out, both in 1911. See letters 47 and 82.

[5] Karl Polányi was presumably bent on a political career. Although he was one of the leaders of the radical students at Budapest University, president of the Galileo Circle, and editor of *Szabadgondolat* (Free Thought), he was never a full-fledged politician, less a Minister of Justice, as stated in Peter Drucker's account of "The Polányis," which is more a figment of Drucker's imagination than a family history. See Peter Drucker, *Adventures of a Bystander* (New York: Harper, 1979), pp. 123–40.

[6] Károly Polacsek, lawyer, uncle of both Irma Seidler and Karl and Michael Polányi.

[7] Károly Réthy, painter.

[8] "Longing and Form," in *Soul and Form*, pp. 91ff.

[9] German philosophical journal. The essay, "Metaphysik der Tragödie," was published in *Logos*, Bd. 2 (1911), pp. 79–91.

[10] Popper's essay, "Zur Aesthetik des Aeroplans", was published in *Die Neue Rundschau* (October 1910), pp. 1477–79.

57. TO LEO POPPER

Berlin
December 10, 1910

My sweet good Leo,

You will forgive me, won't you, for not writing sooner? I was preoccupied with other things, and it seems as if your well-meant analysis of my "coming greatness" has come to pass; in a strange turn of events I am besieged by requests... To begin with: *Logos* will publish my "Metaphysics of Tragedy";[1] I had a talk with Dr. Stein who asked me to write for the *Archiv für Philosophie*.[2] the third concerns Fischer: Heimann is for publication but nothing has been decided yet.[3] Much depends on the jackasses at the *Neue Rundschau,* who right now are reading my Ch.-L. Philippe....[4] [....]

And now I'll take a fresh piece of paper, put aside the literary news, and talk about more important things. You asked me to write about myself. At this moment there could be no duller topic than me, and it is a good sign. I told you before that I feel all right and nothing has changed since, although my physical condition at present is not the best; I have not been sleeping well lately. But it doesn't matter.

It seems that what I started in the spring has been accomplished—the exclusion of "life". This doesn't have to mean asceticism in absolute terms. It merely means that the center of gravity has ultimately and unwaveringly shifted toward "work". What about people? Perhaps yes, perhaps no. Happiness: it may come, or it may not. All of these things float on the surface of life (just as it is accidental whether at the moment I have a headache or not). That is why I cited that English poem[5] that is still valid. You know how much I needed people and human relationships. There were three who touched my essential self: Laci,[6] Irma, and you. The Irma case had a decisive importance for my life: there was someone who was able to touch the inner core of my existence, who meant *life* to me, and who was woven into all of my thoughts and feelings. And then she left (and *how* she left!), and I am alive and moving around. One can die of something like this but once one survives, the case is finished. The kind of "love" that developed—love as life in its completeness—is taken care of once and for all. Do you remember what we talked about in Wengen, namely, that it is not the accuracy of statements and answers—although that may be desirable to a certain point as a possibility of illusion—that guarantees their centrality, it is their suggestive power. Irma's leaving destroyed that possibility for me, not because she left—you are the living proof that one can have a second friend like that—but because of *the way* she left. One's nerves retain the trauma of the transformation of absolute nearness and communion into a state of absolute strangeness. I don't believe I'll ever be open to such influence again. As I said, this doesn't necessarily mean asceticism. Women, even marriage, are in the cards. But the value of everything became different. Thus, my present mood is neither hysterical nor bitter. Once I was *unglücklich* [unhappy]; now I am *jenseits von Glück und Unglück* [beyond happiness and unhappiness]. I am on my way toward my center and I am convinced that nobody will be there to share the experience with me (you know what I mean?) and also that in that area nobody can "help" me (you understand that too, don't you?). The only possible path leads to work. Of course, work is only one path—but it is a unique one. More and more I believe that the Platonic theory of knowledge is correct: all knowledge is remembering—but only the most strenuous work enables one to remember. Even the work that has been accomplished is not valuable in itself (as such, it becomes both objective and independent of me) but is only a *Tathandlung* ("deed-act"), a result of something that *I* did.

As in Fichte's profound scheme: I=action, becoming I by virtue of my own actions. This is the meaning of work for me today. And its value is self-perception, the path to my innermost essence; what I have been given to accomplish is my "self." I cannot know it, only seek it; but the "I" is the search itself.

The tone of my letter tells you that my work progresses. One thing I already see with great clarity: my *ultimate* positing of the question is entirely original, without parallel, as a matter of fact. And yet, it is organically related to that really large-scale work I have in mind. What will become of it? Where do I stand right now? These questions cannot be answered with any certainty. I have to learn infinitely more before I can gain any clarity about the things in my mind and before I can put them down in a way that will stand scientific scrutiny. Little wonder that I don't see clearly where I stand right now. (What I mean by "scientific" nowadays is: "What would Hegel have to say about this?" and not what I meant by it last spring.) More about these things another time, if by any chance I have to reflect on it in connection with another *Problematik*.

Florence, to me, means a place to feel good, physically and emotionally. I learned a lot there. Berlin has nothing to offer me. The time has not yet come when I could appreciate the truly great offerings of Paris. For me, Paris is *also* a city of philosophy. I'll go there only if I can have, for example, a productive conversation with Bergson (or at least when his philosophy doesn't pose a problem for me anymore). Florence is beautiful and kind to me. Perhaps I'll be going there for a few months come spring.

One more "literary" question. What do you think of the following sequence: Introduction–Kierkegaard–George–Philippe–Storm–Novalis–B.[eer]–Hofmann–Kassner–Sterne–Ernst?

God be with you, my son! Write, if only a few lines about yourself. What you wrote the last time troubled me a little bit. My regards to Bé. I have been wanting to write her for some time and perhaps will do so in the near future.

Love and embrace.

Yours,
Gyuri

1 "Metaphysik der Tragödie." See letter no. 56, n. 9. In *Soul and Form*.
2 Ludwig Stein (1859–1930), Hungarian-born philosopher, professor of philosophy in Germany, editor of the journal *Archiv für Philosophie*. Several reviews by Lukács were published in 1911 and 1912 in the journal.
3 S. Fischer Verlag, Frankfurt am Main, finally rejected the manuscript.
4 "Über Sehnsucht und Form: Charles-Louis Philippe," in *Die Neue Rundschau*, vol. 22 (February 1911), pp. 1–40. Thomas Mann, who subscribed to the magazine, read the essay and made extensive notes. The essay proved to be influential in his conception of the novelette, *Death in Venice* (1911).
5 In a letter of November 9, 1910, Lukács quotes a line from "a mediocre English poem": "Others leave me. All things leave me. You remain."
6 László Bánóczi. See "Biographical Notes".

58. TO LEO POPPER

Berlin
December 20, 1910

My dear sweet Leo,

Even before your card arrived, I had in mind to write you one of my "expansive" letters. I'll try to do it today—knowing well that one cannot really deal with certain problems in a letter. To begin with: yesterday evening I was reading Plotinus's aesthetics[1] and found the following thoughts on "intellectual beauty" (i.e., that which is beyond the empirical world):

> To "live at ease" is There; and to these divine beings verity is mother and nurse, existence and sustenance; all that is not of process but of authentic being they see, and themselves in all: for all is transparent, nothing dark, nothing resistant; every being is lucid to every other, in breadth and depth; light runs through light. And each of them contains all within itself, and at the same time sees all in every other, to that everywhere there is all, and all is all and each all, and infinite

the glory. Each of them is great; the small is great; the sun. There, is all the stars; and every star, again, is all the stars and sun. While some one manner of being is dominant in each, all are mirrored in every other.

Movement There is pure (as self-caused), for the moving principle is not a separate thing to complicate as it speeds.

In our realm all is part rising from part and nothing can be more than partial; but There each being is an eternal product of a whole and is at once a whole and an individual manifesting as part but, to the keen vision There, known for the whole it is.

Or at another place:

> Each There walks upon no alien soil; its place is its essential self; and, as each moves, so to speak, towards what is Above, it is attended by the very ground from which it starts; there is no distinguishing between the Being and the Place; all is Intellect, the principle and the ground on which it stands, alike.

I think you can see by now what this means: we have here your *Allteig* [universal matter] concept from the Bruegel,[2] presented as metaphysics, that is, a variation of it in the sense that *Allteig* is *not* something the artist has accomplished thereby fulfilling the deepest human yearnings that cannot be satisfied by any other means, but in the sense that the fulfillment is a *metaphysical reality, "das wahre Sein"* [the essential Being].

This is what all rationalistic philosophies tell us (Plato, Spinoza, Schelling, Hegel, etc.). Therein lies the great problem of their world view, the critique of which I am now preoccupied with—as a road to my own philosophy of art. There exists a profound yearning for the *unity* of the world as it is. (This is the reason why a Bruegel or a Cézanne thinks of himself as a "naturalist.") It is the ultimate aim of all philosophies. The question, however, is not raised by philosophy in a straightforward fashion. The question it asks is: How can unity rise out of plurality? And it gives answers without noticing that the main question has never been asked (I admit, I'm brutally oversimplifying the problem), which is: How can we perceive and experience as One all that plurality contained within it, that which is qualitatively different and incommensurable. We are not talking here about eliminating distances; once we have reached the stage where things are either consonances or dissonances, we have a relatively easy time. The problem is: the distances between diverse phenomena of the corporeal world are so great, they are so far removed from us, from each other and from our cognitive possibilities, that one can establish their being one only by superimposing upon them a seemingly random *projection.* This is done both through philosophies and art. We have to concede that projections are by necessity imperfect (meaning metaphysically, in their relation to the whole, to the extensive complete Being). In science, projection is manifested in the existence of "accidents." (Do you remember what I wrote about this in the *Alexander-Festschrift?*[3]—the laws of the other science=accidents and *vice versa.*) I just read a very clever book on this problem by Boutroux;[4] art takes the easy way out—what it cannot express by technical means doesn't exist. I don't have to prove this thesis to you, do I? [Rationalistic] philosophy goes beyond these units to search for *the* unity. Here enters the great error: in the process of unifying and supplying a *Weltbild,* rationalistic philosophy loses sight of the fact (something that science and true art never do) that it unifies a world that has already been unified, stripped of its heterogeneity and reduced to consonances and dissonances. Rationalistic philosophy is but *unconscious* (and therefore confusedly stylized) *art.* What compels rationalism into becoming art? A philosophy of art and metaphysics—which, by the way, complement each other because both use obscure material, differing only in respect to their signs—is an act of necessity, the crowning act of all rational systems. Thus, we are faced with a tragic situation: the aim is a philosophy of art; the concept of form is the ultimate and decisive concept; and neither can be found with the help of this method, the reason being that what is sought is already unconsciously present in the method itself. If we think this through to its ultimate consequences: rationalistic philosophy *does not need art;* the Being created by it [philosophy], that which is regarded as the Real Being, is in itself *already art.* Art in this way turns into a silly tautology, a poor imitation of reality. (As an aside: this problem lies at the root of all *Nachahmung* theories of the past; they just never discovered the reasons for it.) The tragicomedy of it all: they [philosophies] cannot reach their destinations because they're already there, and so keep running around in circles, trying to get to their own back. You get it?

Now back to your theory. If the world consisted only of one "universal matter" *(Allteig),* we wouldn't need to have art (by the same token, if Being=Thinking, we wouldn't need philosophy).

Your theory had decisive significance for me in that it stated in *concrete* and decisive terms what I had already sensed: namely, a new kind of activity represented by art.

This enables us to arrive at the concept of form. *Form ist eine Erlebnis-Notwendigkeit, eine Kategorie des Erlebens.*[5] This is the only way to perceive the world as something *radically different* and we cannot deal with this knowledge. And science? *"Eine Kategorie des Denkens, eine mögliche und unmögliche einheitliche und uneinheitliche Projektion der Wirklichkeit."*[6] And what about philosophy? If we ask with Kant *"Wie ist Metaphysik möglich?"* [How is metaphysics possible?] we have to give an answer also in the negative, albeit for very different reasons. Why? Because this (rationalistic, monistic) metaphysics is a *contradictio in adjecto,* a projection without a vantage point. (Never mind that it is said: from a universalist standpoint it is all the same.) I put the question differently. *"Warum ist Metaphysik notwendig? Und warum doch unmöglich? Wie muss die Welt sein, dass kein Inhalt in ihr wahrnehmbar und beweisbar und doch notwendigerweise erlebbar ist? Wie muss die Seele geschaffen sein, dass sie dieses muss und doch nicht kann?"*[7] I have no answers (at this point, they're unimportant), only vague notions, but I believe that for the first time I am able to tell you what my book will be about. It will describe the great crisis of this thought from which—I hope—answers may spring. Why am I writing this down? Because I again feel very strongly that you have much to do with my finding my correct path at this time.

I know that this is my road. But I also know that without you (the concept of *Allteig* was only the crystallization of many foregoing things) my progress would have been delayed—maybe indefinitely. For me it appears a matter of fate that I met you, and in this respect I regard myself—don't laugh at me—as your pupil. It is possible that you by yourself wouldn't have come to the same conclusions—and maybe wouldn't have looked at the roots of the problem this way—but no matter. It is quite possible that I am taking your road—only I proceed on it more with the courage [of my convictions] and more "scientifically."

Do you remember that at one point I remarked to you that what I want to do is to stand Platonism on its head? Now I realize that you have done it; you have brought the Ideas down from heaven and planted them in the earth, into the human soul, into the brush of the painter and the chisel of the sculptor. Now we can start rebuilding that castle of the Ideas that lies in ruins because it was built only out of words.

One more thing: what was said may suggest to you that this is really Platonism turned upside down; there, art became superfluous; here, philosophy did. It is not so; art is the fulfillment of man's deepest yearnings. Philosophy has to do with something else: creating a world from this state of affairs (i.e., from the knowledge of what is given as the possibility of desire and fulfillment, of experience, and what is given as the possibility to know. These are the known variables). Philosophy has to state what kind of world it should be in which *this* is known (I see it as a definition of limits and qualities). We have therefore the Kantian question, but we ask it the way he did concerning mathematics, i.e., we take as a given what is really given and look for the circumstances which make it possible. This explains my question: Why is metaphysics necessary—the metaphysical as *Kategorienlehre* and not *Aussage über das Sein!* [propositions about Being]. Or only in an indirect way. Do you understand?

I have written a lot and it is late in the evening; I can't write about anything else today. Next time. Only this much: send me the Novalis[8] in Ms, but try to do it legibly so that I can dictate it. I'll send you back the typewritten version. Fischer decided against publication... after a long hesitation. ... Nothing is happening with it at present. Erich Reiss is a possibility.[9]

I was happy that you answered so quickly. Do it more often, at least write cards. Your situation will surely be changing. What are you doing? How are your days: I mean, aren't you bored that Bé's not there? Or is it better for you? Where is she going? Give her my warmest regards and tell her to let me know about her whereabouts. I plan to go to Italy in April. Are you going to be there? Take your time in answering all these questions—just write soon about your health.

Don't be cross with me for this "pathetic" letter; but I have felt with such a rare intensity the role of fate in our meeting... and one is allowed to be pathetic when it is a matter of fate. I could also tell you something about the book, and that counts. The other part of my letter is more important, though.

Hugs,
Gyuri

1 Lukács used the 1878 edition of Die Enneaden des Plotin translated by H. F. Müller into German. The English-language edition quoted here is *The Enneads* of Plotinus, trans. by S. MacKenna, 3d edition (New York: Pantheon, n.d.), "The Fifth Ennead," chap. 8, pp. 422ff.
2 See letter no. 29, n. 12. and n. 41.
3 See letter no. 47, n. 5.
4 Émile Boutroux (1845–1921), French philosopher, teacher of Bergson.
5 German text. "Form is a necessity of experience, it is a category of experience."
6 [Science is] a category of thinking, it is a possible and impossible, a uniform and non-uniform projection of reality.
7 "Why is metaphysics necessary? and yet impossible? How must the world be that it becomes impossible for the content to be perceived, proved and yet necessarily to be experienced. How must the soul be created that it must and yet cannot do it?"
8 Reference is to the Novalis essay from *Soul and Form*.
9 Erich Reiss, head of a Berlin publishing house.

59. TO LAJOS FÜLEP

Berlin
December 21, 1910

My dear friend,

I have some unpleasant news for you. Szilasi[1] wrote to me today and informed me of the following (I don't want to talk about the personal aspect, i.e., Szilasi's unspeakable behavior): he succeeded in persuading Alexander[2] to edit a Hungarian-language "Logos", with me as intended coeditor. The plan: some Hungarian professors would participate (Beöthy, Riedl, Angyal); some articles from *Logos* would be reprinted but no other translations, and, of course, there would be original contributions. He already contacted Mehlis.[3]

Immediately I wrote Alexander the following (including my personal opinion of Szilasi): that I gave my word to you and I'll act in *complete solidarity* with you. I indicated that I'll consult you and that *your answer will be my answer*. At the same time I specified our standpoint: (1) Concerning translations—both old and new (be it a *Logos* piece or not), as long as it contributes to the establishment of a philosophical culture in Hungary. Since the German philosophical culture was there, the German *Logos* can afford to be a "journal for the philosophy of culture". What we need in Hungary is a "journal for philosophic culture." (2) The contributors should have a new metaphysical and antipositivist philosophical standpoint—not an eclectic one.

Let's take a look at the practical side of the story. If Alexander wants to go ahead with the journal—financially he'd have no problems—then our planned journal is an *impossible venture.* He can get the financial backing, have a steady flow of paid contributors, and a distribution network with the help of the publishing houses, etc., etc. He would even be able to syphon off potential subscribers. As I see it, if he launches his journal, we haven't got a chance. I have a suggestion to make to you: Alexander should be isolated from his environment. One should make him believe that he is a new metaphysician and an antipositivist. It would have a price, of course: he would want to contribute to the journal—but one article per year wouldn't kill us. And he would secure for us the financial backing. The arrangement would have one *conditio sine qua non:* the editorship as a guarantee. I should like to propose (if you wanted to enter into the discussion at all) that the editors should be Alexander, you, Hevesi, and Zalai (Zalai[4] is a good idea, because he is always in [Buda]Pest, is very aggressive and utterly contemptuous of "Hungarian" philosophers), and I. In case we proceed, I would approach Simmel *myself* in order to limit the *Logos* contributions to one or two articles. This way it wouldn't be as beautiful an organ as we had in mind but it'd be financially secure and a feasible venture. Alexander thinks highly of both of us; the journal's fate ultimately would be in our hands.

Now everything depends on you. I repeat, your answer will be mine. I strongly believe that if his journal is founded, ours cannot be realized. Should you wish to go ahead regardless of everything, let me assure you that I am with you *without hesitation* (if I believe it won't succeed, it is only my opinion, and has no role to play in my decision).

May I ask a personal favor? You may be just as mad as I was, but *don't let it show* to Alexander (who simply might have been taken in by Szilasi). It would be unfortunate to make him into an enemy of a good cause; until now, you could always count on Alexander for support in an honest cause. I have my personal reasons[5] to wish to maintain cordial relations with him. Ergo, I recommend our "joining" him but will go along with whatever you decide.

Sincerely yours
György Lukács

1 Vilmos Szilasi. See letter no. 26, n. 1.
2 Bernát Alexander, see "Biographical Notes".
3 Georg Mehlis (1878–1942), professor of philosophy at Freiburg University, editor of *Logos* between 1910 and 1933.
4 Béla Zalai (1882–1915), Hungarian-Jewish philosopher, considered to have been the most promising talent in 20th-century Hungary, perished in WWI. He influenced Karl Mannheim and Arnold Hauser, among others.
5 Allusion is to Lukács's attempt to get habilitated at Budapest University, at which Alexander was one of the most influential faculty members.

60. TO BEATRICE DE WAARD

Berlin
[December 22], 1910

Dear Bé,

How could I not remember last year's beautiful Christmas? It was so peaceful, harmonious, like a family—in the profound sense of the word. Maybe, a family is where one can settle down quietly, where one can interact without exerting a lot of energy and intellectual compulsion, just by being oneself, where all this goes on quietly, beautifully, and as if without purpose. What a pity that this idea of the family is so seldom to be found in one's real family. To be with you was like that.

This time in all likelihood it will be at my place; Herbert[1] will come to Berlin and stay with me. I expect a couple of other people to come by. Ernst Bloch, for example, the German philosopher whom I probably mentioned to you last year. It might turn out to be quite pleasant—but hardly beautiful and harmonious.

I despise Berlin just as you do. Florence generated this change in me. Before, I didn't have sentiments about cities. I mean I admired some buildings or might have been disgruntled by some ugly sculpture. But imagine that a city should evoke physical reactions like a good suit or a great meal! I don't think I've experienced such things before. When I first visited Florence there was so much happening to me. You know all about that. Now I am relatively alone and it appears that my eyes have learned to take in more. It was with almost a childlike pleasure that I explored the city, the streets and plazas, wandering about, and stopping here and there. It all fit well... again I can't think of a better metaphor: it fits like a good suit. It is not that the houses are so beautiful: that is a matter of taste, something one is conscious about. In this case, I mean an almost animal pleasure that can be found in the layout. It comes, for example, from the center of the streets forming a concave dip and having no side walks; in this way, the cross-section of the street, from one house to another, gives the suggestion of a marvelously harmonious, continuous, peaceful, almost circular line so that whenever one takes a step one feels the sea flowing towards one.

Here, on the other hand, the street is an abstraction, means for handling traffic; it resembles ready-to-wear clothes that are too small or too big in places. There is neither unity nor harmony! After I've learned to enjoy a city, Berlin makes me suffer. I'll never again come to Berlin! And then the people! They're so noisy and self-complacent, so without modesty and humbleness—and still so insecure. Inwardly, they're so cowardly and indecisive that they don't even have the courage of their own meanness and stupidity. But you know all that. The way they handled Leo's article at the *Rundschau* is a good example.[2]

And I still don't want to leave right now. The library is very good. I can work here and that is the most important issue. Besides—you know me—I deem it improper to quit something just because it is unpleasant. One has to see things through! I'll be in Florence in the spring. And after that? I'm afraid after that come bad times: existential matters, career, Hungary. My feeling today is that if there is nothing positive possible (Italy or Paris) then everything's the same; Berlin or Budapest, it makes no difference. People don't count. Simmel[3] who was never more available (the last time he made me stay there for over two hours) cannot offer me much anymore; what I could learn from him, I did. Whatever I could at all learn from people, I already have learned—intellectually speaking. Now all I need is "people"—and there are not too many around. Therefore if there are no "real people", I'm indifferent to the difference between individuals. This way, an Edith[4] is more important to me than a Simmel or the *Neue Rundschau* crowd. (By the way, we never discussed it when we were together: how did you like Edith?)

Otherwise there is not much news to tell. I was very glad to hear that your father is on the mend. Give my regards to your parents. What are their traveling plans? If I go to Italy in the spring (April), I could manage to look them up. I'll certainly visit Leo in Gries. Where'll you be? In Paris? Write a few lines once in a while so that we don't lose track of each other. I'm afraid it'll be a while before we meet again. Summer maybe?

I had Aschers[5] send you two books. I wanted to send the first volume of [Meister] Eckhart[6] but it was sold out. Instead, you'll get a German theology (by a disciple of E.), also quite beautiful. The other volume is for Leo.

I wish you both a really beautiful Christmas.

Yours,
Gyuri

[1] Herbert Bauer, alias Béla Balázs.

[2] Reference is to the article, "*Der Kitsch,*" which was first commissioned and then rejected by the magazine. It was subsequently published in Karl Kraus's journal, *Die Fackel,* vol. 12, nos. 313/14 (December 31, 1910), pp. 36–43. Reprinted in Hungarian is a recent slim volume of essays by Leo Popper, *Esszék és kritikák* (Budapest: Magvető, 1983).

[3] Georg Simmel.

[4] Edith Bone, née Hajós (1888–1976), literary translator, physician, first wife (1913–19) of Béla Balázs. Born into a well-to-do Hungarian-Jewish family, she studied medicine in Budapest, Berlin, and Switzerland. Member of the Sunday Circle. Joined the CP, went to the Soviet Union as member of a Red Cross delegation. Lived and worked in Germany under the name "Bone" until the Nazi takeover when she fled to England. Returned to Hungary in 1949 and was imprisoned during the Stalin era. Freed in 1956, she went back to England where she died. Author of *Seven Years Solitary.*

[5] Well-known bookstore in Berlin.

[6] Johann Eckhart, called Meister Eckhart (1260?–1327), Dominican priest, father of German mysticism, Professor of philosophy in Paris, Strasbourg, and Cologne. In his teachings, he combined the mystical and intellectual elements of Thomas, intensified by Neo-Platonic idealism. He wrote sermons, tracts, and aphorisms. At a certain stage of his development, Lukács was deeply influenced by him.

61. FROM FRANZ BLEI

Florence
December 26, 1910

Dear Herr von Lukács,

I cannot begin to tell you how sorry I am not to have been acquainted with your absolutely beautiful essays[1] while I still had *Hyperion.*[2]

The journal of criticism is still very much in the planning stage and the first publication date is so uncertain that I cannot take the responsibility of holding on to your works. If you approve, I will gladly try to place them in the following manner: one of them[3] would be offered to the *Süddeutsche Monatshefte*[4], the other (on Philippe[5]), which at this very time is being read by Dr. Sternheim[6] (of *Logos*), to the *Neue Freie Presse*.[7] Dr. Schnitzler[8] had asked me about the Philippe piece when we last met in Munich. As soon as the new journal of criticism has been launched—which, by the way, will be called *Stendhal*[9]—I will very much count on your lively contributions.

Yours most respectfully,
Franz Blei

[1] Presumably some of the essays later collected in the volume, *Soul and Form.*
[2] German journal, started in 1908, but ceased publication in 1910.
[3] Not identifiable.
[4] *Southern-German Monthly,* conservative magazine.
[5] "Über Sehnsucht und Form: Ch.-L. Philippe" see letter no. 57, n. 4.
[6] Carl Sternheim (1873–1942), German playwright and expressionist writer.
[7] *New Free Press,* Viennese liberal daily.
[8] Arthur Schnitzler (1862–1931), Austrian writer and physician. His psychological novels and plays are well known.
[9] Project never materialized.

62. TO FRANZ BLEI

Berlin
December [?] 1910

Dear Herr Doctor,

Many thanks for your letter. It goes without saying that I accept your offer with pleasure and with gratitude.[1] You may place my essays as you see fit (with the exception of "Ch.-L. Philippe"[2]). Your letter encouraged me to approach you with an even more important question. These essays are part of an essay collection that I would very much like to see published by a first-class German publishing house. Do you think it a possibility that Hyperion Verlag[3] would bring out the book?

As you may know, the financial aspects are of no importance to me; my sole interest is in a first-class edition.

The title of the collection is *Die Seele und die Formen*.[4] The unifying theme of the book is the problem of form; its possibilities are discussed in relation to seemingly disparate and arbitrarily chosen aspects of life and art. The collection as it stands is (I hope) a totality: it covers all areas of literature with regard to the most important problems of form; at the same time, it deals with the problem of *Lebenskunst,* further, with the relationship between form and life. It is in this sense a book and not a "collection of essays". But it also aims at being a "book of essays". The interconnections, its unity, shall be merely immanent; on the surface, the collection may strike one as willful or even contradictory.

I would greatly appreciate it if you would inform me as soon as you can (without wanting to put pressure on you in any way) whether Herr Hans von Weber[5] would be interested in the book. The essays you already know can give you an idea about the rest, which I would send you later. Again, many thanks, dear Herr Doctor,

Most respectfully yours,
Dr. Georg von Lukács

[1] See letter no. 61.
[2] See letter no. 57, n. 4.
[3] The collection was subsequently published by Egon Fleischel, Berlin (1911).
[4] *Soul and Form.*
[5] At that time editor-in-chief of Hyperion publishing house.

63. TO LEO POPPER

Berlin
February 11, 1911

Dear sweet Leo,

I have neglected my correspondence for a long time; lately I have been very distracted and couldn't concentrate. Berlin has become an impossible place for me: so many people and so many nobodies. I don't get anywhere and can't get anything out of it. The book is a lot of trouble; I have to rework some of the translations (Sterne, Storm.)[1] In short, I have done almost nothing. The situation has its positive side, though (it appears that finally my life is in order), meaning that after a six-week break during which I wrote all kinds of things but nothing really good, I took up Hegel again, and *presto:* although I didn't start reading in a concentrated manner, and spent little time at it, within half an hour I found the *"Anschluss"* to the problems dropped six weeks earlier. This means that the great danger I faced in the spring, getting away from my work, is not a problem anymore. I shouldn't fool around with it, of course, and have to see that I make arrangements for an orderly, steady, and peaceful work environment, even if I have to pay for it by moving to Budapest. People have become so unimportant to me that the main thing is to have the comfort, the circumstances conducive to work (food, housing, society, finances); I have overrated the importance of the library in Berlin. What Italy can offer to me—although I wouldn't mind living in Florence for a couple of years—I can get by traveling. *Ergo,* the Great Leveling. I had somebody here who was very useful: Dr. Bloch[2], the German philosopher whom Simmel sent to me once, was the first inspiring intellectual after a long hiatus; he is a real philosopher in the Hegelian mold. Now he intends to move to a smaller German town—possibly to Bonn—and I would have nothing to do there. Of course, if it turns out that I need not or could not *habilitate* in [Buda]Pest within a reasonable time (until I finish the Plotinus[3]), then I would consider the Freiburg "adventure"[4] and Bloch may be able to join me there. But this is neither important nor timely. What is important is that everything is all right with me; once I start thinking that way, things are in order.

Otherwise I have little to report. Baumgarten[5] left for Munich and I don't mind; I still like him very much (and respect him for many reasons), but he was sometimes hard to take. It'll do our friendship good not to be together so often. It is the same with Herbert.[6] It is only with you that things are different. Enclosed is Irma's letter; I found it marvelously lacking in intensity, and it contains a few very good things. By the way, I wrote to her with regard to the dedication. She has no objections, is happy about it (expressed in a curious, in a Freudian way) so that her bad conscience shows. I wrote, namely[7],—as an aside—that the Hungarian-language volume is expanded with two essays, planned long ago. She misread it as "a novel", and of course was afraid that the truth would come out. I'll write to her to put her mind at ease. But the whole affair strikes one as tragicomic.

I am enclosing a funny review of my book.[8] Now let's talk about your affairs, about which I know very little right now. Thanks both to you and Bé for notifying me of your immediate plans. I'll stay here until the 24th or 25th, then will go to [Buda]Pest via Weimar–Vienna. (I'll give a talk in Budapest on the 5th of March on Shakespeare's late style.) Bé should tell me when she'll be in Dresden. It is so conveniently between Weimar and Vienna that it would be a shame if we couldn't arrange a meeting there. I should be around Dresden at the end of February. Tell me about that as soon as possible. How are you doing? How long will you stay there? Are you going to be there around the end of March or beginning of April? (In that case, I'll stop by.)

I am expecting news from you. I hope you don't mind this dry letter but I am afraid it's going to be my new letter-writing style. I don't have to explain to you what's happening and why. Many greetings to Bé.

Yours,
Gyuri

P.S. Bé's letter has also arrived but I couldn't answer it because of that whole circus with the publication. May I ask her forgiveness?

1 *Soul and Form.*
2 Ernst Bloch. See "Biographical Notes".
3 See letter no. 58.
4 Allusion is made to an alternate plan to get habilitated at Freiburg University.
5 Ferenc (Franz) Ferdinand Baumgarten.
6 Béla Balázs.
7 Reference is to an exchange of letters between Lukács and Irma Seidler who expressed her anxiety that Lukács planned to write a novel about their relationship and people might guess who she was (letter of February 8, 1911; in the Lukács Archives).
8 A review in the *Budapesti Szemle* (Revue) by János Horváth (1910).

64. TO MARTIN BUBER

Berlin W 50
Passauerstrasse 22
Monday, February 13, 1911

Dear Herr Doctor,

I have just learned from Mr. M. Heimann[1] that either tomorrow or the day after I could see you in order to discuss the matter of the "Aesthete"[2] for the *"Gesellschaft"*.[3]

I will thus come by tomorrow, Tuesday, between eleven and twelve.

Respectfully,
Yours very truly,
Dr. Georg von Lukács

[1] See letter no. 48, n. 8.
[2] This work never left the planning stage.
[3] *Society*. Series of social-psychological monographs of over 40 volumes, edited by Buber between 1905 and 1912, published by Rütten and Loening.

65. TO MARTIN BUBER

Berlin
Passauerstrasse 22
February 20, 1911

Dear Herr Doctor,

No offense, I hope, but I have to ask you to return my Kierkegaard manuscript.[1] Even if you have not read it yet, please send it to me, as I will certainly leave on Thursday, direct for Budapest. I would be very interested to find out how the work impressed you.

Respectfully,
Very truly yours,
Dr. Georg von Lukács

[1] "The Foundering of Form Against Life. Soren Kierkegaard and Regine Olsen," in *Soul and Form*, pp. 28–41. Lukács's friend, Leo Popper, translated the essay into German from the original Hungarian.

66. FROM MARTIN BUBER

Berlin
February 21, 1911

Dear Herr Doctor,

I am returning the Kierkegaard essay with many thanks. I find it exceptionally clear and solid in its formulation, delineation, and cohesiveness; what impressed me most was the discussion of *choice* and *psychology*. You have undoubtedly come closer to the core of the problem than any previous study. As a supplement, or possibly a correction (see points 1–4), may I call to your special attention the following passages (not in sequence as copied from random notes).[1]

1. What I write here is not even my opinion.
2. (1849) The explanation: the correct explanation, which I keep locked up in my innermost thoughts, namely, the explanation

which contains the real horror of the situation, I will after all never write down.

3. (1843) Had I enough faith, I would have stayed with her.
4. (1837) Oh my God, why did this affection have to strike me just now!
5. (1842) I do not have the time for marriage.
6. Later, I had to regard her as God's punishment of me.
7. I will carry her with me into history.

I was very glad to have this article, which gives such a deserving treatment to a subject of utmost importance to me. If it is not inconvenient for you, I would truly appreciate receiving the journal in which the essay will come out.[2]

Most respectfully yours,
Buber

[1] Buber most likely used two sources available in German at that time: *Kierkegaards Verhältnis zu seiner Braut. Briefe und Aufzeichnungen aus seinem Nachlass*, ed. by Hermann Lund (Leipzig, 1904) and the first volumes of *Gesammelte Werke* (Collected Works), ed. and trans. by H. Gottsched and C. Schrempf (Jena, 1909–1922), 12 vols. See "Diary of the Seducer," in S. Kierkegaard, *Either/Or*, vol. 1.

[2] See letter no. 65, n. 1.

67. TO PAUL ERNST

Budapest
March [?] 1911

Dear Herr Doctor,

I've just now found time to write to you. I talked with Herr Singer, the editor of *Pester Lloyd*, yesterday. He will be happy to publish your short story but not until the Easter issue, because they seldom publish short stories. If you are interested in this kind of arrangement for the Christmas and Easter issues, it could easily be arranged.

Apart from this, not much is new here. I hope to be able to travel to Florence at the beginning of April. When is the performance of your *Brunhild* scheduled in Munich? As soon as you find out, please let me know so that I can adjust my schedule accordingly.

Something else—but please do not think of it as an imposition. Ever since we met, I have been thinking of our discussions about publishing, journals, theater, and so on, and my conviction is growing stronger every day that the triumph of our *direction*—of the good cause—will be possible *only* through a strong alliance. An individual author on his own is just too isolated to break through the indifference and hostility which today surrounds everything that is honest. I know one can break in as an author on his own. And I am not worried at all about your plays (nor about my philosophy of art, just between you and me); but that the cause, as a *cause,* would be able to succeed is an entirely different matter from an isolated triumph, i.e., the isolated success of an isolated author. Now, if your short stories are published by Meyer & Jessen,[2] the scattering of resources will only increase. I truly believe that we now have the first (and probably the last) chance for forming an alliance; Fleischel[3] has the money, power (and possibly the inclination) to become a serious competitor to Fischer and *Rundschau.*[4] I do not know anybody else who could do it. But you know these things as well as I do.

Please give my regards to your wife. I hope to see you soon in Florence or Munich, or somewhere else, as long as we meet soon. As soon as you have finished the play,[5] please send it to me at my Budapest address (VI. Stadtwäldchenallee 20a).

With best regards,
Your
Georg Lukács

[1] German-language Budapest daily.
[2] Verlag Meyer & Jessen, Berlin–Vienna.
[3] Egon Fleischel & Co, Berlin.
[4] See letter no. 37, n. 4.
[5] *Childerich,* a tragic drama about the Merovingian dynasty.

68. FROM KÁROLY (KARL) MANNHEIM

Budapest
March 13, 1911

Dear Sir,

I have come across your writings now, at the beginning—at the very beginning—of my journey and I am very glad.

At the point when the living of an individual life on the one hand and *Kultur* on the other had become problematic for me, I saw every life as an open possibility for the other. Our humanity should help us to perceive that bond that connects us to others and then search on the basis of this perception for the appropriate form which determines the mode of approach between two human beings. I therefore wish to approach you within forms provided by *Kultur*.

It would perhaps be more seemly not to appear before you for now with the first and still undigested document of my life, my essay on the mystics.[1]

Impatience, however, spurs me on to ask you for your opinion, to hear your words and to find out whether you see the path that I am following.

While the fact that every life is an *a priori* opportunity for the other [person] encourages me to ask you more questions, my awareness that one should never violate the rules of modesty holds me back.

And so I shall ask you only that if my essay is of any interest to you and you have the time and inclination, please write me; and I'll make myself available to you anywhere and at any time.

Respectfully yours,
Károly Mannheim

[1] Mannheim's essay on mysticism was believed to have been lost. In 1983, however, the essay was discovered in Mannheim's London house by Mátyás Sárközi, who is writing his dissertation on Mannheim at the London School of Economics; the essay is being translated.

69. TO LEO POPPER

Budapest
March 19, 1911

My dear son, Leo,

Our letters crossed; now it is I who expects news from you, for example, about our next meeting and about whether or not we'll go to Munich together. I hope so. It would be great. You always want me to write about myself. Nothing significant happens to me in [Buda]Pest. I don't work, am spoiled and totally corrupted (in matters of intensity); at this point, if I can't work 7 to 8 hours straight, I don't even sit down to start. The only good thing that I have noticed lately is that idleness doesn't make me nervous anymore. It seems that my hysteria is gone. All I need now is to be able to settle down somewhere where I can get into a good working mood. Something will come out of it, I am sure. It is about time, too!

There is not much going on here. Poor Irma is in very bad shape. It seems that she is finally aware of what we all knew already: her marriage has failed. Besides, they're financially in bad shape too; it is my impression that they both live on the money she earns by teaching courses, etc. Poor Irma! Right now, all I feel is a great pity—and I would like to help her. I don't think that my wish is based on a subconscious feeling of "belonging together". (This is said with a certain degree of caution: we spoke to each other only in the presence of others and didn't have the opportunity for a sincere and intensive talk. Thus I can only assume that this is so.) I'll pay her a visit this week because it is important for me to know where I stand myself. Let me repeat: it would mean a lot to me (in case our relationship turned into a negative one, or in that case even more so) to be able to do something for her. You know me; you can imagine that I have analyzed myself as to my egoistic and hedonistic motives. I would like to be good to her.[1] I am not that—grateful perhaps, certainly correct. Don't protest, my dear son, and don't argue with me. You don't have any idea how much you have done for me. You must know that you have been indescribably kind to me. Whatever I could tell you about it would be mere meaningless stuttering compared to your beautiful songs. Irma is an entirely different case. That the harm she has caused me turned out to be to my advantage is not her doing; she is innocent in that. The fact that it was even worse for her is her misfortune. In only one respect do I think of myself as being (a little bit) good (in the Russian sense[2]) inspite of the horror of the relationship; I concede that "the Queen can do no wrong"![3] It is due to sheer egoism and a yearning for life's pleasures (as a result of my most recent self-analysis) that I'd like to heighten this feeling. And if this is true, it is just as well that she deprives me of this pleasure; that this great and (in spite of everything) pure feeling will evaporate into thin air. All I need is work (life demands it) and not pleasures. If she could only bring herself to trust me and let me do something for her.

I am gabbling too much. Cause for suspicion in your eyes, I am sure. I'd understand your being suspicious but it is unjustified. That's enough of this chatter; it is getting incredibly late. If I have time tomorrow, I'll write some more. If not, I'll mail this as it is. You should not have to wait longer. It is your turn now to answer my last letter even if a few lines only; at least send a telegram about your travel plans.

Tomorrow morning, my boy, I'll have to go and talk to my publisher about the book.[4] More next time!

Hugs,
Yours,
Gyuri

[1] This theme dominates Lukács's "confession", written after Irma's suicide. See letter no. 81, n. 1.
[2] Dostoevskian sense.
[3] Quotation in original English.
[4] Lukács's *Dramabook* was being published by Franklin Társulat in Budapest. Entitled, *A modern dráma fejlődésének története,* it came out in 1911.

70. FROM IRMA SEIDLER

Budapest
April 16, 1911

My dear good friend, Gyuri,

Why don't you write even a few lines? Write me a good, long, real Florence-letter about everybody and everything, about all the people and things I love so much. Nothing special to tell about me: I am sitting at home, working away from early morning—seeing nobody—and my wishes and wants don't go beyond peaceful work. Where shall I send the design for the title page?[1] What are your plans? Where is Edith heading?[2] Write to me; I'm so nervous nowadays. If I don't hear from you, I'll imagine I offended you in some way. Ugh, how strange and rotten this must sound to you in Florence of all places, where it's so easy to cast off earthly worries. I composed a letter before but didn't know your address and was hesitant to send it through the Vedreses.[3] *Don't tell them* about my writing to you. (This is being a bit overwrought, I guess!)

It's heavenly warm here—so much like Easter and spring time. I can almost see you and the Vedreses sitting in the grass *in corpore* after lunch and having the time of your life with some juicy gossip—and I can't be there! Have a great time, all of you. Bye-bye Gyuri. Don't forget to write—and when eating artichokes and peacocks, think of your faithful friend,

Irma

P.S. Write to the Oszlop St. 28. address.
My husband's not here. Nor are Uncle Károly and family. You are not here. Herbert[4] isn't here either. I am telling you this so that you'll see that you just have to write me.

[1] For Lukács's book, *Soul and Form.*
[2] Edith Hajós, wife of Béla Balázs. See letter no. 60, n. 4.
[3] Márk Vedres and family. See letter no. 47, n. 4.
[4] References are made to Károly Réthy, Károly Polacsek and family and, finally, to Béla Balázs.

71. TO IRMA SEIDLER

Florence
[April 18] 1911

Dear Irma,

Your reproach is well deserved, and I don't intend to excuse myself with having started and torn up two letters, etc., etc. The plain truth is that I wanted to write a real "Florentinian" letter but so far have not absorbed enough of the Florentine air. I have not quite attained my peace of mind and I am completely idle. And nowadays I despise myself when I don't work, that is, when—as Edith[1] is given to say—I have only an "inner life," in which case

I can't write at all. The sad conclusion to be drawn from this: I lost my talent for letter-writing. The alternatives are that either I have an "inner life" or—I hate to write this—I work with an intensified, "good" feeling (thank God, never), and then there is nothing to write about. Right now I am in a borderline situation. I settled in my living quarters (i.e., placed my books on the shelves) and tomorrow—maybe tonight—I will sit down to work. I do have at present an "inner life" but not the despicable kind—only a boundless happiness about finally being all by myself, about the long stretch of work lying ahead. (By the way, I plan to stay here until June; are you going to be in Budapest till then?)

In recent months there were too many people around me (inasmuch my "animus" would allow), and I don't regret it because I was able to gain a greater clarity about what is mine and what is not, what life can offer me and what I should expect from it, etc. My insight has become sharper because I used different measuring rods to set the bounds of my self and my existence. It was useful for me and it didn't hurt anyone. The yearning for aloneness grew day by day, though. I have become fully conscious of it only as I said good-bye to Leo in Gries. It is not something I can write about. . . . I couldn't say whether I ever loved Leo more than that time or right now—and whether I was ever happier to leave. I could breathe easier, the world expanded around me, things became more substantial and reasonable; and it seemed to me that the short chat I had with the conductor of the train (about one's rights and obligations) was as meaningful as our beautiful talks with Leo. Please don't misunderstand me! It is not the case of disillusion or loving Leo less—or the few others remaining for me. It is only the feeling growing stronger that the really important things in one's life happen in solitude. One can hardly even talk about them, not to mention making oneself clear or understood. But doesn't friendship pretend to do precisely that? The fact that it cannot make talks with one's friends only idle "chatter". If this sounds to you like the musings of a resigned man, it is not quite true. It may be tiredness, which has very valid inner roots; it has its psychological reasons; the few great and profound sentiments of my life were poured out into a vacuum, into an emptiness without ever being understood or even recognized for what they were (don't misunderstand me, I am not speaking here about unrequited feelings, only about comprehension!). I might be guilty of incomprehension too, of course! Only this much is certain: the feelings offered to me in a beautiful gesture didn't offer life or a prayer, they were an act of giving alms. I have lived on alms and thought I possessed a fortune (which it was, for me). For a long time I kept telling myself that life is like that: it is the inadequacy of life. Today, it doesn't hold true anymore. To put it simply, read Dostoevsky and you'll know what I mean. Today, I see life before me with the same clarity and sharpness that I do literature and I am unable to accept it in its present form, to which my psychic structure condemns me. It is not a matter of despair, though, proven by the fact that I experience its consequences, my solitude, as a redemptive joy. I don't look at resignation to being excluded from life but rather as a discovery *of life,* of *my* own form of existence; it is a life in which adequacy reigns. . . . That is why you have to understand: it was beautiful and very moving to meet you again in Budapest and there was a new relationship between us, which I consider only the beginning. (There are many things of the past to get out of the way, and one cannot make up for three years with a few afternoons.) It was also beautiful, an occasion to weep over, to have those five days with Leo in Gries; and it was nice here with Herbert[2] and Edith. But I am glad to be alone finally. I don't want to get all of you away from me; I just want to be with myself. This solitude is not shutting myself in; I feel (towards people, my people) like a soldier on guard duty, waiting for the order to come to do my best. Our words might prove inadequate to achieve understanding (at least for me), but our deeds can suggest an existing link between us.

But enough of this! It is unseemly to write such a letter from Florence. I have the feeling now that I have arrived here. Until now, it was only a nice excursion with Herbert and Edith. We looked at beautiful things, had a good time together, saw beautiful countryside and marvelous streets. But my Florence is the city of solitude, the city of past times (of last fall, accompanied by the ghost of that first stay, of that unforgettable one).[3] Today I have returned to Florence. Certain things I cannot write about. Not that much to write about people. You'll see Herbert soon, probably right away.[4] Edith goes to Bern. She is in good spirits, better than ever, and one can only wish that it will last; with her, this is always a problem. I should write about the Vedreses[5] but I can only sum up: the more I see of them, the less they mean to me. They're narrow, happy because of their limitations. Strong (I assume), but at the price of vulgarity, or rather, without refinement. And they haven't got what would make up for all this: the human or artistic genius. They are uninteresting. I hate to tell you all this, but I feel it my duty to do so: your emotional involvement with them requires that you see things clearly before you commit yourself further in your attachment. I am convinced that you are both capable of seeing and courageous enough to see things clearly. I even believe that you have known something like that for some time. They perceive things as good, only there is no goodness to be had without (inner!) struggle; what they call their "goal" they got cheap and, because they don't have the true goal, they don't have the true path to travel. They've got a combination of a profound untalentedness and of superficial honesty; their professed "depth" serves to keep from themselves their "cleverness" (not in the positive sense of the word if that word could at all have a positive meaning).

That is more than enough for today. Don't read more into this letter than there is: a temporary nervousness. In a few days I'll be in the middle of my work and although my outlook will be the same, my account of it will change. Please write about yourself! Because of nervousness, I was preoccupied with myself and talked only about me. Now it is too late to talk about you. (It wouldn't be nice and could look like an "afterthought"). But I have to know how you are, what is happening and how.

You'll write about everything, won't you?

As ever, your true friend,
Gyuri

[1] Edith Hajós. See letter no. 60, n. 4.
[2] Béla Balázs.
[3] Reference to the first stay in Florence in the company of Irma Seidler and Leo Popper, on May 28 1908.
[4] Ironically, Balázs and Irma just about the same time had an affair at the end of which, on the night of May 18, 1911, Irma committed suicide.
[5] Márk Vedres and his wife. See letter no. 47, n. 4.

72. TO MARTIN BUBER

Florence, 3 Piazza d'Azeglio
April 20, 1911

Dear Herr Doctor,

Please forgive me for the disturbance but it is important for me to know because of my work schedule whether a decision has been reached on the question of my volume *(Der Aesthet)*[1] for the series *"Gesellschaft"*.[2] I beg you to inform me—provided you want the volume—when I will have to be done with the work.

My Kierkegaard essay[3] has not yet been published. As soon as it comes out, I will take the liberty of sending you a copy. As for the passages, many many thanks! And also for the Chuang-Tzu[4] volume; it has given me much pleasure.

Your sincerely devoted,
Dr. Georg von Lukács

[1] See letter no. 64, n. 2.
[2] Ibid., n. 3.
[3] See letter no. 65, n. 1.
[4] *Reden und Gleichnisse des Tschuan-Tse* (Discourses and Parables of Chuang Tzu) a book on the Chinese sage (Leipzig, 1910), one of many anthologies Buber published dealing with mysticism in religions (Judaism, Christianity, et al.), folklore, legends, ranging from Celtic stories to the Finnish epic, *Kalevala*.

73. FROM MARTIN BUBER

Zehlendorf at Berlin
April 22, 1911

Dear Herr Doctor,

Unfortunately, I was unable to secure the publisher's[1] consent for this specific topic; and I had no choice but to concede the right of veto in order to get these last volumes published in the series.[2] I regret this very much but remain hopeful that one day you will still write this important book. Should you like, I will try to get the Insel Publishing House interested in it.

Your sincerely devoted,
Buber

[1] Rütten und Loening.
[2] See letter no. 64, n. 3.

74. TO MARTIN BUBER

Florence
3 Piazza d'Azeglio
April 24, 1911

Dear Herr Doctor,

Many thanks for the news and for your kind offer of trying to interest Insel in the project. However, the project is tied up with other problems to such a degree that I actually would have had to be really pressured to separate it from other related questions. (This is the reason why the *Gesellschaft*[1] had such an appeal for me.) As for now, I have no idea in what form I am going to do it; thus it would be premature to approach a publisher. (Besides, I have a three-year commitment to offer any new work of mine to Fleischel[2] first.)

Once again, many thanks.

In sincere devotion,
Georg von Lukács

[1] *Society.*
[2] Egon Fleischel & Co., Berlin. The publishing house brought out Lukács's essay collection, *Die Seele und die Formen* (Soul and Form), in 1911.

75. FROM BERNÁT ALEXANDER

Budapest
May 4, 1911

My dear friend,

I am the bearer of bad news: we have failed at the personal voting.[1] Out of 25, there were 13 "no's" and one blank. How could that happen? Gedeon Petz[2] spoke up against the delineation, i.e., definition of the field. He found the designation, "literary aesthetics," both vague and very unusual. He asked whether you would lecture on literature and on what kind of literature (German, French, English). The faculty must have been prepared because it demonstrated its appreciation of the point. Anyway, the faculty behaved with some nervousness and trepidation as the vote-taking and the debate went on. Beöthy[3] stood up in your defense and his own, saying that the expression is not unusual and the definition of the field is entirely legitimate. Medveczky[4] also spoke, and while he was not against you, he voiced the opinion that in a case like this, the faculty has to decide as a separate issue whether or not a (philosophical) *Privatdozentur* [lectureship] could be approved only two years after the Ph. D. This in itself wouldn't have presented a problem had Petz not mentioned earlier that you studied law; thus, the impression was created that you are not really a specialist. Beöthy again defended you, then came the voting; afterwards, Petz looked me up and asked me to tell you that he has nothing against you personally but thought the application premature; hence his comments. According to him, your book[5] rather embittered him; he thinks it unintelligible. I immediately went to your father and informed him. He was beside himself. He said he felt embarrassed because he pressured you into it. He also stated that you won't try a second time. This I'd regret very much. On the contrary, I think that you have to apply two years from now (as the rules stipulate) because the faculty will then act swiftly due to the feeling that they did you an injustice. I could see that Herr Petz himself was sorry about the whole thing; in its own defense, the faculty mentioned your age as a mitigating circumstance for its decision. In other words, you should not take it tragically. If you write to your father, convey to him your feelings, namely, that you don't mind it so much; it would be a great comfort to him. The same thing would've happened to Lipót Fejér[6] had he not withdrawn his application in time. And look, today the faculty extended an almost unanimous invitation to him to become an *Ordinarius* [professor for life].

I have to ask you not to take it too much to heart, not to become bitter; at present, the faculty doesn't know you at all but that will change in two years' time. Your father was here on Sunday and at that time I mentioned to him that I don't expect great difficulties, but that nothing is impossible. Petz seems to have a *very* great influence on the faculty. We tried to circumvent him but it soon became clear that he'd not let us get away with it. By declaring that it is not a designated field, he succeeded in swinging the faculty's decision.

I write these lines in a hurry; about other things the next time. [. . .]

With warm regards, also to Fülep,

As ever,
Alexander

The faculty at the University of Budapest; it voted against Lukács's *Habilitation.*

[2] See letter no. 53, n. 5.

[3] See letter no. 33, n. 3.

[4] Frigyes Medveczky, professor of philosophy member of the Hungarian Academy and the president of the Hungarian Philosophical Society.

[5] *A lélek és a formák* (Soul and Form).

[6] Lipót Fejér, mathematician, who at first had difficulties with his *Habilitation,* presumably both on the account of his progressive views and his being Jewish. See "Biographical Notes".

76. TO LEO POPPER

Pisa
May 19, 1911

My dear boy, Leo,

Just two lines; they are about two timely events: (1) I don't know whether I mentioned to you that *nobody knows* about my *Habilitation* affair;[1] consequently, nobody (not even Karli!) is aware of the failure. This is for your information only. (2) Fülep is interested in articles for the *Szellem.* Why don't you write up your theory of misunderstanding—as an experimental rendering (partially for yourself), so to speak. If you don't intend to submit original writing or a new work, could you translate something ("The Kitsch", for example[2])? In that case, contact F. If you have something unpublished, whatever it may be, he will surely bring it out. If it is a translation, better approach him beforehand.

I'll be in Budapest by Wednesday or Thursday. Write me how you feel.

Gyuri

[1] For the unfolding of the *Habilitation* "affair" see letter of Bernát Alexander, passim.

[2] See letter no. 60, n. 2.

77. FROM LEO POPPER

Görbersdorf
May 24, 1911

My dear Boy,

I have at this very minute received the horrible news[1] from Bé and I am shaken, immensely shocked and destroyed. I stand amidst the darkness in *guilty folly*. And I see you—with great sympathy—all shaken up, trembling and torturing yourself. What can anybody say? I only want to tell you that I am with you in the darkness; and even if I see nothing around me, *I can see you and know that you are pure and shining*.

I embrace you, my dear boy.

Yours,
Leo

[P.S.] Be it only a word, I am waiting to hear from you.

[1] Of the suicide of Irma Seidler. For further references see "Biographical Notes", and letter no. 50, n. 7.

78. TO LEO POPPER

Budapest
May 26, 1911

My dear Boy,

Just two lines so that you won't worry about me. Only this much now: I am alive. And that means I'll go on living. Everything remains in complete darkness. Nobody seems to know anything. Nothing. One cannot even begin to guess the reason.

Concerning myself, I'll have more to say another time. Now only this much: loneliness, which I so desired, is upon me like a life sentence. If anyone could have saved her, it was I... and I did not want and could not. I was her "good friend," I know, but she did not want that; she wanted something else, something more. And I was not ready to act. Hence, the verdict is in.[1]

It is all the same now. My life had meaning only when I took it to her on an occasional afternoon, just as others (better ones than me) take roses with them on a visit. But don't worry about me. In a few days I'll be able to start working, and that is the only thing remaining for me and will forever be in the future.

Gyuri

[1] Lukács, who stayed in Italy at the time, wrote in his diary (May 24, 1911) that Irma's suicide meant "a death sentence on his existence," i.e., the end of meaningful "human relationships". His frame of mind and guilt feelings have been expressed in his dialogue, "On Poverty of Spirit". See letter no. 81, n. 2.

79. FROM LEO POPPER

Görbersdorf
June 26, 1911

My dear boy,

My correspondence certainly has shriveled to almost nothing. I haven't written to you since God knows when. It is very painful but I just cannot do it; nine tenths of the time because I feel very ill, one tenth of the time because I don't dare. Every loudly spoken word, every open-eyed look at the world ends with the realization that I hear the noise of the world and see the lights of the world and then I see myself as a black hole, as a deadly pause. I am longing to see you; now, in these last days I have needed you so badly. But I didn't ask you to come because you're in the middle of your work, and it might not have been good for me either. Since then my ability to speak has improved. It seems—I am at the stage—that my "organism" doesn't mind anymore what I do. Otto [Mandl] was here; I talked incessantly for four days and felt quite all right. From now on, hard times are in store for the Poppers, poor things. Write my boy, a few lines only, what you're doing, how you're doing.

With warm embrace,

Leo

80. TO PAUL ERNST

Budapest
[early July] 1911

Dear Herr Doctor,

I did not intend to write you until after matters had become past events to be referred to . . . ; unfortunately, the present completely refuses to become past . . . What I hinted at in my last letter was the absolutely unexpected and unexplainable suicide of a human being who stood very close to me.[1] There is not much more one can say about it. In consequence, I've become terribly nervous, sometimes apathetic, sometimes overexcited, unable to work, etc., etc. It's better now but still far from being all right. (On top of my nervousness I have anaemia of the brain, resulting in strong headaches.) My works progress at a very slow pace but you will certainly have the article at the deadline.[2]

How are things with you? How was Paris? What are your new plans and the prospects for the old dramas? I can hardly wait to read *Crispin*.[3] If the cholera remains unchecked in Italy,[4] I'll spend the winter in Berlin. We could then arrange a meeting either in Berlin or Weimar; this is my ardent hope. Otherwise, I'll go to Florence for the winter. My essay appeared in *Logos*;[5] you should receive your reprint any day now. I assume that you have read "Brunhild," in the *Schaubühne*.[6]

With warmest regards to your wife,

your devoted
G. v. Lukács

[1] Reference is to Irma Seidler's suicide on May 18, 1911.
[2] Ernst asked Lukács for a contribution to an anthology. The project seems not to have materialized.
[3] *Der heilige Crispin*, a drama by Ernst.
[4] This was the widespread cholera epidemic that Thomas Mann's story, *Death in Venice*, described.
[5] Reference is to the essay, "Die Metaphysik der Tragödie".
[6] Lukács wrote a short essay on Ernst's drama, *Brunhild*, out of which grew the essay, "Metaphysics of Tragedy". See *Soul and Form*.

81. TO LEO POPPER

Budapest
August 7, 1911

My sweet son, Leo,

You have heard nothing from me for a long time and I haven't heard from you either. I don't know what that means in your case. With me, everything is the same. My big problem: I haven't been (and still am not) well and struggle with anemia, nervousness, bad headaches, resulting in a never-before-experienced drop in intensity. If I didn't have to bother with these problems, a large-scale work could've helped me to go through these bad times.[1] I have done little since then. In a few days, I'll send you the most important writing of late, a dialogue entitled *"Von der Armut am Geiste"*.[2] After you have read it, please let me know immediately whether I should publish it or not. Fülep has been asking me to give him something for *Szellem*[3] and I don't have anything else ready. As for me, I can't judge its worth. It is possible that it's quite good, precisely because it is very subjective and not at all "scholarly". I was inwardly compelled to write it (which, of course, has no bearing on its value), and the ideas it contains may one day develop into scholarship but certainly not for another five or six years. The questions themselves are good and secure in their positing—but only within the sphere of objectified experience and not objectifications in the sphere of philosophy. I still worry: isn't it too much of a hybrid as it stands? I just don't know. I am sending it to you and also to Bloch.[4] You shall decide its fate.

By the way, this article will tell you more about my state of mind than any letter could. You'll learn from it how I feel and what I strive to overcome. There is hardly anything else to tell; my life has never been so empty as it is now. At this stage my only wish is for health and for work. I think I'll go to Florence during the winter. If the book needs additional work, I'll get off at Görbersdorf. But don't count on it. I might go straight to Florence (because of my nerves) and only in the spring to the North. Everything is in flux. I would like to meet you, and then again I'd prefer to do it when I'm in better shape. I have my vanity when I am facing you; for the others, the gesture of strength is sufficient, but never for you—you'd know. In my present state, I don't even like myself.

At present, I lead a retired kind of life. I see hardly anybody and don't correspond much. Unfortunately there are some "official" (literary) matters to take care of. This letter was delayed too on their account.

I have just started and have already come to the end of the letter. Please forgive me and try to understand. Write if you can soon, but send your opinion in the form of a "yes" or "no" about the dialogue as soon as possible, please!

Yours,
Gyuri

[1] Allusion is to the aftermath of the Irma Seidler affair.
[2] "Von der Armut am Geiste. Ein Gespräch und ein Brief" (On Poverty of Spirit. A Discussion and a Letter), published in the *Neue Blätter* (Hellerau Germany), vol. 7., no., 5—6 (1912), pp. 67–92.
[3] Under the title, "A lelki szegénységről", the dialogue was published in *A Szellem* in 1911.
[4] Ernst Bloch. See "Biographical Notes."

82. TO LEOPOLD ZIEGLER

Budapest
[August 10] 1911

Dear Herr Doctor,

I hope and trust that you will forgive my bothering you again and with a request at that. A few months ago a few of my like-minded friends and I started a philosophical journal in Budapest somewhat similar in its content and aims to the German *Logos.*[1] The planned fusion with *Logos* didn't materialize although we envisioned our journal to be its Hungarian counterpart and even had some preliminary discussions with some of the gentlemen from *Logos.* Alas, the nature of the Hungarian philosophical culture warrants a different approach. Unlike Germany, no fertile (philosophical) ground exists in Hungary for such a journal as *Logos;* accordingly, we had to devise a simpler and more general approach. For example, we plan to publish translations from pre-modern philosophers whose work is well known by the readers of *Logos;* in our country, even the philosophically inclined lay audience is not acquainted with the thoughts of a Plotinus, Meister Eckhart, and so on.

This brings me to the purpose of my letter, esteemed Herr Doctor. We would like to obtain your permission to translate and print in our next issue the chapter on Kant from your book, *Der abendländische Rationalismus und der Eros.*[2] What I wrote earlier serves as an explanation of why we chose this treatise instead of another of your works, such as for example, one of your contributions to *Logos*. Any knowledge that exists of Kant in Hungary is based on the narrowly conceived and conceptually confused understanding of Kant at the end of the 19th century. Your treatise would serve as a propagation and a preparation for the correct study of Kant. It could have an unconceivably beneficial effect on Hungary's cultural life.

In the hope that your consent will be forthcoming, I remain

Most respectfully yours,
Dr. Georg von Lukács

[1] The journal in question was *A Szellem*. See letter no. 56, n. 4.
[2] The chapter from Ziegler's 1905 book, entitled *Occidental Rationalism and Eros*, was translated into Hungarian by Emma Ritoók and printed in the second issue of *A Szellem*, (I. no. 2. 1911) pp. 215–32.

83. TO LEO POPPER

Budapest
August 27, 1911

My sweet Leo,

Since you have not written a letter to me for a long time now, I am anxiously awaiting a few lines. Karli[1] mentioned that you may leave G.[örbersdorf]. When? It is possible that I have to go to Berlin in September and I could visit you there. But I don't know anything for sure; my work is crawling along ("writing" is not the right word) and there is no telling when it'll be finished.[2] I've decided not to leave [Buda]Pest before my work is done. My pace nowadays parallels yours (10 lines per day) and I still feel as exhausted as when I used to write 10 pages a day. You can see from this that my state of mind is anything but good. [. . .] I am sitting at my desk, waiting for the sentences to come along, although the whole thing is all complete in my thought (and that is the disgusting part of it), even to the point of boredom; it is disgustingly complete in my mind. At this rate, I'll need 2,000 years to finish my work.

You will find humor in this situation. I was never so liked and loved by my family as now—at the worst stage of my life. Before, I used to see them only at the dinner table, at meal times, and upon finishing, I used to excuse myself by referring to the work to be done. But now (and you know well this puritanical streak in me!) I would consider it posturing if I stated that I have to run to work. Since I cannot work anyway, it would be striking a pose to send Mici away when she comes in to visit me in my room—I am doing nothing, after all. It would be a pretense not to accompany my father on his walks, etc., etc. It is posturing even to show how nervous and irritated I am; and I despise myself as well as my life. Not to mention that one can *encanaille* oneself by complaining to the wrong people. One disregards the basic rules of good manners by being unjustifiably ill-humored among the merry crowd if one is not toiling away on *the work (das Werk)*. The best way is to become like other ordinary people, that is, to become a lesser man (as regards goodness and usefulness). After all, by what justification is one entitled to supercilious remarks and tone?

Ergo, for the first time in my life I am a nice and good little boy. Do you find that funny? I do. Although I don't have my reasons for it. You know what? This reminds me of our old times together when we discussed humor and you said that I don't have a sense of humor. Now I do! My previous conviction is vindicated: when I am shit, a piece of dirt, lying on the ground, I'll have found my sense of humor.

I would like to tell God that I don't want any of this. But he hasn't been open to my suggestions lately. Had I become convinced that he has withdrawn his support for good, I'd take the consequences. But I do have "ideas," the system is coming along, built up little by little; only I can't seem to force myself to work.

What do you think of the skirmish between Kerr and Kraus?[3] Don't you see that this vindicates my professed opinion of them? Essentially, both of them are superficial idiots; as thinkers, they are "kitsch"-makers; as a moral force: nil, zero. (They have a stylistic value and a sense of humor.) Kraus makes me nervous by his constant irritation with the trivialities of life. If the churlishness of the Imperial Court can elicit such pathetic reaction from him, he will never be able to rise to the occasion. Pathos is justified only if it accomplishes something, if it helps to penetrate the interior and the depth of things. Oh yes, we do find policemen in Hegel's philosophy of right but only as asides, as illustrations, and only after Hegel described God's relation to the world. I had to say this because you and others perceive a thinker lurking in this gentleman [Kraus], and don't see that he is merely a journalist of smart (but often manneristic) style who is often witty but more often offensive. He may be a notch above Kerr—cleverer, more entertaining, and of wider horizon—but it is not a qualitative difference.

Ady[4] as a journalist is a million times more valuable.

Well then, write me once in a while. Something maybe about the *Armut*.[5] At any rate, send back the manuscript if finished with the reading and the Dostoevsky book as well.

God be with you!

Gyuri

[1] Károly Polányi, who visited Leo Popper in the final stages of his illness, along with another friend, Henrik Herz. Lukács never again visited his friend, who was dead in less than two months after this letter.

[2] Reference is to *Die Ästhetik der 'Romance.' Versuch einer metaphysischen Grundlegung der Form des untragischen Dramas,* which remained a fragment. A shortened version, entitled "Das Problem des untragischen Dramas", appeared in *Die Schaubühne,* no. 9 (1911).

[3] Alfred Kerr (1867–1948), Germany's leading theater critic, noted for his impressionistic style as well as for his viperous reviews based on personal animosities; Karl Kraus (1874–1936), Viennese journalist, founder of the one-man journal, *Die Fackel* (The Torch), from 1899 to 1936. His satirical thrust was aimed at the Press, Church, military, hypocrisy, the advertising industry, among others. His writings explored the relationship between language and behavior; for him, corrupt language meant corruption of thought as well as corruption of private and public action. Author of *The Last Days of Mankind* and *In These Great Times*.

[4] Endre Ady. See letter no. 15, n. 3.

[5] *Von der Armut am Geiste* (On Poverty of Spirit).

84. TO PAUL ERNST

Budapest
[September ?] 1911

Dear Herr Doctor,

The news about the *Jahrbuch*[1] makes me see red. I can already see that I'll be forced into purely "scientific" philosophy. Whenever one opens an issue of a yearbook or journal, one is horrified by the spiritual *(geistige)* decline of Germany: there is an overwhelming fear of profundity and reflection. Sch.[effler]'s[2] remark about the "practicality" of things belongs to that category. What could be more practical, I ask you, than to tell your readers: become conscious of your own self! You cannot change the external world; build a new world out of yourself![3] That is what my article contained and I find it more practical than all that talk about *Gartenstädte* and *Reihenkolonien,*[4] concepts offered by the philosophical dilettantes who think it will solve all aesthetic problems. It really looks as if Kant and Hegel lived in vain for the Germans. Almost nobody in Germany today seems to know that such a thing as *Selbstbewegung des Geistes* exists, that one can act *only* on the *Geist*. And what is more: nobody wants to know! They believe in the redemptive force of the "practical" solutions. But why do I tell you all this when you already agree with me.

Many thanks for the review offer! Please send me your address in Zurich so that I can send you the book.[5] What do you think: shall I send (review) copies to [Wilhelm von] Scholz and Stoessl?[6]

One more practical question—if you don't mind! It is of some importance to me that I find a line to scholarly-philosophical journals. I learned from your previous letters that you talked to Simmel about me. Would you give me your impression? Can I approach him with such questions? (It has to do with placing several of my essays.)

Next week I'll probably travel to Berlin to take care of some business matters. After that, it is Florence—probably until summer. If you write, please use my Budapest address; my parents forward everything.

Have a pleasant trip!

Your sincerely devoted,
G. v. Lukács

[1] Reference is to a planned project. Ernst and Karl Scheffler planned the publication of a *Yearbook* which was accepted in principle, by the J. C. B. Mohr publishing house in Tübingen. Later, the firm offered compensation in order to get out of the contract.
[2] Karl Scheffler. See letter no. 6, n. 4.
[3] The same idea is at the root of Lukács's essay on Kassner in *Soul and Form*.
[4] Allusion is to the propagation at that time in Germany of the "healthy" environment and way of life.
[5] *Die Seele und die Formen.*
[6] Wilhelm von Scholz (1874–1969), German neo-classical dramatist, writer

and critic with a mystical bent. Author of the play *Die Juden von Konstanz* (1905) and *Die Gedanken zum Drama* (1905); Otto Stoessl (1875–1936), Austrian writer, essayist and journalist. For a while, he was a contributor to *Die Fackel*, Karl Kraus's journal.

85. TO PAUL ERNST

Cap Martin
Hôtel près Menton
October [?] 1911

Dear Herr Doctor,

Thank you very much for the review;[1] a lot can be expected from a Georg Lukács! The other reviews that came today similarly demonstrate complete incomprehension but not without a certain decency of tone—but then again, it might just be a sign of the cowardice and lack of conviction so characteristic of our times.

Our meeting in Genoa was in a certain sense both strange and significant. I have neglected Goethe for some years; this time I took along his *Wilhelm Meister* and read it, together with the novella from the *Wanderjahre*,[2] and was entirely overwhelmed. Now I am tackling the *Wahlverwandtschaften*[3] and plan to read the rest as well. From this perspective I appreciate even more the tone of your short stories. You seem to resume the grand tradition of the *German* novelette. To be sure, I cannot as yet define the essence of the German novelette, but it seems to me that its *punctum saliens* lies in its great breadth, in its atmosphere, which makes it possible to enclose a plentitude of meaning, inner depth, a comprehensive and highly differentiated social picture, and an ethical sensitivity, all of which cannot be found in the simpler and more robust French and Italian stories. Just as you as a dramatist (as I see it today) return to the tradition represented by Schiller and Hebbel (and thus Alfieri[4] is nothing but a pretext), your prose fiction shows remarkable fidelity to the Goethean tradition that ended with Keller's[5] death. All in all, I believe that "Der schmale Weg zum Glück"[6] comes closer to a work like *Wilhelm Meister* than you yourself may have realized. I first saw this trend in the work of Pontoppidan;[7] as soon as my short essay on him (Feb. 1910) is published, I will send it to you. I now view your new short stories differently (I mean those you read to me in Genoa. I haven't received the book[8] yet; it might be lying around in Florence with my other books that have not been forwarded to me yet), namely in a significant and most fortunate context. This short story as well as your tragedy now constitute a cultural value for Germany, while your old style was more of the purely artistic and aesthetic kind.

The weather continues to be bad. I will leave for Florence some time next week; if possible, I will visit Frau Schorn in Genoa. Kahn[9] and his wife will probably travel to Florence at about the same time. He still has not regained his peace of mind; I don't know what is going to happen.

I am enclosing a few stamps for Walter.[10] My father will send him more from Budapest.

Give my warmest regards to your wife.

Cordially yours,
G. v. Lukács

[1] Not identifiable.
[2] *Wilhelm Meisters Wanderjahre.*
[3] *Elective Affinities,* Goethe's novel from his Romantic period.
[4] Count Vittorio Alfieri (1749–1803), Italian dramatist.
[5] Gottfried Keller (1819–1890), Swiss-German writer, author of *Martin Salander* and of the *Bildungsroman, Der grüne Heinrich.*
[6] *Narrow Path to Happiness,* Ernst's novelette.
[7] Henrik Pontoppidan (1857–1943), Danish writer. Among his works: *Hans im Glück.* Lukács's review appeared in *Aurora* (1911).
[8] Reference is to *Der Tod des Cosimo,* a collection of short stories by Ernst.
[9] Harry Kahn (1883–1970), German essayist, translator, at that time editor at Egon Fleischel & Co., the publisher of *Soul and Form.* Their friendship dates from his work on Lukács's Ms.
[10] Son of Ernst by his second wife, Lilli.

86. TO MARTIN BUBER

54 via dei Robbia
Pensione Consigli, Florence
November [?] 1911

Dear Herr Doctor,

I have asked my publisher to send you a copy of my book;[1] and although I cannot expect the subject matter of the whole collection to interest you as greatly as the Kierkegaard essay[2] did, I do hope that the volume proves to be an enjoyable reading. I am eager to hear your comments on the book (and I hope that such an opportunity will present itself), but this is not why I am writing to you. Rather, it is to express my deep gratitude for your two books, *Baal-Schem* and *Rabbi Nachman,*[3] both of which I didn't get to finish until last summer for several reasons.

Baal-Schem especially was an unforgettable experience! What a pity that there is not more of it; it is almost impossible to believe that nothing more survived! Do you know of any other editions (in German, French, or English)? Or do you think, revered Herr Doctor, that you will in the future undertake an enlarged edition? I should think that, as in the case of the Indian texts,[4] it may not be possible to put a complete edition together? There are so many things, such as, for example, the ethical aspects of reincarnation, that one would like to become acquainted with, that is, with the whole range of historical tradition.

Most respectfully yours,
Dr. Georg von Lukács

[1] *Die Seele und die Formen.*
[2] See letter no. 65, n. 1.
[3] Reference is to *Die Legende des Baalschem* (1908) and *Die Geschichten des Rabbi Nachman* (1906), published by Rütten und Loening, two of the numerous volumes devoted to Hasidism, written between 1904 and 1963. Lukács's interest was both deep and genuine, as their publication coincided with his discovery of his "Jewishness". His enthusiastic review on Buber's work entitled "Zsidó miszticizmus" (Jewish Mysticism) appeared in the Hungarian magazine *A Szellem* (Spirit), in 1911.
[4] Lukács alludes to the collection of *Sutras.*

87. TO PAUL ERNST

Florence
[November] 1911

Dear Herr Doctor,

I have a favor to ask: enclosed you will find my short obituary of Leo Popper. The *Neue Rundschau* first accepted it and then returned it to me. Can you think of a journal that would print it? I know that Scheffler[1] doesn't like my writing but he thought very highly of Leo Popper. Maybe he would print it in the *Kunst und Künstler?* (Leo Popper was a contributor to the journal.) If nothing can be done there, can you think of something else? How about Stoessl[2] in the *Fackel?* (Leo Popper contributed to the *Fackel* too.) I must admit I would like that solution least. In general, I don't care whether my work gets printed or not but I know that nobody else will even write a line about Leo Popper and so it is important to me.

Did you receive my book? How did you like it? Fleischel notified me a few days ago that the book is out but I don't have a copy yet.

Following your advice, I will have a copy sent to Stoessl, but he should be alerted to it.

When will I have the opportunity to read *Ariadne?*[3] Did the novels come out in the meantime?[4] I haven't heard anything around here about Germany.

My work is still not progressing well. For over a week I had such rheumatic pains in my right shoulder that the writing is nothing if not an acrobatic act.

With warm regards,

Yours respectfully,
G. v. Lukács

[1] Karl Scheffler. See letter no. 6, n. 4. In his letter to Ernst of November 15, Scheffler rejected the Ms and wrote among other things that although he deeply respected Popper, such an obituary cannot be printed. "It is an impossibility to write this way—even about a dead person," he wrote, "it is not an obituary but a theory of art." The obituary was published in German in the *Pester Lloyd* in Budapest: "Leo Popper (1886–1911). Ein Nachruf," no. 339–40, pp. 560–61.
[2] Otto Stoessl. See letter no. 84, n. 6.
[3] *Ariadne auf Naxos* (1911).
[4] *Der Tod des Cosimo* (1911).

88. FROM JÓZSEF VON LUKÁCS

Budapest
November 17, 1911

My dear son, Gyuri,

Your good wishes are greatly appreciated; I am well and rather satisfied with myself.

The publication of your book gave me great pleasure;[1] it is a beautiful edition too. It is also nice that you have received 500 marks as an honorarium; I want to impress on you that the money is *yours,* that is, don't use it for everyday expenses which are my duty to meet. You have to get used to the idea that you have to accumulate some capital, and you should start with moneys you receive in the form of honorariums.

The book you ordered has arrived and I have asked Mici to forward it to you. I talked to Gajári on behalf of Balázs.[2] He was being very officious. In the meantime, I reminded him of the matter and he promised to look into it and treat it with appropriate good will. As soon as I hear from him, I'll let you know.

Saturday—that is, yesterday—was spent in the important mission of going to see the Poppers[3] (on the basis of Otto Mandl's letter); and I talked to them on behalf of Bé.[4] The reception was even worse than expected; the old man doesn't want to accept any obligation and denies that it was Leo's wish. Even if conceded that it was Leo's wish, he'd want no part of it, first, because Bé isn't ill; she didn't get anything fatal from Leo, and her parents are well-to-do. He has made inquiries, so he said, and was told that her father is solvent. Second, Bé is to blame for the premature death of Leo because she shlepped him to Berlin, and Leo, in order to please her, led an irrational life. Bé knew well—because he, the old man, told her so—that Leo was so ill that marriage was out of the question. If after that Bé chose to maintain their relationship and got engaged, she has to take the consequences. He therefore rejects all responsibility; should she fall into poverty one day, and turn to him, he'd consider helping her. Naturally, I didn't volunteer the information that we have been supporting her all along. I restricted my remarks to recommending that the Poppers should think it over because every human being has some obligations toward others that are more important than those required by law. I don't believe the old man will give in, and for him the only significance of Leo's death lies in the fact that he doesn't have to pay for his cure anymore. [....]

During our discussion the old man mentioned that Leo confessed to him something that has to do with you. Thinking that it is about the money we sent to Bé, I remarked that you would not discuss money matters. But it came out gradually that you had previously lent 1,000 Kronen to Leo which he wants to give back to you. If you agree, I'll tell him when I see him that the next time he should give me the money and you'll then give it to Bé. On that occasion, I'll also inform him that you, that is we, sent monthly support to Bé on a regular basis and will continue to do so until she gets well enough and won't need it anymore. Should he stick to his standpoint, I'll tell him coldly that I will sever all connections with him and no longer wish to know him. I assume that poor little Mici will turn to you for advice on what she should do. I don't think that a break in our relationship should be of consequence to her. She can go on taking cello lessons for which she pays handsomely; the old man is not interested in anything but money.

I'll answer Otto Mandl's letter after I have heard from you; similarly, only after I hear from you will I inform Polányi[5] that my intervention was in vain.

Many loving embraces and kisses from your

Father

[1] *Die Seele und die Formen.*

[2] Béla Balázs was constantly in need of money and the Lukácses often helped him out. They also approached Bernát Alexander and others, to find a teaching position for him. The reference is to Ödön Gajári, formerly Bettelheim (1852–1919), journalist, lawyer, later member of the parliament on the ticket of Count Tisza's "Liberal Party". After 1884, steady contributor to *Pester Lloyd* and other newspapers. Founded *Az Újság* (The News), a daily advocating Tisza's political line, in 1903; hence, Lukács *père*'s appeal to him.

[3] David Popper and his wife, parents of Leo Popper. See also letter no. 96.

[4] Beatrice de Waard.

[5] Karl Polányi. See letter no. 96.

89. FROM MARTIN BUBER

Zehlendorf/Berlin
December 3, 1911

Dear Herr Doctor,

Many thanks for your thoughtfulness in having sent me your book. I have already begun reading it—and with great pleasure. I admire its finesse and cohesiveness as well as its beautifully balanced way of argumentation amid the torrent of *Problematik*. That you found my "Chassidica"[1] satisfying, I was very happy to hear. I must confess (I cannot keep it from you)—and I hope that your feelings for the work will not be negatively affected—that in *Baalschem* the innermost motifs alone are "authentic". I refer to the stories only, naturally, since the sayings quoted in the foreword are exact translations of the original.

The same is true of the last two poems of *Nachman*. For this reason, you can see why a collection of texts as you envision is such a tricky affair. I could, I suppose, put together a slim volume of aphorisms—I have, indeed, given it some thought—but the bulk of the text of the stories would yield certain motifs only. Should you come to Berlin (when will that be?) I will do an on-the-spot literary translation of a few texts for you. You will then have a better understanding of my attitude and the situation itself. On top of that, there are no other "Chassidica" in Europe beside my books and a few folksy pamphlets. The broad historical tradition of Hasidism you spoke of is dead—gone. Its renewal can come only from the very narrow confines of the human brain.

With warm greetings,
Yours faithfully,
Buber

[1] "Hasidic Tales." Buber's Hasidic writings, *The Legend of the Baal-Shem* and *Tales of the Hasidim,* were published by Schocken, and *The Tales of Rabbi Nachman* by Avon Books (1970). The first complete translation into English of a significant part of "Chassidica" was published in 1970: *In Praise of the Bal Shem Tov,* transl. and ed. by D. Ben-Amos and J. Mintz (Bloomington, Ind., 1970).

90. TO FRANZ BLEI

Florence
[December 10]1911

Dear Herr Doctor,

My most sincere thanks for your letter. I am looking forward to reading your detailed criticism of my book,[1] a difficult, if not impossible, task to accomplish in a letter. That is why I am very glad about the review you promised, independently from its effect on the reception of the book.

Since you showed interest in my ongoing work, may I send you one of my most recent works?[2] I believe it'll be only the first in a series of ethical-religious treatises, while my first book remained in the realm of the metaphysics of art.

Last winter you were kind enough to offer your mediation at the *Süddeutsche Monatshefte.*[3] I would accept it gladly for this work if you deem it likely that it can be placed at the *Süd. Monatshefte*. If not, I would like to ask you to return the MS at some future date.

Most respectfully,
Your sincerely devoted,
Dr. Georg von Lukács

[1] *Die Seele und die Formen*. In fact, only a short announcement appeared in a little magazine, *Der lose Vogel* (The Loose Bird), (January 1912), p. 36.
[2] *Von der Armut am Geiste* (On Poverty of Spirit). See letter no. 81, n. 2.
[3] See letter no. 37, n. 5.

91. FROM BERNÁT ALEXANDER

Budapest
December 11, 1911

Dear Herr Doctor,

Your letter was most welcome in that we finally heard from you. The day of your visit I was not back yet; in fact, I returned from my trip that very night. Had I met you then, I would have implored you in person not to settle abroad but to come back as soon as possible or necessary and get your *Habilitation* at the University here. I find it typical that just the other day one faculty member remarked—at the Committee meeting on a similar case—that not even in your case did we waive the three-year waiting period between the doctoral degree and the *Privatdozentur* [lectureship].

In other words, people remember your case as having failed on account of the missing three-year waiting time. This was the obvious reason for his "nay". Another person told me that he simply cast his vote with Petz;[1] when I explained things to him he was a little ashamed of his action. In conclusion, we have to give it another try. I am almost certain of a smooth passing this time, and it would do you good to be guided in your work by the requirements of teaching. I am very sorry that we don't see eye to eye in this matter.

The Hungarian language publication of your article[2] created a general uproar. Since I had read it in German before, it wasn't until now that I looked at the Hungarian version. I must say that the Hungarian text is not particularly good. It's high-sounding but not particularly clear. Hevesi[3] told me the other day that Balázs[4] translated it. If so, he won't get any praise from me for the job. (As to Balázs, I got something for him[5] and I wrote and told him so. For weeks, he didn't even answer my note. Then he wrote that his address had changed in the meantime but didn't give me the new one.) [. . .]

I am glad to hear that you are preoccupied with logic these days. I look forward to reading something from you. When is the 2nd issue of *Szellem*[6] due?

Haven't heard anything regarding your book.[7] I learned only this much from Gyula Vargha,[8] that it's in print. I haven't been to Franklin for a long time. I assume that it will be distributed with the others on their list.

Cordially yours,
Bernát Alexander

P.S. If the address is misspelled, you are the one to blame. Tell me, is my writing really as illegible as yours?

[1] Gedeon Petz. See letter no. 53, n. 5.
[2] "A tragédia metafizikája," published in *A Szellem* (March 1911); "Die Metaphysik der Tragödie" in *Logos* (1911). See "Metaphysics of Tragedy," in *Soul and Form.*
[3] See letter no. 4, n. 2.
[4] See "Biographical Notes".
[5] Balázs in his diaries often mentions his "Bohemian poverty," and around October 1911 records the generosity of Lukács's father, who sent him money to Paris. Balázs had no job at that time and many of his journalistic pieces were rejected. Alexander presumably was asked to help to find him a teaching position.
[6] *Spirit.*
[7] *A modern dráma fejlődésének története*. See letter no. 69, n. 4.
[8] Gyula Vargha (1853–1929), member of the Hungarian Academy of Sciences and one-time secretary of the Kisfaludy Society. From 1901, he was Director of the Hungarian Statistical Office. He dabbled in poetry, but his main writings are on banking and credit.

92. TO MARTIN BUBER

Florence
December 20, 1911

Dear Herr Doctor,

My initial impression is in no way affected by the fact that the Baalschem legends are not "authentic," and I quite understand your position as not only a possible but as a necessary one. Essentially, my wish is not a cry for more! If it is impossible—as it appears—to prepare an edition of Hasidic texts similar to the Indian texts edited by Deussen,[1] we, all of us for whom the books were a great experience, at least want to possess everything that is available and can be edited. That is why a volume of sayings that you hinted at (or, as I want to believe, promised) for me would be a truly welcome gift.

I have written a rather short review of the two volumes for the Hungarian philosophical journal, *Szellem*[2] (roughly translated: Logos). The editor of the journal, Mr. Lajos Fülep,[3] a connoisseur of Italian and Spanish mysticism, is very much interested in the volumes. Could you ask your publisher to send him a copy? His present address: Florence, 6 Piazzale Donatello.

It is very unlikely that I will come to Berlin in the forseeable future, the enticing prospect of your reading to me the original texts notwithstanding. I am thinking of staying on in Italy for the time being; I just don't know when I will get to Berlin.

I am very pleased that my book impressed you, and hope that the collection as a whole has not diminished the effect of its parts.

Respectfully,

Your sincerely devoted,
Dr. Georg von Lukács

[1] Paul Jakob Deussen (1849–1919), professor of philosophy at Kiel, one of the most prominent European Indologists. Edited, translated, and interpreted the Upanishadic system of thought. Lukács refers to the following volumes: *Die Sutras des Vedanta* (1887) and *Die Geheimlehre des Veda* (1907). At that time, Lukács was interested in the concepts of transmigration. See P. Deussen, *The Philosophy of the Upanishads* (New York, 1966).

[2] *Spirit*. The review mentioned, "Jewish Mysticism," was translated into German and English by Judith Marcus and printed in her book on *Georg Lukács and Thomas Mann. A Study in the Sociology of Literature* (Amherst, Mass.: University of Massachusetts Press, 1986).

[3] See "Biographical Notes".

PART TWO

1912—1920

93. TO LEOPOLD ZIEGLER

Florence
January 1, 1912

Esteemed Herr Doctor,

Many thanks for your friendly lines. In the last sentences of your letter you expressed your wish to see my scattered notes on the diverse manifestations of form collected in a sort of aesthetics of literature. I fully share your sentiments and hope for their realization—but the "when" remains highly indeterminable.

It is unlikely that it escaped your attention—being the kind of reader you are—that the essay (more specifically, my essay) contains a kind of ironic dogmatism, so to speak, an apodictic with "reservations". Consequently, it can be but—in Hegelian terms—a "moment;" only the individual case which it deals with can lend life and fundament to its (temporarily only intuitive) apriorism. But this will become impossible in a system. And so we are confronted with enormous difficulties in terms of epistemology, philosophy of history, etc., etc., especially since little has been done in regard to an aesthetics of literature—as you yourself pointed out. How could we then contemplate the writing of an aesthetics at the present stage?

The issue which contains your Kant-chapter is just about out;[1] the same issue will bring a short bibliographical note on your works *cum* an informative note—as you requested—on the changes that occurred in your views in reference to the Hartmann book.[2]

Most respectfully yours,
Dr. G. Lukács

[1] Reference is to the second and last issue of *A Szellem* (Spirit). The "Kant-chapter" was entitled, "*Kant és a metafizika mint a transcendentális kategóriák tana*" (Kant and Metaphysics as a Theory of Transcendental Categories), translated into Hungarian by Emma Ritoók, pp. 215–32. The same issue contained Lukács's short introduction to Ziegler, the philosopher: "Leopold Ziegler," *A Szellem*, vol. 1, no. 2 (December 1911), pp. 255–56, signed: L. Gy.

[2] The work in question: *Das Weltbild Eduard von Hartmanns* (1910).

94. FROM KÁROLY (KARL) MANNHEIM

Budapest
January 5, 1912

Dear Sir,

I have not written to you until now because I felt that I didn't have the right to bother you with the chaos of my present days and questions and because I was waiting for all the questions and motives in my mind to find a satisfactory solution in formulations which I could submit to you.

I am nevertheless writing to you now and presumably at great length, on the one hand because my problems are already taking a definite shape and are thus undoubtedly linked to somebody, and, on the other, because you encouraged me to write to you about the events of my life so far. This is certainly necessary in order for me to ask your opinion about whether you see in the postponement of my problem so far the orderly process of creation, and in my determination to continue an organic and necessary growth.

I wish to begin with my solutions to my present questions, which cover a wide range and are the foundation of all that follows. Then I wish to proceed toward the core of my *Problematik* which becomes not only problematical but also timely in my essay in progress.

Questions such as "Does God exist," every question that looks for causes, and all similar philosophical questions which I would call theological have moved farther and farther away from me.

It does not make sense to move along the causal chain. Asking for the cause is already unproductive in its emphasis; and the one who first asked "Who created this world?" deserved an answer such as the moon, lightning, or what have you.

Is it at all possible to get an answer of a different sort to that kind of question? If we ask for a cause, we can answer with a cause; that is the best we can do.

I do not wish to abandon God, only I find unworthy the feelings which drive us to seek and to know Him, to turn to Him this way.

God—or whatever I might call Him—is in me *a priori;* all one can strive for is "To get from Him to Him".

I believe that the great Renaissance scholar, Cusanus,[1] suspected as much; but I have not really studied him yet. His starting point was that there is self-knowledge only; but since the part is at the same time also the whole, we get to know the whole by knowing ourselves.

To make conscious what is unconscious at the beginning, to find oneself through living, to get to know ourselves through others, and conversely others through ourselves and everything as if it were ourselves—this is the path of the soul from itself to itself.

Thus we may speak only of our life, of its most hidden tendencies, and we can find them in magnificent self-knowledge, declaring their unequivocal and unchangeable order.

And we must believe that our truth is not merely a subjective caprice but unequivocal and, in the last resort, identical [sic!]. This is the great community of man, our great togetherness.

This, our creed, is more than knowledge, because knowledge always springs from doubt; this is certainty itself, it is experience in the most profound sense, provided by the direct order of experience.

"The cognition of Life is more than Life, the cognition of the Laws of Happiness is more than Happiness itself" (Dostoevsky).

I believe that it is here that we must seek the common root of all forms, I believe that it is in this [cognition] that every true form professes community with every other: the drama, poetry, the novel, philosophy.

And the fact that the one is a drama and the other philosophy comes only from the different approach to the same thing.

It is therefore possible for the problems of philosophy, let us say, those of the medieval mystics, or of the ancient Indians, to live on, to develop further, to find resolution in the novel or in the life of a Dostoevsky.

That the lives of those who live so far away from one another, who know nothing of each other, should be linked this way in spite of their thousands of differences is only possible through their having had to face the same thing, their own life, Life itself.

To discover this identity that others have bequeathed to us in their own forms is the task of philosophy. That this can be discovered as immanent in every life and shape is due to the nature of forms.

Form can find content, an unequivocal content, in us alone, because form in itself does not have life due to its material and external nature.

And since we face externals all our lives and that is where our lives take place, the problem of immanence is the most important problem.

It follows inclusively from the permanent flow of the outside world that truth and all our goals must be immanent and the fulfillment can only be in fulfillment itself [sic!].

The search for immanence behind the form and at the same time the assertion that in the final analysis every form is chancelike, that is the position of philosophy. (I call philosophy what I see in its original tendency.)

As necessary as it is that for the critic "form should be the only reality," it is just as necessary that for the philosopher, who perceives in an even more abstract way than the critic, forms should have only a necessary but ultimately self-negating existence vis-à-vis the immanence instilled in them.

This idea would render the critic helpless and thus useless, driving him to the greatest sin that can be committed in life, negation.

Only philosophy can take on this task because its original tendency is the final synthesis. And since the final synthesis is only possible in complete abstraction, its only reality can be the soul which, as such, is the final abstraction. For the philosopher the soul blends so much with the light of abstraction that he can face it only in the direct perception growing beyond all its shapes.

This is why every philosophy in the final analysis has its roots in mysticism. (The mathematicism of Spinoza is in the last resort the most extreme mysticism.)

Philosophy can accept only a single certainty, which it brings along from this self-cognition as a memory: that life and afterlife can exist only in the soul.

The critic and others setting out from different directions may attribute such a life also to the forms; as, e.g., the Romantics did, they may also speak of the "folk-soul".

But philosophy considers reality a single thing, the soul which leads directly to self-perception.

It is at this point that a second important problem of philosophy enters the scene, and the further fate of philosophy depends upon the answer to it: it is the problem of permanence.

The problem of permanence could be formulated as follows: "Is a permanent, immediate confrontation with our soul and our life possible?"

The tendency of every genuine life contains the affirmation of this, and thus all strivings and actions immanently carried this ideal in themselves.

Monks withdrew into their caves and Indian ascetics searched in their own way for the same ideal that Dostoevsky, e.g., considered attainable in the deepening of every single fact of the life surrounding us.

But the earthly order of things and of life nevertheless makes impossible a permanent confrontation in the original meaning, desired by the mystics, who are immersed in themselves. And it also teaches us the lesson that those who retired into themselves erred in that they believed that the further they removed themselves from earthly things, the closer they would get to heaven; but it was precisely Dostoevsky who demonstrated that the more tenaciously we hold to the earth the closer we come to the heavens.

This solution to the problem of permanence also marks the path of the further evolution of philosophy.

Since permanent confrontation with our own soul and life is impossible—and all the more so since we may seldom perceive the nature of our own life and when we do it is only for brief moments that are like miracles, and all that remains is memory – philosophy as well is also a form only in its further continuation, and precisely for this reason we have to apply the criteria of form to it [philosophy].

It is at this point that philosophy divides into metaphysics and ethics.

Criticism must confront metaphysics and ethics in much the same way as any other form; therefore, such a question as, for example, "Is it of one material" might contradict its original tendency [sic!].

This brings us back to our point of departure, i.e., that philosophy is just as much a form as everything else. Its roots have the same origin as any other, but it differs in its path and in its method; and this is exactly what assures it a separate existence among forms; i.e., that its path is synthesis and its method is the final abstraction.

The peculiarity of its path and method, the so-called great consciousness which manifests itself in the fact that it's always seeking clear tendencies, makes that impossibility possible, which no other form may speak of, from which all other forms start, that it [philosophy] finds at the end of its path, in the final abstraction, i.e., the soul.

The fact that the truth for philosophy is the existence of the soul, of oneself, on the basis of direct experience—that is the only unconditional reality, a truth which takes precedence over all our inquiries and appears only at the end of the road. This follows from the order of our life.

Since our life and our truths manifest themselves within the framework of space and time, what is in fact the basis of everything occurs *a posteriori.*

Since it is paths that lead us to truths, time is needed to travel them.

One of the most particular attributes of philosophy, which follows from its formal nature, is that its basic tenets are *a posteriori–a priori,* in other words, the results occur at the end of the road, which, due to their importance and the experience contained in them, should precede everything else and should be written into our philosophy as the first sentence, as an *a priori* certainty.

The close relationship of philosophy to criticism should already be clear from what has been said so far.

Both philosophy and criticism look for interconnections (but no causes. Many people think erroneously that what is feasible in the natural sciences is appropriate here as well) and their joy is the pure idea.

The main difference between them is that criticism has (and must have!) at the beginning of the road a single reality, form; and consequently its path is analysis, while the path of philosophy is synthesis. And that is why its single reality appears at the end of the road as a result.

(It is obvious that in speaking of philosophy and criticism we mean clear tendencies, and they should not be confused with philosophers and critics who are necessarily men made of flesh and blood, and in whom, as in everyone who creates, the process of synthesis and analysis run parallel all the time, complementing each other, in order to fulfill each other.)

Whether somebody chooses philosophy or criticism to express himself depends just as much on his individual disposition as whether one's writing is lyric or epic.

I do not want to generalize and can speak only for myself, however; I feel one thing, that the path of criticism will undoubtedly lead to philosophy, and I need criticism for the sake of philosophy, because philosophy, being synthetic, cannot nourish itself and occurs as the integration of a certain degree of differentiation.

I have written all this to give you an account of the development of my ideas on the one hand, and on the other, in order to erect within this framework a parallel picture of the timely need for the treatise I am about to write.

I wish namely to write about Dostoevsky.

It is not only because I feel that I should be able to pose my problems and my questions through a study of his work, but also because I feel that a knowledge of his life promises solutions. I feel that his life and his world are very much akin to ours in all their vicissitudes, their lack of fulfillment and distortions.

I feel that his fate can provide either negative or positive answers to things that disturb us now.

I feel there are two men who are very much a part of our times: Dostoevsky and Ady.[2] Is there anyone else whose lives can teach us more than theirs?

I know that their lives were fulfilling for them, but their fate cannot be the same as mine.

Therefore what I write about Dostoevsky must be a biography in the true sense of the word.

When I think of him, I am unable to imagine any greater reality than his life; therefore I am certain that my writing will be a criticism.

It must not happen, indeed it is impossible from the beginning, that anything in this letter should be repeated in the biography in much the same way as I have done here. I wish that piece to have a single reality, and that is Dostoevsky.

I want to know and I want to resurrect that frosty Petersburg sun in which Dostoevsky walked, which was right there and then, and the torture of the soul which he felt on a night that could only exist for him. I want to know those things as if they existed now and in me.

I never could attribute my interest in history and the men of the past merely to an aesthetic interest. And I can never see history as anything other than something that comes from the necessity of our present life. And consequently, if I return to Dostoevsky, I do so only because I know that he must become a factor in my life.

The nearness of life and my bond with him sufficiently justify, I think, my need to study him.

It would mean a great deal to me if you'd send me your opinion of the work I am about to begin.[3]

Please forgive me and excuse me for having troubled you with such a long letter and for adding a perhaps inopportune request. I certainly do not wish to abuse your kindness.

Respectfully, your devoted
Károly Mannheim

P.S. Allow me to tell you, Sir, how much I appreciated your interest in my affairs. I should like to give you a brief account of what I did since our last meeting, inasmuch as it may be of interest to you.

I called on Professor Alexander[4] after he came to Budapest, and he received me very kindly, which I attributed mainly to your kind introduction, which I would like to thank you for on this occasion.

I told him my business and he approved every item. He too could not see how ancient Indian philosophy could be implemented; nevertheless, he agreed with my choice of such a special study.

I have maintained contact with him and gave two papers in his Kant seminar; in the latter, I risked an independent opinion. He received both papers sympathetically. He also asked me to criticize a paper on Eucken[5] which was given in a seminar of advanced students. I have done this.

I am progressing slowly in my study of Kant but—I believe—I am really understanding him. I have already developed three longer trains of thought in this connection; they may develop into a future treatise on Kant.

Nor do I find my philological studies as dry as I had expected and I am convinced that, if understood properly, philology could also be delved into more deeply than is presently done, e.g., by Herm[ann] Paul.[6]

I have also studied Middle High grammar which I'll need when translating [Meister] Eckhart.

I really look forward to the next issue of *Szellem,* even more so now since you promised an essay in it which I suspect will mean a lot to me.[7]

I have received the proofs of the translation[8] and duly returned them corrected within a few days.

It would please me very much, Sir, if you would tell me whether you have published anything recently, either here or abroad; I only know of the article published in the Christmas issue of the *Pester Lloyd.*[9]

You made me very happy with your book published in German.[10] It was especially interesting to read it all again in German and to notice the difference the changes made.

[1] Nicolaus Cusanus or von Cues (1401–1464), German late-medieval theologian and philosopher, Cardinal of Trier. Among his works: *De vision dei* and *De docta ignorantia.*

[2] Endre Ady. See letter no. 15, n. 3.

[3] Project was abandoned.

4 Bernát Alexander.
5 Rudolf Eucken (1846–1926), German philosopher, professor at Jena. Proponent of Neo-Idealism. Author of *Mensch und Welt.*
6 Hermann Paul (1846–1921), German philologist and professor of German. Author of *Deutsche Grammatik.*
7 *Spirit.* The second and last issue of the magazine came out in January 1912.
8 Hegel excerpts on the essence of philosophical criticism, published in *Szellem,* no. 2, pp. 187–201.
9 "The Gallic Danger" (original title: "Die Romanische Gefahr") in *Pester Lloyd* (Budapest), no. 305 (1911).
10 *Die Seele und die Formen* (Soul and Form), published in 1911.

95. FROM MARGARETE VON BENDEMANN

Berlin
January 25, 1912

Dear Herr Doctor,

I preferred not to write until after I had finished reading every single word of your book;[1] and because different things held me up, it was not possible until today. In the course of an initially slow but then ever increasing tempo that consummated the getting-acquainted process, I have come to love your book. I have lain with it for such an extended period of time that I would very much like to tell of my experience—but not to you; that would prove too difficult for me. I am thinking of writing a short review essay[2], if it is agreeable with you, after the impression it made on me becomes sufficiently objectified. As of now, the music of the whole composition is still so much in my ear that there was no time for it to be condensed into a rational discourse.

With your suggestion in mind, it was not difficult for me to perceive the individual essays as stations on a road; and still, the effect of the whole was not in the form of a developmental unity; and the individual essays conveyed their own message so strongly that I finally could accept them as simple way-stations. Beside the opening and the closing essays, my particular love belongs to the Novalis and the Ch. L. Philippe essays; but I have learned much from the others as well and they gave me immense enjoyment. However, I keep racking my brain about the—obviously formal—necessity of the girl in the Sterne essay.[3] My feeling is that something definitive was intended with her inclusion, but I just cannot see what. Perhaps this can serve as a symbol for the limits of understanding between human beings, even in the case when the presence of another person elicits and enhances everything the giver has to offer. I don't know whether I understood you correctly.

But instead of talking about your book, I should express my heartfelt thanks for it. As for myself, I can only wish that in some form at some future date I'd be able to communicate to you what it meant to me.

I would welcome an opportunity to discuss certain aspects of it in person. For the time being though, I don't see my being able to go to Florence; your book has awakened in me long-buried longings for the Florentine landscape. We are moving to Rüschlikon on the Zürich Lake on April 1st and thus will be a great step closer to Italy. And you too may find that the distance from us has become shorter!

I would gladly send you some of my own works but nothing is in print yet; I've been hesitant to expose you to the reading of a manuscript; it can be very tiresome. An article of mine, written a few months earlier, will appear in the next issue of the *Frank.-[furter] Z.[eitung]*.[4]

I ask you to forgive my long silence and want to thank you again.

With best regards,
Yours,
M. v. Bendemann

[1] *Die Seele und die Formen.*
[2] The review appeared in the September 5, 1912 issue of the *Frankfurter Zeitung.*
[3] See *Soul and Form,* p. 124ff.
[4] "Der esoterische Charakter in der heutigen Kunst," in the January 31, 1912 issue of the *Frankfurter Zeitung.*

96. FROM KÁROLY (KARL) POLÁNYI

Budapest
January 27, 1912

My dear little Gyuri,

From the following you'll understand why I am writing this letter now, in the late evening hours. You can see, can't you, why for weeks I didn't want to read what you wrote about Leo.[1]

I told at least two hundred people the lie that I have read it already, but in fact I was afraid to; so I kept putting it off. You know how much I loved Leo; to hear your voice talking about him—to whom you were so close—was more than I could bear.

Today, finally I read it—it was forwarded to me by Bé[2]—at least four or five times. It helped me greatly and I am happy to be able to tell you so. You have accomplished a difficult and noble task and Leo would be the first to understand that it has brought us closer together.

Ever since, I have been preoccupied with remembering Leo. I have reread many of your things and have seen their virtues and shortcomings in an entirely new light. A short article that appeared in the March issue of the *Schaubühne* ("The Untragic Drama")[3] is particularly suited for reappraisal.

My dear Gyuri, I am more loquacious than before and don't torture myself so much anymore. My friends, those whom I saved up in all my humbleness and respectfulness for better times, will soon learn that through this experience I have come to comprehend what life is all about.

My morose nervousness is gone and I am free again.

You too have grown in statute in my eyes; I have been following your progress with bated breath. Each increment of it is part of the measuring of the world, and the time of plenty which I saw you in, endows you with special richness.

I have gotten rid of most of my vanities and now I exist in the jungle of the ones that remain.

The others I don't even miss. The well-accomplished poetic work is akin to that: the self-limiting of a poet is glorified by the fact that the sacrifice ceases to be seen as one.

I think of Leo very often; it comes easy. I have visited the Poppers[4] many times since. The man is an aging *coquette;* the woman, the poor thing, is completely broken. She now sees things and configurations she never even imagined. Her attention, which used to revolve around costs and expenses, now focuses on Leo. She jealously guards his writings and pictures, his thoughts and words. My frequent visits have been very slow in producing results. Yesterday—*finally*—we could sit down and start sorting out Leo's things. They were for a long time in mothballs and only now has she been able to bear going through his belongings. (The particular humor in some of these episodes—anticipated fully by Leo—made me think at times that the joy of being proven right would bring Leo back to life.)

She destroyed Leo's letters. I burned the few remaining ones.

Only the correspondence with Bé, with you, Otto, and Heini[5] were saved. I sorted yours out and will mail them to you tomorrow.[6]

I have found many, many papers, full of notes, lines, fragments, most of which I knew. Among others were the completed "Dialogue,"[7] and the Cézanne and Seghers fragments.[8] Also the diaries,[9] and so on. I will reread the dialogue and if I find it good, I will send it to Kraus[10] for publication. I might also prepare my thoughts on it in a separate letter, and then we can decide about its fate (after sending you the manuscript). Do you agree with that?

I could give the Cézanne and Seghers fragments to Bé for copying together with the notes and other things (pictures, etc.). Do you agree with that?

As to publication (in the form of collected essays): only a simple, not a fancy edition... but with a good publisher. [....]

Bé will spend February and March in Davos. The Poppers will send her 200 francs for that purpose and they do so gladly—finally. There must be a special kind of pressure that would compel them to do such a thing gladly. More and more, their lives resemble of a Pre-Raphaelite painting.

As you know: good Jews don't add yeast to the *Allteig*.[11] At one time, when P. Altenberg[12] wanted to have the word printed *"Alltag,"* the printers printed it *"Alltäg"*. All the better! The theory of misunderstanding[13] would thus advance two steps at a time: *"Du, schreibs ma Alltäg mit ei?"*[14]

Dear Gyuri, bye for now. Write if you have the time, but in any case give me an answer to the above questions.

Your father sure is an Englishman![15]

I am going away for a few months to prepare for my law examinations. Will do my studying in the Harz mountains, where it is cheap and there is quiet. My address remains: Bécsi Str. 4.

Your sorely tried friend,
Karli

[1] An obituary, entitled "Leo Popper (1886–1911). Ein Nachruf," published in *Pester Lloyd* (December 18, 1911), pp. 5–6. Reprinted in Karl Kraus's *Die Fackel* (1911) 13: 339–40.

[2] Beatrice de Waard. See "Biographical Notes".

[3] Original title, "Das Problem des untragischen Dramas," in *Die Schaubühne* (March 2, 1911), pp. 231–34.

[4] David Popper, the famous cellist, and his wife (Leo's parents).

[5] Otto Mandl. See letter no. 48, n. 6. Heini is Henrik Herz, also of Budapest and also a mutual friend of Popper, Polányi, and Lukács. See letter no. 24, n. 6.

[6] These are the letters that Lukács saved and from which the selection for this volume was made.
[7] Written in German in 1906, the full title is "Dialog über die Kunst" (A Dialogue about Art). Published in Hungarian in the slim volume of collected essays by Leo Popper: *Esszék és kritikák* (Budapest: Magvető, 1983).
[8] Cézanne MS not found. The fragment discussing Hercules Seghers (1589–1645), Flemish painter, has survived.
[9] Not found.
[10] Reference is to Karl Kraus. See letter no. 83, n. 2.
[11] For *Allteig,* see letters no. 29, 41, and 49.
[12] Peter Altenberg (1859–1919), alias Richard Engländer, Austrian writer, master of the impressionistic miniature prose. His works, such as the collections *Wie ich es sehe* (1896) or *Neues Altes* (1911) are delighted and/or resigned vignettes of the everyday life of the people in *fin de siècle* Vienna. His poem for his 60th birthday *Lebensenergien,* describes the *"Alltag-Mensch"* as the opposite of a poet, idealist, a dreamer.
[13] Allusion to Popper's intended "theory of the necessary misunderstanding" between the work of art as realized and the perception of the same by the public. Lukács found the concept useful in his *Heidelberger Philosophie.*
[14] A play on words, using Viennese dialect and capitalizing on the phonetic similarities among the words, *Alltag* (every day), *Alltäg* (same in Viennese dialect), and *Allteig* (universal matter). Translated: "Say, how does one write everyday, with an 'ei' [i.e., egg]?"
[15] Meaning: he's a gentleman.

97. TO PAUL ERNST

Florence
February 15, 1912

Dear Herr Doctor,

Didn't want to write until the matter of the child was settled.[1] Meanwhile, the *consiglio di famiglia* will take place on Monday, due to the proverbial and complicated slovenliness of the Florentine authorities. As soon as I receive the documents, I'll forward them either to you or to Frau von Schorn.

Your letter has reached me here since the bad weather forced us to curtail our stay on the Riviera; I also abandoned my planned trip through Southern France. I met Frau v. Sch[orn] only once in Genoa; the weather was so unpleasant that I was eager to be back in Florence as soon as possible.

I still haven't received your book.[2] What I had to say about the "typical German" novelette[3] was, of course, very vague and written in haste. I happen to believe, though, that there's some truth in it. Regardless of how general and unclear our formulation of the concept of form may be, history cannot be excluded from it. For this reason, it has to be incorporated into the concept. Granted, it is extremely difficult (i.e., if done without cheating) and again we are faced with the question: how can forms have a history? That they have one, namely, is a given fact. If, therefore, we draw the principle of movement into the concept of form, wich enables us to add meaning to this connection, we'd either be (like those stupid Modernists) giving up the idea of meaning or of Eternal Form, or else life in its totality (in which after all the forms move) would have to appear to us as something dreadfully empty, into which fall the distorted shadows of meaning that forever remain out of our reach. This way, all questions point toward the philosophy of history, and thus, toward the realm of the practical. If we establish the formal possibilities for the German form, does it mean that German reality will be accorded a meaning and Germany's efforts an aim? But nobody in Germany today is interested in such questions.

The Pan affair was to be expected;[4] I am still going to send you the two articles and their brevity might be their asset.[5]

I am thankful for your mediating in the Balázs business.[6] How did you like his works?

My greetings to your family.

Respectfully yours,
G. v. Lukács

[1] Allusion is to Ernst's long-standing affair with Else von Schorn, née Apelt (1874–1946), and their son, Karl, born out of wedlock in 1912. In a gesture of friendship, Lukács acted as an appointed guardian (that obviously required financial and social standing) until the parents could marry after Ernst's drawn-out divorce proceedings in 1916. The matter had to be taken care of in Italy in order to save Ernst any embarrassment and/or social ostracism, since he still was married to his second wife, Lilli, and they had a son, Walther. Frau von Schorn was a widow.

[2] *Der Tod des Cosimo* (Berlin, 1911), a collection of short stories.

[3] See letter no. 85.

[4] *Pan,* the second German journal of the same name (1910–14), in which Ernst tried to place some of Lukács's writings without success. Several of its editors left the journal under a cloud.

[5] "Zwei Wege und keine Synthese" (Two Ways and No Synthesis), German language MS, unpublished; and the review, "Novels of Pontoppidan," published in Hungarian in *Aurora* (1911).

[6] Dramas of Béla Balázs which Ernst tried to recommend for staging at the Düsseldorf Theater.

98. FROM KÁROLY (KARL) MANNHEIM

Budapest
March 3, 1912

Dear Sir,

Recent circumstances have kept me from doing any work whatsoever. Please accept my apologies for the delay in thanking you for your kind letter.

I have to confess that I am aware of the importance of your recent letter as well as your remarks concerning all of my affairs so far. Thus, I implore you not to think that I want to engage in polemics with you when I comment on some of your observations. My only wish is to reformulate my own vague notions in accordance with the original intent.

In the lines you quote in which I discuss the heterogeneity in forms as but deriving from differing perceptions of the same entity, it was not my intention to focus on the problem of the difference of forms but rather to emphasize the unity of forms existing outside and beyond themselves.

I readily admit that the word "differing" has nothing to do with the solution to any problem.

I was much more aware of the dizzying abyss over which I was treading than of trying to deny the existence of a problem whose significance was brought home to me in all of your writings.

Although I am clear about the relatedness of my statement and your standpoint, I was unable to decide even when writing to you what your views are with regard to the following *Problematik*. Thus, I would like to pointedly confront you with the question: is it at all possible to raise the question within the framework of an individual life whether, from the perspective of the sphere of the soul, the artistic formation (process of creation) is only incidental and not fully complete? (And I don't mean the reciprocal and unequivocal relationship between diverse forms and what is beyond form.)

Is our philosophy in accord with our primary perception of the ordering of things, that is, truth, if it allows—as do the mystics—the positing of the statement that *in the final analysis* every form is its own negation?

I believe we cannot be unduly concerned with those who, by opting for complete withdrawal, have reduced this proposition to the point of negation by drawing false conclusions and cannot see that this truth only helps to confirm that the forms constitute for us the only possibility—the only path—to the fulfillment of mysticism.

Inasmuch as I understand philosophy as being the expression of our attitude toward concrete totality, the essential element of the philosophy of contemporary man is the expression of his relation to things and thus to form.

It would be a lie in my opinion to assert that our sense of reality vis-à-vis both things and forms is as strong as that of the pre-Socratic Greeks. It's precisely the loss of this strong sense of reality that has brought us face to face with the abyss within ourselves.

I have to admit to you, Sir, that neither my studies nor my thinking have progressed to the point where I can really grasp what you say in connection with the problem of being (with reference to the problem of permanence.)

I can see from the inorganic and inadequate nature of my objections at the reading of your lines about this problem that they give a general demonstration of the fact that a certain truth has not become sufficiently part of our life and blood to allow us a worthy response.

Unfortunately, and for the reasons referred to at the beginning of my letter, I have not done much on my Dostoevsky[1] study and cannot therefore say when I will be able to send it.

For some time now, I have been looking for the Cusanus[2] edition you recommended but it is out of print. I keep searching for it in second-hand bookstores.

In case of need, there is an original Latin version in the university library.

Thank you again for your kind letter and my apologies for the delay in answering it.

Respectfully yours,
Karl Mannheim

1 The planned Dostoevsky study never materialized. See also letter no. 94.
2 Nicolaus Cusanus. See letter no. 94, n. 1.

99. FROM EMMY LEDERER-SEIDLER

Heidelberg
May 17, 1912

Dear Gyuri Lukács,

(Forgive me for writing you this kind of a letter and for writing in Hungarian, but I can't help it for reasons that have to do with certain associations...)[1]

I am very surprised and very glad.[2] Still, I have to ask you not to come by today or tomorrow either. May 17 and 18—you understand (you know, don't you, that nothing can be added to the emotional load of these two days)...[3]

You understand also, don't you, that anything that would divert my attention or make my involvement more intense would put a great burden on me, even if the diversion in itself would be a welcome or a pleasant one.

I want to be *"gefasst"*[4] (I know how you like this word!) when I meet you. Until then, though, it is absolute solitude for me.

How about a *Sunday* visit? I'll let you know for certain by Saturday evening or Sunday morning at the latest.

Until then, both of us send our warmest regards.

Yours,
Mrs. Lederer, Emmy Seidler

P.S. I was told in Budapest that you never received my letter sent to Florence. I was very unhappy about that for several reasons and was thinking of asking you to inquire about it at the post office but decided against it (why, I can explain better in person as with everything else...)

[1] Allusion is made to her sister's death and to Lukács's relationship to her.
[2] The Lederers encouraged and welcomed Lukács's decision to settle in Heidelberg.
[3] The first anniversary of Irma Seidler's suicide.
[4] Composed.

100. FROM GEORG SIMMEL

Den Haag
May 25, 1912

Dear Herr Doctor,

Your kind letter reached me during my travels. In the coming days I am going to drop a few lines to Lask[1] so that you can visit him and mention my name. On the other hand, I would not recommend that you go to see Windelband;[2] first, he is an extremely busy man and in addition, there are good reasons why I don't think that any good would come from it. Should you for some very specific reasons insist on it, let me know (at my Westend address) and I will send you a letter of introduction.

Do you happen to know Dr. Salz,[3] *Privatdozent,* of Heidelberg University? He is truly a fine and interesting man; if you wish, I can write him also. Herr Bauer[4] was in Berlin recently and I was able to see him only once before my trip and enjoyed my visit with him tremendously. He seems to be developing into an independent and mature individual.

My wife sends you her best regards.

Yours truly,
Simmel

1 See "Biographical Notes".

2 Wilhelm Windelband (1848–1915), outstanding historian of philosophy. Founder and head of the so-called Baden or Southwestern-German School (also called "axiological school") of Neo-Kantianism. Professor at the University of Heidelberg. Also taught at the universities of Zurich, Freiburg and Strasbourg. Main works: *Geschichte und Naturwissenschaft* (1894) and *Geschichte der neueren Philosophie* (History of Philosophy, 1891), 2 vols.

3 Arthur Salz (1881–1963), political economist, professor at Heidelberg University. Emigrated to the United States and became professor at Ohio State University (1939–52).

4 Reference is to Béla Balázs, whose name originally was Herbert Bauer.

101. FROM EMIL LASK

Heidelberg
June 11, 1912

Dear Herr Doctor,

It is unforgivable that I did not thank you before today for your kindness in sending me your book[1] with the enclosed note. I hope you won't judge me too harshly if I tell you that I was not well for a while and then had to take care of several important official matters. I am quite exhausted still. Nevertheless, I don't want to put off our meeting any longer. You approached me in such a kind and friendly way that I grew quite impatient to meet you and have a good talk with you. If you can spare the time, may I ask you to come by tomorrow, Wednesday afternoon, around 5 : 30 p.m.? I would be very happy if you could make it. Let us discuss everything else in person. My best wishes.

Very truly yours,
Emil Lask

[1] *Die Seele und die Formen* (Soul and Form), published by Egon Fleischel & Co., Berlin, 1911.

102. FROM BERNÁT ALEXANDER

Budapest
June 24, 1912

Dear Doctor,

I have been so busy for the last two weeks that I didn't have the time to write, or rather I had the time for everything else but my correspondence. At last I am free, that is, until before the dinner starts in the room next to mine...

To tell the truth, I did not have anything to write about. Although I took a quick look into your book,[1] I wasn't able to sit down and read it systematically. I'll take it along and report on it. Here in Budapest there were some fierce attacks from certain philological quarters: a gentleman signed only as "R" wrote about it in the *Irodalom*[2] and Jenő Vértessy in the *Filológiai Közlöny*.[3] I will respond to these critics and also to the tone of their attacks.

I had already talked to Gedeon Petz[4] a few weeks ago. Although I have not been able to "tame" him as yet, I think I succeeded in making him more receptive. I have to proceed very cautiously but I trust I will reach my goal ultimately. Since the matter is not urgent for you either, let's wait a couple of months; we must wait anyhow because the Committee won't meet before October. We will perhaps be successful with the personal vote[5] in November. Béla Zalai too failed at the personal vote.[6] I was his sponsor but forgot to report right away that he was born a Calvinist. At the same Committee meeting, a geologist (Vadász) also failed at the personal vote but he really is a Jew. The faculty is extremely nervous every time the question of religious affiliation comes up. It may sound strange but it was the appointments in *mathematics* that did it to us. The appointment of Lipót Fehér [sic!][7] created the impression that now the Jews are ready to take over the university. At the same time, at Kolozsvár,[8] there were two Jewish mathematicians appointed.

Thank you very much for the report on your work. A young student of mine, A. Fogarasi,[9] is also at Heidelberg; he is a great admirer of Windelband and adores Lask.

I am sure you know that Fülep was here to get his doctorate (summa c.l.) only to take off immediately.

I will be leaving the day after tomorrow straight for Bozen and from then later on will move somewhere higher, maybe to Ober-Bozen. I will send you my address from there. Until then, my Budapest address will do since they forward everything.

(Vedres[10] was also here for a short visit.)

I plan to go to Levanto some time in September at the recommendation of Fülep.

As ever,
Bernát Alexander

[1] *A modern dráma fejlődésének története* (The History of the Development of the Modern Drama), 2 vols. (Budapest: Franklin Társulat, 1911).
[2] *Literature*.
[3] *Philological Journal*. The review appeared in the May 1912 issue.
[4] See letter no. 53, n. 5.
[5] Lukács by that time decided to try to get his *Habilitation* at Heidelberg University.
[6] See letter no. 59, n. 4.
[7] Lipót Fejér. See "Biographical Notes".
[8] Cluj-Napoca (Transylvania), now part of Romania.
[9] Adalbert Fogarasi later used the name Béla Fogarasi (1891–1960); studied

philosophy in Budapest and Heidelberg, translated Bergson into Hungarian. Member of the Sunday Circle and from 1919 member of the Communist Party.

10 Márk Vedres. See letter no. 47, n. 4.

103. FROM FERENC (FRANZ FERDINAND) BAUMGARTEN

Freiburg
July 8, 1912

My dear friend,

The groundwork is laid for you. It will be very helpful that Simmel praised you in his letter and even more that Lask wrote about you in enthusiastic terms (to Rickert or Cohn),[1] praising your adherence to the redemptive doctrine of epistemology. You are not a savage *(Wilder)* any more for them.

Until now, that is what you were in spite of—or because of—your book and article. Rickert and Cohn apologized for their silence as follows: they could not give their written opinion, because they read only part of your work. Both of them liked the Storm essay best (Cohn must be the source of this opinion because Rickert is not smart enough for that kind of misunderstanding).

Rickert finds your *Logos* article[2] "too feuilletonistic". They are very eager, though, to make your acquaintance and expect your visit. I was told to write you to this effect. In the meantime, Cohn will set about reading your book.

I have told them a lot about you. Steppuhn,[3] the mystic private genius (he is a mystic) also promised to read your book.

As Knapp[4] is given to say: people are too dumb to understand people like us. We have to educate them. That's what you'll have to do. It should be easy for you to impress those gentlemen. Cohn might be the only one to understand you. By far, he is the most intelligent. *Summa summarum:* you should live here for a while in order to lay roots. Then a *Habilitation* should be easy to attain—it would prove impossible from afar. I think it very likely that if you're here in person, you'll make the same impact as on Simmel and Lask—and we would be assured of the success of your habilitation efforts.

Around here, they read books only if they know the author. So much for the objectivity of German professors. Every one of them has staked out a circle of interest and doesn't bother himself with other interesting things.

If possible, get a letter of introduction from Weber to Rickert; he is Rickert's idol.

Best regards,
F. Baumgarten

[P.S.] I am returning today to Badenweiler; I spent only 24 hours here.

1 For Heinrich Rickert, see "Biographical Notes". Cohn is Jonas Cohn (1860–1947), professor of philosophy at Freiburg University.
2 "Metaphysik der Tragödie." See letter no. 56, n. 9.
3 Friedrich Steppuhn (1884–?), Russian-born philosopher and mystic who lived in Germany. His fate is unknown.
4 Georg Friedrich Knapp (1842–1926), German economic theorist of the historical school. Taught at the University of Strasbourg. His works were on theory of money and agrarian politics.

104. FROM MAX WEBER

Ziegelh.[äuser] Landstr.[asse]
Tel. 1401
July 22, 1912

Dear Herr Doctor,

Yesterday I sat next to Windelband[1] (not accidentally) and mentioned your name during a conversation with Gothein.[2] W. then made a few remarks concerning your essay,[3] unimportant in their content, not unfriendly, but as expected; the concept of *form* holds *no* interest for him *whatsoever* and he became quite brusque at that point in the discussion. I made some cautious remarks, *as few as possible,* above all, mainly regarding you personally: that you were essentially a *systematic thinker* who left his essayistic stage behind him, etc. He listened, politely as is his wont, but obviously *without* any real interest. So I decided not to press the matter further, as it would not have served your interest. I know him well in this respect, you see!

I can only *reiterate* my views on the matter: if you are in a position to submit a *finished* work, not just a chapter, but something that in itself is "complete," your chances for a positive outcome[4] would improve greatly. For me to have tried to find out yesterday whether or not there are *objective* factors[5]—of which you are fully aware—that would render your chances *nil,* would have been a futile exercise and, in effect, would have made things worse.

In any case, I do hope to be able to talk to *Rickert*[6] about it during the holidays (this coming October). He won't make any trouble.

With the highest respect and kindest regards in the hope to see you soon,

Yours,
Max Weber

1 Wilhelm Windelband. See letter no. 100, n. 2.
2 Eberhard Gothein (1853–1923), political scientist, historian, and economist. Taught at the universities of Bonn and Heidelberg; was respected as a prolific and truly interdisciplinary scholar. Founding member, together with Weber, Simmel, Sombart, Toennies, and Troeltsch, of the German Sociological Society in 1910. Among his works: *Ignatius von Loyola und die Gegenreformation* (1895). Friend of both the Webers and of Lukács.
3 Presumably an essay from the collection, *Soul and Form.*
4 Allusion to Lukács's aim to take his *Habilitation* at Heidelberg University and to obtain a position of Lecturer *(Privatdozent).* Max and Alfred Weber along with Gothein were backing the effort and tried to enlist the help of distinguished faculty members. A "systematic work" on the aesthetic was to pave the way for an academic career. Hence Weber's admonition.
5 Reference is to the prevailing atmosphere in German academic circles that made it difficult for foreigners (or for Jews) to have their *Habilitationsschrift* accepted.
6 See "Biographical Notes".

105. FROM ERNST TROELTSCH

Heidelberg
August 1, 1912

Most honored Sir,

I am greatly indebted to you for sending your book, *Die Seele und die Formen;* I feel deeply honored. I didn't want to express my thanks until I read at least a substantial part of the essays. Therein lies the reason for the delay in my answer.

If I understand you correctly, you intended to penetrate contemporary intellectual life and its most significant types in order to arrive at your own position in the reigning odd mixture of decay and forward-looking political-economic forces. At any rate,

I myself have read the essays from such a perspective; for me, the purely literary-artistic aspect is not a vital question of enhancement; I view them as merely consequences... Judged from this viewpoint, the essays on Novalis and Storm contain very fine, highly perceptive, and to-the-point observations. That is how I have always perceived Romanticism! Your views on Storm, on the other hand, say something entirely new for me and I find it very convincing. I suspect that the other essays, those I haven't read, will prove equally rich, stimulating, and enlightening, but I don't want to postpone my thanks any longer. I hope I'll be permitted to make your personal acquaintance and to tell you more adequately what your essays mean to me.

With the highest respect,

Your most grateful,
E. Troeltsch

106. TO MARGARETE VON BENDEMANN

Budapest
September 25, 1912

Esteemed Frau von Bendemann,

It has taken an inexcusably long time to answer your letter, but I was hardly able to appropriate your precious offering before another arrived,[1] forcing me into renewed introspection and abstinence from expression. The time has come at last to thank you for both of them; and even though my words of thanks may be brief (because compressed), they are no less warm.

I find it very difficult to answer the letter you sent me at Scheveningen.[2] The written word—be it a letter even—is to such an extent a messenger only of the suprapersonal sphere that it won't allow us (without disturbing adequacies) to touch upon the most personal matters. Moreover, we have never met in person and this renders it almost impossible to perceive "nuances" *(Accents)* that constitute its real meaning. It will perhaps be possible for us to meet in person and I have some reason to be hopeful. I'll probably go from Heidelberg—where I am going to stay during the winter—to Bern, which would present me with the opportunity to look you up provided you are still in Rüschlikon. This would give us a chance to discuss matters in person, the way it can never be done in a letter.

Yet, I must be grateful for your letter because even though some of our views may differ, I could glimpse from it something essential, namely, your feelings toward Ernst Bloch. I am now convinced that if you could get together once again, all the misunderstanding would come to naught.

It becomes even more difficult for me to express myself adequately when I want to convey to you my gratitude for your review of my book and for sending me your own book *(Vom Sinn der Liebe)*. Until now, very few people have been able to grasp with the same force and certainty what is most essential in my book, as you did. What right have I to expect—much less demand—that appreciation and understanding be accorded this book, which amounts to even less than a beginning? (Only an objectively accomplished act of the mind [Geist] can have such a claim.) The book is, after all, full of intuitive knowledge of what will come (for me), from ideas whose development and aim I can only now see clearly myself—after the work itself as well as its form have become alien to me. And yet, you have been able to grasp it as an objective totality and to comprehend the most important element of the work: my concept of form. For that, I want to thank you deeply; I hope to express my gratitude for the trust you have afforded me in a more appropriate way by soon presenting you with a more accomplished work. It gave me great pleasure to see you pointing to the role of history as well as to the significance of the introductory and closing essay. If I voice my disagreement with you on one point, it doesn't mean that you have misinterpreted the book as it stands, but rather that for once you have been less clairvoyant in discovering what lies ahead amidst the chaos of the present, I mean your interpretation of "faithless mysticism". You have made a "personality trait" out of the conditions that I work under or generally those who write such books. The absence of a final, unsurpassed end makes for the despair of the book, but—at least I now feel—it beckons to one from afar, here and there, in the book. In your interpretation, this aim is beyond reach and as such is a historico-philosophical "fact" that is characteristic of our times. As for myself, this aim is definitely not beyond reach (and was thought to be the case when I wrote the introductory and closing essays of the book). If it proved to be unreachable for me, it would not constitute a fact from which one should draw conclusions in regard to the essence of metaphysical sentiments; it would merely be a sentence passed upon me (and only upon me), upon my not having a calling for philosophy.

By refusing to believe in the possibility of an answer to the ultimate and all-decisive questions, whereby all of our categories would loose their constitutive meaning and everything (our proclamations about what is "above us" and "beyond us") would remain within ourselves and become reflexive, one gives up the definitive responsibility for the severity of the concepts, which can only be accomplished by a hierarchical incorporation into the absolute system. I took care that nothing was left unexplored in my essays to avoid this danger. Everything in them that is seemingly all-too-subjective, "poetic," or of a fragmentary nature was engendered by the effort to be unequivocal, pointed, and responsible although *not yet* possessing the self-evident responsibility inherent in a perfected system. The ethics of the essayistic form is despair, originating in the ancient schism of this form.

Thus I have arrived at the point that enables me to gain an overview of your book and to state the most essential points of my criticism. (As said before, I find this form of communication very restricting. If I could talk with you, you would see—indeed, you couldn't help seeing—from the warmth and animation of my presentation, how much your book means to me—that regardless of the seeming harshness of my tone, it is generated by the love I have for your book and by the respect for the conviction that gave rise to it.) But to come to the most important point right away: your book stands midway between the essay and the system. By its striving to go beyond the essay, it abandons the pointedness that was born of "despair," having only an immanent effect and having been created *ad hoc;* yet it was not able to reach the rigor of the responsibility of a hierarchy, of a system. I believe you have already begun to see what I am driving at: the position, the positing of love as a mediator, as an intermediatory interval, born out of true, philosophical sentiment, with the ultimate clarity missing. The "Above" and the "Below" have been worked out with decisive clarity while the topography of the super- and subordination does not have the—sheer artistic-space-creating—evident and unequivocal character which the archsentiment, out of which it arose, must have possessed. "Life" is the most manifold and uncertain concept of any terminology and consequently severity is called for in case something is constructed upon it. Because what is authentic and "to-be-taken literally" turns into something "metaphysically inauthentic" in the concept of "life"; that way, ambiguities are created as are variations and illicit complications which are held together by a fundamental sentiment that failed to take shape and in which the authentic and the metaphysical become one.

And the supreme concept of "God" reveals a similar hovering between two possible meanings. It never acquires form; nothing is solid or unequivocal that would amount to a definitive thing. Just as one must speak in unequivocal terms of the purely sexual aspect of love, with all of its earthly ballast and carnal insufficiency, in order to execute the transcendence to clarity, to the not-quite earthly, one must speak of God in the same fashion—unequivocally, unmetaphorically, and with full responsibility. Or one must not speak of Him. You have—if I am allowed to use the expression—a medieval-Catholic disposition and will, along with a dash of modern-Protestant "sentimental" theory of knowledge, which avoids the ultimate (questions) and remains at the level of "yearning". This attitude affects me as an external inhibition, i.e., as acquired and not yet left behind. It is precisely your pure honesty, the beautiful feminine depth of your disposition and will that forces me to tell you all this openly and without hesitation. All of these characteristics lift you well beyond and above the more or less witty, yet essentially self-satisfied unauthenticity of our epoch and the irresponsibility of its philosophers. But what is missing in this book is the ultimate decision, the ability to speak about everything the way a child dares, in its artless innocence, to acknowledge in all naiveté its real sentiments. Your book seems to me to be a work of transition, from the essay to the system, complete with the waverings of an incomplete transition; it is also blessed with the tranquil light of ultimate maturity and inner perfection.

It would be highly inadequate and almost an offense to speak now of insignificant details and other matters. From what I said you must have discerned what your book as a whole meant to me (both as an act and as a hope). You can see, can't you, how strongly it affected me in the midst of indifference towards so many other things which remained alien to me. I hope to have the opportunity to talk with you about this and other matters as well. May I ask you to ascribe everything that might have sounded alien and/or offensive to you to the fact that we have not made each other's personal acquaintance.

Sincerely and most respectfully yours,

Dr. Georg von Lukács

[1] Reference is both to her letter (no. 95) and to a subsequent review that appeared in the *Frankfurter Zeitung*.
[2] Lukács spent the holidays at Scheveningen in the company of Ernst Bloch. Margarete Bendemann informed Lukács about her strained relationship to Bloch and presumably the reasons for it.

107. FROM ALFRED WEBER

Heidelberg
November 8, 1912

Dear Herr Doctor,

You were very kind to have sent me your collected essays;[1] right now I have time only to thank you.

It gave me great pleasure to learn that you are in Heidelberg at present. I should like to ask whether you'd consider it appropriate to express my thanks and convey my impression of your work to you by asking you to join us one evening at my home? There will be just a small gathering of friends. You'd then meet Dr. Salz[2] and his wife.

Respectfully,
Alfred Weber

[1] *Die Seele und die Formen* (Soul and Form).
[2] See letter no. 100, n. 3.

108. FROM GEORG SIMMEL

Heidelberg
[?] 1912

Dear Herr Doctor,

Since I am going to spend a few days in Heidelberg, I wouldn't like to miss out on the opportunity to see you again after all this time.

I suggest that we meet tomorrow, Saturday, at 9 p.m. in the evening at the Café Odeon. I hope that the date meets with your kind approval.

Cordially yours,
Simmel

109. FROM MAX WEBER

Heidelberg
Tuesday [January 28, 1913]

Dear Herr Doctor,

No need to worry![1] I will keep my questions on a *very* general level. The reason you haven't heard from me before was that in the meantime there was a slight *possibility* of our filling the second position here, which has been vacant for decades, with *Simmel.*[2] This is now a *moot issue;* nothing will come of it. On the other hand, Windelband has *just* requested that the position of an *Extraordinariat* be given to Lask; and the faculty will go along with that. (This is, of course, *strictly* confidential and has to remain between us.) Thus, we now have, so to speak, one less candidate in philosophy and that makes things easier—*perhaps.*

It is a fact that W.[indelband] does nothing without first consulting Lask. *I myself* will also ask him about your case. It goes without saying that he has nothing *against* your *Habilitation.* However, it is questionable that even Lask could persuade Windelband, who is *very* old and whose basic principle is *"Quietà, non movere,"* not to move.

Most respectfully,
Max Weber

[1] With regard to the planned *Habilitation* colloquium. See Appendix.
[2] Georg Simmel. Weber had tried at least twice in the years after 1910 to bring Simmel to Heidelberg but met with rejection.

110. FROM MAX WEBER

Heidelberg
January 29, 1913

Dear Herr Doctor,

If you are free tomorrow *(Thursday)* at 5:45 p.m. for a few hours, I would like to ask Professor *Troeltsch*[1] to come down and join us.

Would you be so kind as to give me a call?

Until then,

Most respectfully yours,
Max Weber

[1] Ernst Troeltsch. See "Biographical Notes". Troeltsch and the Webers moved into the house formerly owned by the Fallenstein family on the Ziegelhäuser Landstrasse in Heidelberg, in 1910.

111. FROM FELIX BERTAUX

Limoges
January 31, 1913

Dear Sir,

I read *Die Seele und die Formen* with the greatest of admiration. Since I was accorded very limited space, I could not say as much as I'd have liked to about your book for the *Nouvelle Revue Française* (Jan. 1, 1913).[1] Herr Andler,[2] by the way, introduced you to the readers of *Parthénon*[3] and did an excellent job of it.

May I use this occasion to ask you to respond to a questionnaire put together by Jean-Richard Bloch[4] for *L'Effort?* You will find the text enclosed.[5] By now you have a following in France who will listen to what you have to say.

I was also thinking of asking you for permission to reprint your essay on Stefan George in the *Nouvelle Revue Française.* I would be glad to do the translation[6]. Would your publisher be agreeable?

I am looking forward to your answer and ask you to consider me as a great admirer of your essays, which have given us original insights.

F. Bertaux

[1] "Lettres allemandes," in *Nouvelle Revue Française,* vol. 1 (1913), pp. 168–71.
[2] Charles Andler (1866–1933), professor of German literature at the Sorbonne at that time.
[3] *Le Parthenon,* bimonthly journal devoted to politics and literature. The review in question, "La vie de l'âme et la genèse des formes littéraires," appeared in vol. 2 (1912), pp. 1031–48.
[4] Jean-Richard Bloch (1884–1947), writer, editor of the journal *L'Effort Libre.*
[5] The questionnaire intended to address the problems that at that time preoccupied German artists and critics. It asked specifically, for example, about the chances of the realistic novel (re Thomas Mann), about Neo-Romanticism (Hofmannsthal) and Neo-Classicism (Paul Ernst) or aristocratic individualism, the Stefan George Circle, the more relevant literary efforts of a Dehmel, etc. Lukács's answer, written in German, has so far been published only in Hungarian. See *Ifjúkori művek (1902–1918)* (Early Works [1902–1918]), (Budapest: Magvető, 1977), pp. 587–93. See letter no. 113.
[6] The essay. "The New Solitude and its Poetry " in *Soul and Form,* was not translated and reprinted at that time.

112. FROM BÉLA BALÁZS

Budapest
[January] 1913

Dear Gyuri,

Thank you for the 50 Kronen which I received some time back. Actually the reason for not having written earlier is that I wanted to be able to tell you something definitive with regards to the *Mystery Plays.* Nothing but a condescending review in the *Hét.*[1] Not a line since then. Nowhere. Even my book of poems[2] elicited a livelier reaction. The case is hopeless. They declared me nil. I don't even rate a scathing critique. It would be very useful if you'd manage to write at least a review in the *[Pester] Lloyd.* The effect on me is as expected: I am becoming bitter and have time on my hands (which I don't need). I'm in no hurry to do anything because the question is ever present in my mind: what is the point? This is not good because it sounds like a persecution mania has slowly formed in my mind. (In your terms: "inner life," because, after all, persecution mania is at the root of everything. I was told that Mihály Babits[3] is going to write an essay in *Nyugat* about *you and me,* the relationship. I would guess that will have its unpleasant consequences, but I won't let it go by without a response! As a matter of fact, I am discovering more and more my penchant for disputes, indeed, even some talent for it. In the last issue of *Nyugat* I have already given it to Dezső Szabó.[4] The past year I have learned to write well and I'll use my abilities to slap a few faces... For what else can it be used?)

I must say that in the meantime a new generation has grown up, as an outgrowth and fossil of the "generation of the twenty-year olds"[5] who sort of formed a sect around us; it is rather a secretive one, also passive, untalented, but well-meaning. But they are around; I have met them in the catacombs of the coffee-houses. They are mostly young men from the province. They say that "all of us claim to be the students of Georg Lukács." The sectarian spirit, the conscientiousness of a caste, is palpable. They state that Ady[6] could satisfy only one segment of their lyrical needs and that I am the greatest poet. Regardless of my complete agreement on this point, they make me sad for the simple reason that they make such a cause out of me, and a pitiably hopeless cause at that. There is one person who is crazy about my *Mystery Plays,* Ernő Vajda,[7] who praised your *Dramabook* in an enthusiastic but untalented way. He will write a review in the *Élet,* a religious organ.[8] (My book is only in one window: in the religious bookstore in Szeged. I'll send it to Prohászka.[10]

I don't feel very well, physically, either. I have transcribed the *Deadly Youth*[11] but had the feeling that the corrections and additions didn't improve it; just the opposite: it is too verbose now. (Just think of it: it was written a year ago and here I am still pussyfooting around with it.) Do you want to read it? I suspect that you are up to your ears with it. . . .

How is your book coming along? I mean, the chapters? Will you have time to write the review? If it inconveniences you, just tell me. I'll then ask Lorsy.[12] It is all the same to the *Lloyd* people. The only important point is that the *Lloyd* is read in Germany and if you'd written it, I could distribute it there. (Give my regards to Bloch!)[13]

Servus!
Herbert

1 *Week*. Hungarian literary weekly. Balázs's collection of mystery plays was entitled *Misztériumok* and was reviewed in the November 13, 1912, issue. See letter no. 117, n. 1.
2 *A vándor énekel* (The Pilgrim Sings, 1910).
3 Mihály Babits (1883–1941), poet, writer, essayist, Hungary's prominent literary and progressive-liberal-humanist spokesman between the two wars. From 1931, he became editor of *Nyugat*. He wrote a critical article in *Nyugat* in 1913 entitled "Dráma," pp. 166–69.
4 Dezső Szabó, novelist; Balázs's "Válasz Szabó Dezsőnek" was dublished in *Nyugat* (1913), pp. 79–80.
5 Balázs was thinking of the young, progressive generation that coalesced around the Thalia Theater and Lukács, between 1904 and 1908. Among them were László Bánóczi, Sándor Hevesi, and Marcell Benedek.
6 Endre Ady.
7 Ernő Vajda (1885–1964), journalist.
8 Presumably never written. The journal was *Life*.
9 A large city in Hungary, close to the Yugoslav border.
10 Ottokár Prohászka (1858–1927), Catholic bishop, foremost representant of modern Catholicism. His books addressing the concerns and attitudes of young people were widely read in Hungary at that time.
11 The drama was published first in 1917.
12 Ernő Lorsy (1889–1961), journalist of progressive persuasion, who worked for *Pester Lloyd*.
13 Ernst Bloch. See "Biographical Notes".

113. TO FELIX BERTAUX

Heidelberg
[March] 1913

Dear Sir,

Forgive me for not being able to answer your questionnaire in full. If one were to deal with every single problem exhaustively, one would have to write an essay on each; a "yes" or "no" answer would no doubt be of little interest to you. Therefore, I will attempt to summarize my views briefly on those items which, in my opinion, are the most important ones, and will refer to individuals and trends only as examples and illustrations.

The most striking feature of contemporary German literary life—recognized with sadness by everyone seriously concerned about the matter—is its disorientation and lack of ideas, regardless of the obvious talent of many individual writers. Today's Germany does not have a *poet laureate* whose influence would go beyond a small coterie of the like-minded, of the "initiated". Even if an artist is accorded a great success once in a while, it is by accident and/or because of a specific conjuncture of things and therefore it doesn't have a lasting effect on the life work of the individual artist, not to mention its affecting the successful outcome of certain spiritual *(geistige)* aspirations or the search for style (and one can hardly separate the two). To be sure, the artists of the truly great epochs of Germany were also cut off from society and dependent on their *petites églises;* but a circle such as the Romantic School represented the Germany that mattered. The poets and writers were lonely to a certain degree because Germany in those times could produce only small groups in which its deepest aspirations and ultimate meaning could find their objectification. Goethe and Schiller—indeed, Hebbel and Wagner, somewhat later—represented the whole of Germany. Today—this development has been most strikingly visible since 1879—the Germany that "matters" is a big country, reaching far and wide, but there is no trace in it of an inner spiritual and intellectual unity, a common orientation, which becomes evident only in the form of muted yearnings and open despair, or in the ruinous fate of real talents. So far, nothing positive or decisive has been undertaken to overcome all this.

Naturalism represented the last unifying movement. Social despair, a revolt against the existing order of things, and materialism turned metaphysics has engendered works of art which harbored the possibility of affecting the entire nation (the young Hauptmann, Thomas Mann). However, the recognition that this *Weltanschauung* had essentially a defensive-oppositional and negative character, and was internally hollow, surfaced at the very moment when more was needed than merely giving form to despair or resignation. When the need was felt for a positive significance—be it a hero or an elevating destiny—that would be capable of uniting people in a state of joyous emotionality, it was unavoidable that this *Weltanschauung* and its form-giving energy declared bankruptcy. It is difficult to formulate briefly the ultimate cause of this disillusionment; no doubt, it is due to a large extent to the fact that the socialist sentiment owes its pathos only to the strong emphasis on an abstract *ought*—the demand of the future—that is, the very same sentiment is able to inspire only works that are protesting the existing but cannot say anything about the Being—be it empirical or metaempirical; art, after all, doesn't know what to make of a mere "ought". Consequently, the human and artistic development of these young writers had to take them beyond their youthful sentiment if they wanted to avoid being stunted; and so, the largest segment of the Hauptmann generation became sterile. Hauptmann himself, who became a more profound man and a more powerful artist, today stands alone in every sense of the word; nowhere can one discern an unconscious stream, an unspoken longing that would come alive, whose redeeming word could match his work. What the earlier, artistically weaker works of Hauptmann's youth could achieve has been denied his more mature works, namely, to become the cultural-philosophical meaning and the spoken expression of an epoch. In his case, this resulted in a tragic conflict; others, provided they remained artistically honest, drew the consequences and became mere aesthetes, aiming at "atelier-effects".

Since this movement of the 1890s, there has not emerged a new encompassing trend to hold things together in Germany. On the one hand, some tried (unconsciously) to make a virtue out of necessity: the lonely and self-reliant individual is now considered to be the ultimate value that mankind can produce. But contrary to the general belief that to be a personality is to be true to Germanness, this tendency too turned out to be fruitless. Not only is there an absence of really great talents (personalities of the stature of a Baudelaire) but also a lack of culture *(Kultur)*. Since there can be no individual *in itself* and *for itself*, extreme individualism is always a movement *à rebours*, and the enemy is missing in today's

Germany. That abstract totality, that overwhelming power of the general which stands in opposition to the individual is in itself entirely indecisive, colorless, and without direction, only a dull rejection of the High Ideal; thus, opposition to it is bound to be barren. The new German individualists went into the desert and ended up in the coffee-houses. They were either carried away by their accidental success, whereby their previously deep and honest sufferings on account of alienation turned into *Virtuosität* [brilliance], (as is the case with Hoffmannsthal) or, because they remained undetected, they succeeded in preserving their loneliness but because of the situation often became eccentrics, freaks (as in the case of a Peter Hille[1]). On the other hand, attempts have been made—often in strong faith and with holy conviction—to break out of this individualistic isolation; aristocratic as well as democratic circles and movements have emerged, trying with considerable enthusiasm to create for the sake of the creative minds a milieu of like-minded people and at the same time making visible to the "masses" the path to true art. All these movements, however, suffer from philosophico-historical happenstance and the lack of ideas that follow.

This is not to deny the relatively positive and partly useful character of their efforts; what should be pointed out is why they ultimately have to remain barren. The reason for a lack of ideas in the democratic movements lies in the presupposition that they intend to offer "good art" to the "masses," thereby elevating the masses with the beneficial effect of eliminating, at the same time, the aesthetelike isolation of the artists through their lively contact with a broad and receptive public. A decisive fact is (necessarily) overlooked, namely, that the "tragedy of culture" today is not due to the separation of the artist and public, which could be helped by a really effective and purposeful organization, but rather to the causes of this very fact. The underlying cause is that Germany today is not in possession of a profound and fruitful *Weltanschauung* that would encompass and embrace both the artist and the public and which consequently would mean that both work and its reception would be attuned to each other, as if they were made of each other. Thus, any effective artistic organization would only promote what is an *a priori* necessity toward a faster empirical realization. As an underlying fact also, the work of today's artist is engendered by loneliness, by a state of *Auf-sich-Gestelltsein;* and there is (or can be) no corresponding readiness to receive it. Therefore, any effect on the public at large will always be accidental, a matter of *Bildung* but never a real necessity, namely, that the receivers could recognize their innermost longings expressed in those works. The aristocratic circles of Germany suffer from the same lack of ideas, albeit in a different manifestation: through the impact of a great personality upon his disciples there is supposed to emerge a community that is called upon to transcend the directionlessness of the times and to gather the shattered forces. The original sin of each and every one of these movements is that without themselves being religious they operate with certain religious presuppositions that effect a complete confusion in essential values (instead of bringing about the desired clarification). In constructing the foundations of the circle as a master-disciple relationship, the personality of the master is canonized; the master, who, to be sure, is a very talented man who is imprisoned by and suffering in his times, limited by himself and his times, is elevated to the role of the supreme guide from past to future times. But because this relationship is not an objectively-superpersonal (i.e., a truly religious or philosophical) one, the role of such an accidental personality is exaggerated beyond all proportion; his capabilities as well as his limitations receive a metaphysical and historico-philosophical meaning, which absolutely determines the values of the past and the present and becomes the signpost of the future. This, however, doesn't help to overcome the existing misery, the lack of an all-embracing sentiment, since such a movement has no universality that can mobilize forces. It stands and falls with the valuation of a single personality. And such a personality—unless he really is a prophet, or a true messenger of God—can never comprise all contradictions in himself, shoulder all the suffering and thus point the way to salvation. Therefore, such movements must remain aesthetic, but in projecting their structure into the religious sphere they also succeed in bringing confusion to the aesthetic sphere; their atelier-esoteric character acquires a false accent and their evaluations come to take on even more of a subjective-arbitrary nature than those of their counterparts (i.e., the canonization of the limitations of a personality). They become dogmatic without possessing dogma, and they lose their original aesthetically colored receptivity without displaying anything other than the image of a personality—in the last analysis, something impressionistic. They waver between an admiration for the Middle Ages and Caesar-worship (with some Bergson mixed in); they can neither lead nor be led. They deliver themselves to one man in a way that would only be appropriate for an idea; they lose themselves and don't gain anything supra-individual. The accidental character of a significant man is made into an eternally valid and exemplary case—such an exaggeration will show up precisely the accidental character of such a career, i.e., it becomes embarrassingly clear that its nature is merely an individual and a searching one, and not an affirmative one that should be canonized. I hope I don't have to emphasize that the above does not apply to Stefan George, *the poet*.

It is fortunate that in Germany the dissatisfaction with today's disoriented state of affairs as well as with the unsatisfactory attempts to deal with it grows steadily. The significance of the dissatisfaction, the yearning for a real *Gemeinschaft,* is in its accent on sentiment, which lies somewhere other than in the renewal of the arts; it lies rather in the hope for a reawakening of German philosophy and religiosity. Because here and only here lies the opportunity for a German *Kultur* (and as its necessary consequence, a German art). Germany has never possessed a culture in the sense of France or England; in its best periods her culture was but an "invisible church," the all-penetrating and *Weltanschauung*-creating power of philosophy and religion. The last culturally effective force in Germany, naturalistic-materialistic socialism, achieved its effect because of its hidden religious and *weltanschauliche* elements, a *Weltanschauung* of a metasubjective nature that could at the same time become a deeply personal experience. It proved to be insufficient in the long run, and we have arrived at a stage of abandonment and in search of a *Gemeinschaft*. To be sure, the search is often still very "personal". Mostly, the search is not for the great *Gemeinschaft* that is to come but rather an attempt to discover metaphysics suitable for the present conditions of the disoriented individual only; consequently, the confusion may even increase. But the opposite trend is also again alive. After a long period when German philosophy was an affair of scholars and could not assume a culturally leading role in spite of its tremendous scholarly achievements—after a period when its cultural philosophical direction (e.g., Dilthey) represented a noble, essayistic receptivity—the will has awakened for a system as a symbol of culture and as a receptor of culture. The day when that philosophical Renaissance (which today is not much more than a hope) blossoms, when the system to come will not be only a scholastic-methodological summation of the possibilities of knowledge, but the unspoken religiosity of our age given voice as the real answer to its problems—then again we can have hopes for a German *Kultur* in which literature will mean more than a list of prominent artistic personalities, isolated from each other and from the public. One must not forget that the great age of German literature was also the age of the great German philosophy. The forms in which Germans could express themselves are the tragedy and the epic *(Parsifal, Wilhelm Meister, Faust)*; these forms become purely aesthetic in their ultimate completion but presuppose a living metaphysics to their genesis. The purely aesthetic talent of the Germans is perhaps less pronounced than of other peoples; on the other hand, they have more depth of creative power than any other nation. We can only hope without stating anything for certain that we are at the threshold of the awakening of such a *Deutschtum.* To be precise, in the field of philosophy we have only hopes and promises but no deeds; as far as religious movements are concerned, we don't even have clear hopes, and we can't know whether or not "down there" in the social movements there exists a real readiness for cultural values to come. The only accomplishment that in this sense can be called a fact is the life-work of Paul Ernst. He rises to the heights and above all other German writers of our epoch, not purely by his literary talents—there are quite a few who are his equal—but by his deeply felt ethos which transcends the purely contingently personal fates of his characters. His tragedies are given form as if there existed again a German culture, a culture that has absorbed all of the essential past and hence can point to the future. He is the only one who was not driven by the advancement of socialism as a central cultural force into an aimless individualism, rather, he has preserved everything that was alive in the past as an organic component of what is to come. A renewal of German literature cannot emanate from him (and he knows that best); his forms would become aestheticized by his "disciples". He can only be an example of the fact that the Germany of old, the land of Kant and Goethe, of Schiller and Hegel, is awaiting those who would awaken it to a new life.

(unsigned)

[1] Peter Hille (1854–1904), German writer, member of the Bohemian circle of Berlin, author of the novel *Sozialisten* (1889).

114. FROM MAX WEBER

Heidelberg
March 6, 1913

Dear Herr Doctor,

Mr. Gaston Riou, who is the bearer of this letter, is with the *Figaro* of Paris, the author of a book (with an introduction by Faguet)[1] on "Aux écoutes de la France à venir,"[2] and is associated with the people belonging to the "Jeune France";[3] he is a Protestant. His paper sent him here to prepare a similar volume on Germany which would *essentially* consist of interviews. He is especially interested in contemporary religious and assimilated trends. I have never granted an interview before but must admit that this extremely pleasant and attentive gentleman whom I received at the urging of Troeltsch (and who also visited Windelband, Rickert, and others) deserves to be made an exception. In spite of my hair-raising French, the conversation was a pleasant one. After having told him a few things from my perspective, he insisted on meeting you too; actually, during the conversation I happened to mention your name as representing *one* of the types of German "eschatologism"[4] and in that sense being at the opposite pole from Stefan George. I presume it won't pose a problem for you to grant him an hour or so of conversation. *First of all,* you could tell him who of the *young literati* in Germany are worth talking to (one should be somewhat "generous" here as he should experience the average too). You can arrange, *if you'd like,* not to have your name appear in the publication and you can keep yourself as far in the background as you wish. But then again—why do that? I cannot avoid being mentioned.

I hope to see you soon.

Respectfully yours,
Max Weber

1 Emile Faguet (1847–1916), professor of literature at the Sorbonne.
2 Correctly, *Aux Écoutes de la France qui vient* (Paris: Grasset, 1913).
3 French intellectual movement with a program called, "Gesta Dei per Francos". See Gaston Riou, *Lettre aux Jeune France* (1912).
4 The Webers' opinion was recorded in Marianne Weber's biography: "These young philosophers [especially Lukács and Ernst Bloch] were moved by eschatological hopes of a new emissary of the transcendent God, and they saw the basis of salvation in a socialist social order created by brotherhood . . . The ultimate goal is salvation *from* the world, not as for George and his circle, fulfillment *in* it." Hence Weber's comparison. See M. Weber, *Max Weber . . .* (p. 466).

115. FROM MAX WEBER

Heidelberg
March 10, 1913

Dear Herr Doctor,

Wednesday, 5:00 p.m. would be a good time for your visit, until about half past six (when I have to dress and go to pay a visit). My wife will *not* be back *before* Saturday. Monday of the f.[ollowing] w.[eek] we expect guests, so we can agree on a future date only after that.

Chapter One[1] I've read, that is, I've glanced over it. I can accept your basic thesis, on the basis of what I have seen so far. As for *Fiedler,*[2] he has at least made the *attempt* to think in terms of a kind of "logic of the visible" *(sichtbar),* that is, going beyond what can be experienced. It is only that such a restriction can never result in a universal conception of "art". After having seen aesthetics approached from the standpoint of the receiver and more recently from that of the creator, it is a pleasure to see that the "work" itself is given a voice.

I know neither Riegl[3] nor Popper,[4] to my shame. (I have not as yet had the opportunity to read Broder Christiansen.[5] You don't cite him at all. Rickert[6] seems to think highly of him.)

I am eager to see how it will be when your concept of *form* emerges. After all, "formed life" is not *only* the *value*-containing *(das Werthafte)* element that rises above the experiential, but also the *erotic* element that dips into the deep and outermost corners of the "dungeon" in "formed life" as well.[7] It shares the faith of the quilt-laden with all formed life; and in the quality of its opposition to everything that belongs to the sphere of the "form alien" *(formfremd)* God it is close to the aesthetic attitude. Its topographical position has yet to be determined, and I am quite curious to see *where* it is going to be located in your work. The presentation (of your material) is clear, at least for me. But on the other hand, I have already halfway forgotten the *train* of thought. I read too fast.

Auf Wiedersehen!

Yours,
Max Weber

[1] "Die Kunst als 'Ausdruck' und die Mitteilungsformen der Erlebniswirklichkeit," in *Heidelberger Philosophie der Kunst (1912–1914).*

[2] Konrad Fiedler (1841–1895), German mentor of artists and an art theoretician. Lukács extensively quoted from his work, *Über den Ursprung der künstlerischer Tätigkeit. Schriften über Kunst.* 2 vols., ed. by H. Konnerth (München: Piper Verlag, 1913).
[3] Alois Riegl (1858–1905) Austrian art historian and professor of art history at the University of Vienna beginning in 1897, coined the term "artistic intention" or "art will" *(Kunstwollen)*. Author of *Stilfragen: Grundlegungen zu neue Geschichte der Ornamentik* (1893) and *Spätrömische Kunstindustrie nach der Funden in Österreich-Ungarn* (1910). Influenced Karl Mannheim and Arnold Hauser.
[4] Leo Popper. See "Biographical Notes".
[5] Broder Christiansen (1869–1958), German philosopher and aesthete. Weber refers to his essay, "Das ästhetische Urphänomen," in *Logos* (1911–12), pp. 15.
[6] Heinrich Rickert, Jr. See "Biographical Notes".
[7] The reference point is Lukács's *Heidelberger Philosophie der Kunst (1912–1914)* in wich he wrote: "*der Kerker [dungeon] der eigenen Individualität hat sich zu einer Welt geweitet–ein Kerker ist sie dennoch geblieben*" (p. 31).

116. FROM MAX WEBER

Heidelberg
March 22, 1913

Dear Herr Doctor,

Hard as I tried, I've found it impossible to read the *entire* chapter two[1] again before my impending trip. My poor head just doesn't function anymore.

In Chapter 1, there is for most readers a discernible "leap" *(Sprung)* at the point at which you state: *Should* it be that art was a true reflection of the world of *experience* (I might add, not necessarily of each and *every*), then art would become a means for a knowledge of God that was thus ascertainable.[2] It seems to me that it is hardly possible to eliminate the problematic nature of the category of "the world of experience" *(Lebenswirklichkeit)*. That would lead to endless complications.

But it is precisely at *this point* of the discussion that one becomes aware of its *unfinished nature*.

This problem aside, I find that this time the writing is *very* concise and logical and—in direct disagreement with Lask's opinion[3]—*not too* detailed. Rather, at times it is a bit too abstract ("carpet").[4]

One thing is certain: the more material you have to hand in, the better your chances for success in a situation fought with difficulties.[5]

I am in want of the *necessary* energy and time to even *try* to get down to a discussion of your thesis.* I am all done in.

With warmest regards,
Your,
Max Weber

* My impression is a very strong one, and I am quite convinced that the statement of the problem is definitely the correct one—at last!

[1] Reference is to the first version of the projected *Aesthetics,* intended to be the introductory part of Lukács's general system of philosophy. Outlined during his stay in Florence (1911–12), it was revised (1916–18) and then abandoned in 1918. The MS was discovered after Lukács's death. It was published in German in two volumes as *Heidelberger Philosophie der Kunst, 1912–1914* and *Heidelberger Ästhetik, 1916–1918* (Neuwied: Luchterhand, 1974). Weber had alluded to his trip to Ascona on Lago Maggiore, where he spent the springs of 1913 and 1914. According to Marianne Weber, the small town "provided a refuge for all sorts of strange people who dropped out of bourgeois society... adherents of the disciples of Freud ... anarchists and communists," in *Max Weber: A Biography,* ed. and trans. by Harry Zohn (New York: Wiley, 1975), pp. 486ff.

[2] *Heidelberger Philosophie der Kunst,* pp. 36–37. Allusion is to the Schellingian concept of art standing at the "summit" of the "philosophical hierarchy" (p. 16), i.e., the concept of the unity of philosophy and religion.

[3] Emil Lask. See "Biographical Notes".

[4] See "Teppich als Paradigma" (Carpet as a Paradigm), chapter 2, *Heidelberger Philosophie der Kunst,* pp. 92–98.

[5] Reference to attempted *Habilitation.*

117. TO LAJOS FÜLEP

Heidelberg
[Early May] 1913

Dear Friend,

I was pleased to hear from you, at last, even if it was not all that good (re: work). I wonder if you have or are interested in a connection to *Pester Lloyd?* It is by far the best-paying (relatively) and the most decent (again relatively) paper in Budapest. How are your connections—if any—to Italian papers? I went to Budapest for the Balázs première[1] and came back disgusted—with people, friends, and enemies (most intensively with the two former).

That is why I don't have great expectations for *Szellem:* partly because there are only a few of us—and it is to be feared that we cannot maintain the continuity, partly because in Hungary there is such suffocating indifference that even if *Szellem* were to be a well-functioning magazine, its long-term success would by no means be certain. Who can we count on as contributors? I am working on my aesthetics and would gladly give a chapter of it to the magazine although it might prove too long. (It's very unlikely that I'll write articles any time soon.) Hevesi[2] has become an opera director. Emma Ritoók[3] needs two years for an article. Balázs wrote something that would fit the magazine only by accident. All we have left is Zalai[4] and Fogarasi (and the latter is not a sympathetic choice for you). F.[ogarasi], by the way, wrote quite a good article for the *Athenaeum* on the "voluntaristic theory of judgment".[5] This is not to discourage you, only to point out the difficulties to you. If you think that we could put together a fall issue, I'll ask Balázs to translate a chapter of my work in progress. As for the financial side: I am ready and willing to cover a deficit up to 200 or 250 *Kronen,* but not more, not even as an advance. This year I've had unexpectedly high expenses and expect considerably more. If you find a way to do it, the sum is at your disposal.

The gossip you mentioned[6] is characteristic of [Buda]Pest, whoever the inventor was.

I am now working on my aesthetics (this turns out to be the book I mentioned to you last winter). I hope to have the first volume in publishable shape in a year's time. (It is planned as a two-volume work, approx. 500–600 pages each.) Consequently, I can't do much traveling. I am even thinking of settling down... For one thing, it is easier to travel if one doesn't live in a transitional state. But where and when? I don't think I could settle in Italy for good, after all. Budapest is absolutely out of the question for me. This presents real psychological problems. I'd like very much to go to Rome but I'd need 2–3 quiet months for that. I'll go to Italy in the fall but it is uncertain whether I'll get as far as Rome. Will you be there in September?

I hope I'll hear from you more often in the future.

With friendly greetings,

Yours,
György Lukács

[1] Presumably the April 20, 1913 matinée, consisting of two Balázs "mystery plays": *Bluebeard's Castle* and *The Blood of the Holy Virgin*. The former was used as a libretto by Béla Bartók for his one-act opera.
[2] Sándor Hevesi. See letter no. 4, n. 2.
[3] See "Biographical Notes".
[4] Zalai. See letter no. 59, n. 4.
[5] Béla Fogarasi, "Az ítélet voluntarisztikus elmélete," in *Athenaeum* 1, (1913), the house organ of the Philosophical Society. See letter no. 102, n. 9.
[6] Fülep's letter of April 20, 1913, mentioned that he was accused of collecting money for *A Szellem* (from Lukács and others) but was using it for maintaining his lifestyle.

118. FROM GÉZA RÉVÉSZ

Budapest
May 24, 1913

Highly esteemed Herr Doctor,

I have been planning to establish here at home a philosophical society[1] which would be a gathering point for those young men seriously interested and/or engaged in one or another area of philosophy. Many times I have been asked in the past to undertake such a venture but only now do I see an opportune time for it. In my opinion, only those who have a serious interest in philosophy or psychology and have proven it by publication in the field should join. We would thus be spared the company of those who read and write about philosophy purely as dilettantes and obstruct any serious work. I was thinking of the following as prospective members: Zalai, Szilasi, Fogarasi, Enyvári, Ritoók, Szemere, Fülep, you, and myself.[2] We'd probably get a few more requests to join. Everyone who'd pay could become a supporting member. The Society could start up in the fall and then we could entertain the thought of launching our house organ; such a publication is badly needed here. I have made inquiries at several printing houses and believe that we could manage financially a medium-size journal. One printing house especially (where one or two of my personal friends are executives) made a very good offer. Later, we may be able to launch a German-language edition. I've talked about it to one of my friends who heads one of the most prestigious publishing houses in Leipzig and he also mentioned a very acceptable prize. Of course, we can think of such ventures only after the Society has been formed and is on a secure footing financially.

I should like to ask you whether or not you'd consider joining our society; if yes, please let me know. Next weekend I'd like to call together an exploratory meeting and would appreciate your answer by then.

My sincere regards and respects,

Yours,
Géza Révész

[1] The Society was never launched. Some of the younger men mentioned joined the existing Hungarian Philosophical Society under Bernát Alexander. Their house organ was *Athenaeum* (1892–1944). Révész himself became in time a coeditor of *Athenaeum*.

[2] Béla Zalai. See letter no. 59, n. 4. Vilmos Szilasi (see letter no. 26, n. 1.) left Hungary in 1919 and lived first in Germany and then in Switzerland; after WWII, he became professor of philosophy at Freiburg University; Béla Fogarasi. See letter no. 102, n. 9; Jenő Enyvári (1884–1969), was a librarian in Budapest; Emma Ritoók, see "Biographical Notes"; Samu Szemere (1881–1978), philosopher and Hegel translator; Lajos Fülep, see "Biographical Notes".

119. FROM ALBERT SALOMON

Heidelberg
May 27, 1913

Esteemed Herr Doctor,

Is it convenient for you if I come by Friday afternoon, about 6 p.m.—or at any other time of your choice? I think by that time I will have finished with the copying. "Ariadne"[1] keeps me preoccupied.

Yesterday I went in to Gundolf's[2] lecture; whenever I listen to him I have the unfortunate sense that he has proclaimed Goethe as a *Lebensideal* and believes himself to be its realization. Besides, his Goethe interpretation based on hedonism and Bergson is very disagreeable. The whole lecture flows past one like a river and one cannot retain anything of it.

I have read Claudel's[3] *Verkündigung*. More about it in person. Only this: after I read the drama, I decided against attending the performance. I would feel like the impure in the temple; I'd keep thinking that I should not be allowed to hear this because only the pure and the believers are entitled to it.

Wish you the best and send my greetings,

Yours,
Albert Salomon

[1] Drama of Paul Ernst. Presumably Salomon copied the text for himself.
[2] Friedrich Gundolf. See letter no. 34, n. 4.
[3] Paul Claudel (1868–1955), French diplomat and Catholic dramatist, famous for his baroque manners and return to dramatic verse. His mystery play, *L'annonce faite à Marie* (1912) was translated into German by Jacob Hegner. The performance Salomon refers to was staged in Hellerau at that time.

120. TO PAUL ERNST

Heidelberg
[Early June] 1913

Dear Herr Doctor,

Unfortunately nothing came of my planned trip to Hellerau. I have too much to do and too many diverse things to take care of and can't afford the time. I regret it even more because I don't foresee any chance for a good talk in the near future. I am here until the end of July. After that I'll be going to an Italian sea resort. In September–October comes Florence and Rome. Are you going there?

As far as Claudel[1] is concerned, our opinions differ. There are certain parts of it which simply cannot (in principle) be given form; and because he wanted to do so, he wrote a bad drama. However, his going beyond the possibilities of form (with its consequences—compositional failure) is not due to dilettantism, but to a religious inwardness that strains the boundaries of the poetic. What could be given form, has been accomplished.

Last week, Kahn[2] paid me a visit. He talked at length about his plans for a journal which you know about. Do you think that such a plan can be realized? Nowadays, I have very little interest in anything purely of a literary nature (unless it involves the ultimate questions). Personally, I am involved to such a degree in working out my systematic philosophy that I have become quite incompetent in such (practical) matters. I understand Kahn's impatience but cannot share his sentiments.

Balázs[3] wrote today concerning the reworking of his translations. He is negotiating with a theatrical publisher and needs your help badly. I told him to approach Kahn and Greiner[4] and to write to you. Would you be so kind as to negotiate the matter with Greiner in case Kahn has no time or interest in it?

Brunhild was staged in Dürkheim on the 15th, but since the performances are not advertised publicly, I had no advance knowledge of it. If the next performance fits my schedule, I'll go.

Please give my regards to Kahn if he comes to Weimar (and please don't mention the affair of the *Habilitation,* which won't come up for another year, anyway). What are your summer plans? Is there any chance that we can meet?

Kindest regards from your,
G. v. Lukács

[1] See letter 119, n. 3.
[2] Harry Kahn. See letter no. 85, n. 9.
[3] Béla Balázs. The translations in question were not undertaken.
[4] Leo Greiner (1876–1928), German dramatist, translator.

121. FROM MAX WEBER

Rome
Hotel Tordelli
Piazza Colonna
October 3, 1913

Dear Herr Doctor,

We are staying at the Albergo *Colonna* (see above)—a *hotel garni*. Inform us of the time of your arrival.[1]

With warm greetings,

Yours,
Max Weber

[1] As Marianne Weber reports in her biography of Weber, the Webers went on their last joint Italian journey that fall, visiting Assisi, Siena, Perugia, and Rome, where Lukács joined them. Lukács stayed there with the Webers about two weeks.

122. FROM YELENA (ANDREYEVNA) GRABENKO

Budapest
October 15, 1913

Gyuri darling,

Do you know what I am thinking of now?

I just came home from a walk in the hills. What did I find there? Nothing! A glimpse of a few roofs, trees losing their foliage, and blue skies. I was walking slowly, following the windswept leaves.

Then, suddenly, I felt like fainting—my God, where am I, what am I doing here, and why?

Truly, the French language has bewitched me so much[1] that I have lost touch with my Russian past; but that is my real self and I know I'll have to pay for this one day. When I went to Bellaria, it meant redemption for me; now it destroys me. Do you believe me when I say that if I speak Russian again I'll scream out of despair? You know, since I have been to Bellaria, I haven't spoken one word of Russian; and whenever I hear a Slavic language I begin shaking, even if I don't understand a word? You now have a cold and so you know how it feels: I am a stranger to my own self and everything is so muddled; it feels like having an eternal cold.

You alone were the reality for me, because our souls sensed each other behind the languages we spoke.

But if I now imagine that you are surrounded by people, you too become obscure for me, you are not real either; you have become "they". I have the feeling I too am *they,* if I speak *their* language, live their kind of life. You wrote to me about Edith.[2] I love her and I know she loves me too, but she too has become *they.* I try to tell her everything, I feel I can tell her everything but I sense that she doesn't understand me. I despise myself because I speak a language alien to me and I have become alien to myself. I have learned to understand only here why I am a good human being, and why Edith isn't, and what "goodness" is, the goodness you told me about.

I guess you are really good; it is impossible that you are not, or at least you are always good when you talk to me. If I imagine you otherwise, I get a chill.

When you said to me that you have become an uncomplicated man, I felt so happy; I can't tell you how happy. Anybody who is good, has to be uncomplicated—has to be simple and truthful toward others.

But that is not all I want to tell you. What I wanted to tell you is that suddenly I was thinking of going to Russia, to the place which I never thought I'd go back to. I will marry Zagorodny[3] and forget everything. Whenever I turn inward, I know with a certainty that as soon as I see Russia, Zagorodny, and family again, my past will come alive; I could even work. I don't even care about Marusja.[4]

You see, I tell you everything. I even ask you to tell me what you think about my plan? I know I am cruel. I am at my cruelest toward you, because you are the closest to me, because you alone reign in my soul, Gyuri darling, my only friend. I am afraid to go to Heidelberg. Heidelberg means a decision, a finality—something we associate with death. If I can't stand it, I can always go away, change things, but one doesn't go toward death, into nothingness; one fears it. It may surprise you when I say that I am not afraid because I could succeed—rather than the other way around.

That is it. Oh, yes, something else. I don't know why but I have the feeling I am in the throws of death. Physically. Maybe it is the climate. Maybe it is because I have lived too much, maybe only my nerves. I sometimes think, *it* may come quickly. Already my correspondence disturbs me. Take it easy, darling. Maybe I am just plain stupid. I am telling you all this so that you will see I tell you everything. But I am sure I shouldn't stay here. I cannot imagine anything more dreadful than to die in Hungary. I don't hate Hungary, but I don't love it.

Sometimes I would like to meet a few simple people. I met Kende[5] and was happy after that.

Goodness me, the stupidities I write to you! I am afraid you won't like my letters.

Perhaps, to say the same for you, I shouldn't write any letters. I, for example, can't stand Zagorodny's letters. It may easily be that you feel the same toward mine.

I went to the Museum with Edith yesterday. I was very happy. I wanted to go today too, but Edith said we have to go to the doctor. It seems she has forgotten all about that and now I am nervous. Don't write her about it; I left a note behind for her. I am at the end of my paper and don't want to begin a new page. I am afraid of my stupidities but then I don't want to part from you. Hold me tight. Speak to me so that I can feel you.

Gyuri, my *sikidii,*[6] how I would like to see your eyes; are they smiling? Of course you are smiling; you have to be smiling. Forgive me, I have written too much. But tell me if you are happy? Are you well now? Are you glad that you are with the Webers and in Rome? I wish you happiness. My god, you are so good to write so soon. How I love you, but I'd like to escape. Besides Salov and Zagorodny, you are my only other friend; but, you know, I feel differently towards them. My sikidii. I love you. Kiss your necktie.

Yelena

[1] Yelena's letters were written in (an extremely poor) French. After having fled Russia, she was living in Paris for a while in great poverty, where she met some of Lukács's closest friends such as Béla Balázs, Hilda Bauer (Balázs's sister) and Edith Hajós (Bone), Balázs's wife.
[2] Edith Hajós.
[3] Her fiancé in Russia.
[4] Presumably a girlfriend of Zagorodny.
[5] Zsigmond Kende (1888–1973), physician, one of the founders of the Galileo Circle, a friend of Karl Polányi and the Balázses.
[6] Nickname.

123. FROM YELENA (ANDREYEVNA) GRABENKO

Budapest
October 29, 1913

My *sikidii,*

I wonder whether I'll be able to write this letter; I have a headache, a cold, and am in such a state that I always worry about every line I put down, because I am so stupid. My only consolation is that you very often deal with people who are stupider than you.

But I have to write because I have to ask you to address your future letters to Swabian-Hill and not to Jolan Street. (Edith said that you know the address.) We will live there with Edith. We talked about it yesterday. She doesn't work nowadays; I'm afraid she will go to pot. The truth is that it is all physiological; she has to leave. I know this state very well: one suffers the torment of the pain of pains, tearing at one's hair; nothing can please—and the cause is a folly, the fact that the two natures are unsuited. As if we couldn't be more human. Tear up my letter, darling. I promised Edith that I'd stay with her at least for two weeks. We visited the place today. It is very painful to move there under such circumstances. At the bottom of my soul, I am desperate. I feel as if I have promised myself for marriage. It disturbs my equilibrium and my work. But... the matter is even sadder, because now I'll receive your letters a few hours later.

I still don't know, darling, when is the earliest that I can go to Heidelberg—if you still want me to. As soon as I begin living with people, the confusion sets in. I, who am the most punctual person possible, become unpunctual; I become lazy and my fundamentally ascetic nature turns into a hedonistic one. I keep observing myself and wonder where my willpower went; when I am by myself, I certainly have plenty of it.

Do you know what the secret of Edith's punctuality is? That she is never on time. But that is not what I want to write about. More precisely, I don't have anything definite to say to you; I am so attached to you that I can't think, work, or write (luckily, I can sleep, thank God!). I am waiting. And then I am so tired that I fear you won't come. Do you understand me? The autumn is so beautiful now in Hungary that I would like to fall in love. But then it would not be you I would want with me here, under the trees. I wish I knew why—maybe because I am tired, I want only you but by the time you arrive I will be incapable because the waiting will have exhausted me. (Maybe I felt like that only today, because of the headache, just like the last night in Venice.) I feel that I am profoundly attached to you; we almost form a symbiosis, and that scares me.

I had an attack of nervousness last night. I dreamed that Herbert wrote a bad poem, you criticized it, and they threw you into a dark dungeon. I ran there, saying that it was not serious, that you'd be out in two weeks. Then I noticed the mold on the door and asked about it; the answer was that it was the moisture. I started screaming that it'd be fatal for you! I screamed, pushed and pulled on the door and wanted you to hear me; because if you heard me, you'd be so agitated that you'd be running up and down and keeping yourself warm. I woke up yelling and Gyuri, Gyuri, I was so scared.

So I didn't see you, darling. I would like to see you again. It's dark now, I can hardly see. I have to finish. I don't write about art. I think what you wrote about was beautiful but I am not in the state of mind to think about it. I am restless, I run around, search out people (there are too many of them). I don't understand myself anymore, neither my physical nor my emotional state.

Something has happened to my willpower. Maybe I just have a cold. You too are so alone. I would so much like to put my head on your knees. Don't you feel that would drive away the loneliness and everything dark and uncertain? You would become a little—the way you put it—frivolous; that is such a deep and comforting thought. And of course you are such a little ass, darling, if you call that frivolity. Sikidii, I love you, I hug your head, hold it to myself, kiss you behind your ears: I do so love your ears. And I kiss your mouth, once, and then again and again. It is more than a thousand times, isn't it? And I hold up my nose for you to kiss; it'll make you merry.

My angel, my life, forget everything. It is not a sin that you love me. When I think of it, you have always made me happy; and it is not our fault that we are the exclusive source of happiness for each other.

I smile at you and hug your legs even if you don't love me anymore and don't desire me. You shouldn't mind about me because I'm full of vitality and even if you don't want me, life is still ahead of me; and if you want me, it is the same case, except that it is nicer.

And if you hold on to me and then leave me, that too is life and life's offering. My child, I hold your hands and I can't take leave of you; I am not strong enough. Do you want to come with me to Edith's? No? I would like to say something infinitely moving to you but can't find the words. I am just very close to you.

Yelena

124. FROM MAX WEBER

Heidelberg
November 6, 1913

Dear Herr Doctor,

May we trouble you *once again* (and for the last time!)? I asked the "Manifattura di Signa"

(1) about their *"prezzo ultimo"* for the *Wagenlenker* (statue)

(2) about whether the things (the statue) will be *insured ("assicurato")* and how much it will cost.

It looks as if they could not decipher my letter or my Italian was simply too poor. I would be *very* grateful—if it is not out of your way—if *you* could simply buy it *for us,* provided it won't cost more than 450 lire, including the insurance.

The payment will be sent *immediately* after receiving word from you. The statue should be sent only after you receive the money, with the freight c.o.d. If it is at all *possible,* I wish, of course, to be insured against breakage during transportation (they did it for me in Florence in the past, so it can be done).

Forgive me for this renewed bother. I would be *very* thankful for the favor, if you can manage it.

I recall with true pleasure the days spent together in Rome, although I was in a less receptive mood this time. I was preoccupied (with my ongoing work) and the changes that were so visible all around us[1] disturbed me greatly. Our stay was too short.

Warmest greetings and many thanks, also from my wife,

Yours,
Max Weber

1 Marianne Weber recounts their last trip together in Italy, although she does not mention Lukács. The changes Weber refer to are described as follows: "Rome had undergone an ugly transformation. There were obtrusive new buildings, particularly the frosty white and gold marble monument, the expression and symbol of a united Italy... Even the *Siegesallee* in Berlin was better. As though made by a pastry chef, it not only ruined the old Piazza Venezia, but ... by shifting all dimensions it overwhelmed the capitol behind it." In *Max Weber. A Biography,* trans. and ed. by Harry Zohn (New York: Wiley Interscience, 1975), p. 504.

125. FROM MAX WEBER

Heidelberg
November 7, 1913

Dear Herr Doctor,

My *letter* is taken care of; the firm *(Manifattura)* just wrote. I do hope that you have not yet gone to any trouble. Once again, my heartfelt thanks for your kindness.

I am anxious to know whether we will have you here again in a few weeks or does Rome prove to be a stronger magnet?[1]

Greetings from my wife,

As ever,
Yours,
Max Weber

1 Lukács left Italy a few days after, and before returning to Heidelberg he visited his family and friends in Budapest, informing them of his impending marriage to Yelena Grabenko. He was back in Heidelberg by December.

126. FROM JÓZSEF VON LUKÁCS

Budapest
May 25, 1914

My dear son, Gyuri,

For days I have been meaning to answer your kind letter of May 20, but was unable to find the time to do so. I am hereby returning the letter from Düsseldorf[1]; I cannot honestly say that I am sorry for the negative outcome. It seems that they were only interested in somebody who was a great scholar but would not cost them anything—or at least, not much, i.e., somebody who took the job because he was ambitious. In my opinion, only a university has a right to expect someone to work for so little, and I am pleased that you intend to save yourself for an academic career. How I would love to see you have a *Privatdozentur* at a university!

Mici informed me that your marriage[2] has come to pass, after all. I wish with all my heart that all the hopes and wishes that you have had or now entertain shall be fulfilled; nobody will be happier than I when that happens. But since I can see that for you marriage is only a burdensome formality that has nothing to do with the essence of things, I would like to think that should you come one day to regard it as a mistake, you would deal with it as you did with the marriage ceremony, that is, you would regard the necessary steps to dissolve the marriage also as a formality.[3] You should never forget the essence of things: your happiness and individual well-being come first.

And now allow me to make a serious comment about your wife's behavior. I can understand and appreciate an aloofness that in certain circumstances and to a certain degree may be the sign of an aristocratic attitude. But her negative approach to your family, to your father, mother, brother and sister, in the past as well as right now, after your wedding, is something else again. Her discourteous and contemptuous behavior makes me think that she does not wish to become a member of the family; she merely wants to be your wedded wife. It is admittedly a legitimate standpoint, although a highly unconventional one. In this regard, I have by now so lowered my expectations that I can live with it, although only if the attitude is reciprocated.

Please let me know when your wife intends to visit her parents in Russia.[4]

I must also ask you to let me know how much extra expense you have had so far this year, so that I can adjust your line of credit with the bank there. As I see it, there is only 2,800 left at your disposal out of the 10,000 marks deposited on your account for the year of 1914. Though I think that your yearly expenses should not exceed 10,000 marks, I want to make sure that you always have at least that amount at your disposal. I have to have, therefore, your expenses for the year so that I am able to raise the line of credit.

Once again, I wish with all the warmth of a father's love and a friend's sentiment that your hopes and expectations for the future are fulfilled and that your happiness may compensate for my heartbreak.

I affectionately embrace you,
Your Father

[1] Reference is to a letter by Leopold von Wiese, dated April 17, 1914 in which there is mention of a plan of the city of Düsseldorf to establish an Academy of the Performing Arts and of the possibility of a Visiting Lectureship in Philosophy for Lukács: the plan was dropped by the city shortly after that.

[2] To Yelena (or Jelena) Andreyevna Grabenko, "daughter of Andrey Michailowitch Grabenko, *semstvo*-secretary [civil servant] of Cherson," according to Lukács's curriculum vitae of 1918. Lukács reminisced shortly before his death about his reasons for marrying her: "Situation in Heidelberg: the existence of a 'free floating intellectual' with adequate financial means. Necessity of marriage because of the war: J. G. is Russian, her only protection: Hungarian citizenship. Her love affair [with that musician] is imminent. The three of us living together. Inner separation amidst physical proximity. Real solution: friendly parting but only after the war". (Transcript at the Lukács Archives in Budapest.)

[3] The marriage was formally dissolved in 1919. She visited Lukács in Budapest during the 1919 Commune and her (erotic) adventures with several of the young radical intellectuals there were well-known. Lukács's father helped her escape to Vienna after the collapse of the Commune.

[4] See note 2.

127. From MÁRIA (MICI) LUKÁCS

Pörtschach
[June], 1914

Dear Gyuri,

I have thought of writing to you for a long, long time, but since I didn't want to send you the usual conventional lines, I have kept putting it off ever since my arrival here. I can't hide from you the fact that I am very upset by your—and by Ljena's[1]—behavior, that you haven't found time to write a line since our meeting in Vienna. Yet, I neither can nor want to play the game of being at loggerheads, especially with you. This doesn't mean at all that I approve of what you are doing and the way you do it. I am not speaking about myself—I am only thinking of Dad. You have always preached that we must spare him additional aggravation within the family, so that no grief should gnaw at his heart. To what purpose? So that he can continue providing for us. Let's be honest: this was the sole motivation. You have to admit that one cannot find a more understanding, loving, and generous man. He did everything for us, and never cared about whether it was good or bad for him. I'll try with all of my energies to reciprocate his generosity, somehow. You, my dear boy, have always been his pride and his future. And on the first occasion that he asked you for something, not to get married yet, but to wait a couple of months (and I believe this was the very first time that he ever asked you for something), your resolutely refused to consider his request. You did it in the knowledge that he would resign himself to the fact as he has always done in the past. But you shouldn't have ever made him feel that it is the money—not exclusively, but largely—that keeps your nexus with the family. I cannot help it if my attitude toward life is very petty-bourgeois; I can't accept that someone who is not wholly independent should not have any obligations towards the family. No matter what you say, you should feel obliged to give Dad the great pleasure of becoming a *Privatdozent*. I consider it a moral obligation on your part. I tell you: if you had seen how sad and downcast Dad was in the past few months, you couldn't help but reflect upon it and then move energetically toward finishing your *Habilitationsschrift*. I don't have much to tell you about myself, and anyway I am too agitated to write more today. Write quickly and I'll also tell more about my problems, how I am struggling with the situation of having a new nursemaid!

With love,
Mici

[1] The Hungarian spelling of Yelena Grabenko's name.

128. FROM GOTTFRIED SALOMON

Strasbourg
July 3, 1914

Esteemed Herr von Lukács,

Ever since I read your *Von der Armut am Geiste,*[1] I have felt a strong desire to meet you; our shared love (for Philippe, Kassner, and Kierkegaard)[2] is a strong bond. I will be giving a talk in Heidelberg on the 16th of July at the Sociological Society (on the "Typology of Religiosity"), and I would be more than glad to have a session with you—a minilecture or a pre-presentation discussion of sorts—because I can sense your leaning toward mysticism; I think that this would be a quick way to gain a certain degree of intimacy. What counts here is neither the ideas nor the form but rather the direction (of interest). I openly admit that you are among those I respect the most.

Gottfried Salomon

P.S. Would you be so kind as to write to me (or let me know through intermediaries) when my visit would suit you; I will be in Heidelberg on Saturday and Sunday, Gaisberg-Str. 21.

[1] *On Poverty of Spirit.*
[2] All three essays included in the volume, *Soul and Form.*

129. FROM KÁROLY (KARL) MANNHEIM

Berlin
July 25, 1914

Dear Sir,

Please rest assured that your letter has given me great pleasure and that I feel deeply honored by your commission.[1] My prompt answer should indicate to you that your cause—in which you allow me to partake in a modest way—comes first and my affairs take a back seat: I come straight to the matter of translation and postpone any report of my own progress. But this much should be said: during the long silence that followed our acquaintance, your writings and personality played a much greater role in my own development than you could possibly imagine.

I gladly accept the commission because it means I will undertake a work toward which I don't feel indifferent; that helps reassure me that I will do my best. I am also aware of the difficulty of the task, which raises some doubts in my mind about whether or not my best efforts can satisfy you. But this is something you must decide; until your decision such anxieties only serve to stimulate me.

First of all, may I ask you how much time I will have to do the work? When do you expect to finalize negotiations with Diederichs,[2] or to be more exact, when do you want me to start with the translation? As to the details, I would be interested to know which chapters are mine, or to what extent I can rely on the text of the *Drama history* that I have right here with me; and, finally, at what point would I have to consult the changed manuscript? But all these questions can be raised in the course of future correspondence, after we have come to a final understanding and can begin with the work.

May I ask a few personal questions, because I prefer to hear answers directly from you. Have you published any papers in German or Hungarian journals since the publication of *Von der Armut am Geiste?*[3] It is rumored that you are working on an *Aesthetics;* when could I read some of it? I am immensely interested. My last question: Are you going to stay in Germany for good?

This time I have kept silent about my own affairs, but I fervently hope that even before a visit to Heidelberg I shall be able to break my silence either by writing a letter or through personal talk—a silence which is solely due to my awkwardness.

I await your kind answer and remain,

Faithfully yours,
Karl Mannheim

P.S. I shall stay here until September 1; from then on my address will be: Budapest, V., Sas Str. 19.

[1] The translation in question was to be the rendering into German of Lukács's Hungarian-language book, *A modern dráma fejlődésének története* (The History of the Development of the Modern Drama), but the war interfered. It was not until 1981 that the work came out in German, as volume 15 of the *Georg Lukács Werke* (Collected Works) (Neuwied–Berlin: Luchterhand Verlag). See letter no, 41. n. 7.

[2] Eugene Diederichs, publishing house in Jena.

[3] *On Poverty of Spirit.*

130. FROM KÁROLY (KARL) MANNHEIM

Budapest V.
Sas Str. 19
November 14, 1914

Dear Sir,

The reason I bother your with a few lines today is that I don't want our rapprochement to be interrupted again on my account.

I do not know whether you received the letter I sent you from Berlin. It may easily have been lost amidst the disorders caused by the outbreak of the war.[1] It is also conceivable that you sent an answer which I never received because I left Berlin soon afterwards.

Having returned to Budapest, I thought that the question of translation was moot since the war intervened; therefore I have started to work on my dissertation,[2] which will tie me down for quite a while.

I beg you to keep your benevolent interest in me either until I visit you in Heidelberg or until you come to Budapest.

Hoping that you will drop me a few lines and let me know whether you have received my letter or not, I remain respectfully,

Yours,
Karl Mannheim

[1] Since the letter in question (July 25, 1914) was in Lukács's possession, he obviously received it.

[2] "Az ismeretelmélet szerkezeti elemzése" (A Structural Analysis of Epistemology). Mannheim wrote his dissertation under Bernát Alexander at the University of Budapest where he received his Ph.D. with *summa cum laude* in 1918. It was published by Athenaeum, the publishing house of the Hungarian Academy of Sciences, the same year. A revised version was published in German in the *Kant-Studien:* "Die Strukturanalyse der Erkenntnistheorie" (1922).

131. FROM BÉLA BALÁZS

Budapest
February 28, 1915

Dear Gyuri,

I am leaving tomorrow for Szabadka for my medical check up. After my military discharge—which I fully expect to get—I will have to remove myself to the quiet of a sanatorium.[1]

And not only to take care of my bad heart. Need one month absolute rest. I want to start a new life. It is connected to what we discussed in our letters, to the necessity of action. I am preparing for the moral war.

To begin with, I want you to know that I have broken all ties with *Nyugat*[2]. The immediate reason: they passed over the fourth installment of my diaries from the front in favor of another report. True, such things have happened in the past; but this time it just gave me an excuse to walk out in a polite way, without a fight. Have curious prophetic inclinations these days! I have, however, no new ideas. We have discussed all these things at length, haven't we? But as I see it now, I have *to act* and become the *kind of person* others can follow and believe in. I have come back to the idea that we have to organize all the honest people and start a social ethical caste war—or this country will rot. Moreover, I think that our new spiritual generation has to get organized internationally, in the name of the Holy Spirit—the way workers and women get organized. There are so few of us, and we cannot achieve anything without an international movement like Catholicism or Protestantism; that should be our answer to this war. The movement should resemble a union, a fraternity of kindred spirits—mostly personal friends—in one word, a sect. That alone can provide a meaningful framework for your moral activity. You have to assume a leading role![3]

For a while it looked as if there was in the offing a specifically Hungarian solution to our problem. Lajos Fülep[4] paid me a visit and outlined his ideas about a Hungarian Philosophical Society—somewhat modeled upon the Italian "circolos"—complete with a journal devoted to philosophical and cultural issues. (He also wants to include literature.)[5] The whole thing was supposed to attain its unified style through the spiritual *Weltanschauung,* etc., etc., as was the case with *Szellem.*[6]

I was very happy about all this, especially when I heard that certain practical steps had already been taken in the form of negotiations with City Hall, with Wildner[7]—you know how smart Fülep is and he even has a job there! But that is not all: hardly had Fülep left when Emma Ritoók[8] dropped in and she, too, had a plan for a new "Revue". Originally it was planned by Fülep—or so she says—but it came to naught after a big quarrel with Fülep because he made extremely rude remarks about her new novel.[9] She also informed me that until now Fülep has had a very low opinion of me and spoke out against my cooperation in the new "Revue" in any form. Now he seeks me out. Maybe he has come to me only because he wants to gain access to you through me. The situation is as follows: we need such a Revue but Fülep is not to be trusted—and possibly is not even the best man for it. You know how it was with *Szellem*... [...]

Edith[10] sends her regards to you and Ljena; she too wants to see you both. What are you both doing with yourselves? How is Ljena feeling nowadays about her Russianness? Has she heard from her brother, Mischa?[11]

Servus! Herbert

[1] Out of short-lived patriotic feelings, Balázs volunteered for front duty, was wounded in action, and returned to Budapest to recuperate.
[2] *The West*. See letter no. 7, n. 1.
[3] The movement as envisaged by Balázs never materialized. With a group of friends, however, he initiated what has become known as the Sunday Circle. Referring to their preoccupation with "*szellem*" *(Geist)*, the group called itself "*szellemkék*" (little spirits).
[4] See "Biographical Notes".
[5] *circolos* (Ital.) means Clubs.
[6] *Spirit*. See letter no. 56, n. 4.
[7] Ödön Wildner (1874–1944), writer, cultural critic, sociologist. Editorial Board member of *Huszadik Század* (Twentieth Century). From 1911 on, he held the position of educational director at City Hall.
[8] Edith Bone, née Hajós.
[9] *A szellem kalandorai* (The Adventurers of the Spirit), published in 1921. The final version gives a caricaturized portrait of the group around Lukács and also has heavily anti-Semitic undertones.
[10] See "Biographical Notes".
[11] Brother of Yelena, Lukács's wife, presumably fighting in the Russian Army at that time.

132. TO PAUL ERNST

Heidelberg
[March ?] 1915

Dear Herr Doctor,

I have been wanting to write you for a long time but was waiting for your new drama to arrive[1] in order to respond to that too. What's holding it up? How was the production received and when will it be published? I would welcome any information.

It has been so long since I have heard anything at all. What is the situation with the divorce? I believe I wrote to you far back in January that the letter has been sent to Florence.[2]

Finally, I have started working on my new book on Dostoevsky[3] (and have put the aesthetics aside for the time being). The book will go beyond Dostoevsky though; it will contain my metaphysical ethics and a significant part of my philosophy of history. It would be a sheer impossibility to describe it in a letter; I'd welcome a hearty discussion with you especially about some problems concerning the epic form, which comes up in the first part of my book. Thus, an exchange of views would be very valuable and most useful. But what can one do? As soon as I have a sizeable part of the manuscript, I'll send it to you and ask for your opinion.

In connection with this project I have a favor to ask you. The *Berliner Tageblatt* printed a new novel by Ropshin[4] as a series in 1910, entitled *"Der fahle Ross"* [The Pale Horse]. It's of great importance to me that I get hold of this novel (re: psychology of Russian terrorism, about which I'll have a lot to say when discussing Dostoevsky); the library here doesn't have back copies of the paper. My book dealer wrote a letter to the paper on my behalf without even receiving a reply. May I therefore ask you to use your connections at the paper (you must know some people there; I believe you used to write for it) and ask for the 1910 issues as if you needed them yourself? I am sure they won't deny your request and it is really important to me. I beg your forgiveness for this imposition, but I am in need of them and can see no other way to get them.

How is Fr. von Schorn doing? Please give her my warm regards.

Cordially yours,
G. v. Lukács

[1] *Preussengeist* (1915).
[2] See letter no. 97, n. 1.
[3] The Dostoevsky project was abandoned; the introductory part was later published under the title, *Die Theorie des Romans* (The Theory of the Novel).
[4] Ropshin, born Boris Viktorovitch Savinkov (1879–1925), son of a judge in Tzarist Russia, he joined the Party of Socialist Revolutionarists in 1899. He was a poet, novelist, revolutionist and terrorist, and took part in the assassinations of Von Plehve, minister of interior (on July 15, 1904) and that of the Grand Duke Sergius (on February 4, 1905). Became assistant minister of war in the 1917 Provisional Government. After November 7, 1917, he organized rebellions against the Bolsheviks. He lived in exile in Paris several times during his revolutionary career. Returned to the Soviet Union in 1924, and was captured. His death sentence was subsequently turned into ten years' imprisonment. He committed suicide shortly after by throwing himself out of a prison window. Author of *Memoirs of a Terrorist* (New York: Albert & Charles Boni, 1931); *The Pale Horse* (New York: Alfred A. Knopf, 1919).

133. TO PAUL ERNST

Kepplerstrasse 28
Heidelberg
April 14, 1915

Dear Herr Doctor,

Many thanks for the information.[1] Regardless of how much I would love to go to Berlin—if only to be able to see you again—it is impossible right now. You see, important as the book is to me, it is not worth having my writing interrupted. In the meantime, my wife has read to me the Russian book in German and will provide a sample translation of some of its key passages for me. It will have to do for now, especially since I am not interested in the book as a work of art. It is the ethical problem of terrorism that matters most to me and the book is an important document in this respect. (Its author was one of the well-known terrorists who took part in the assassination of von Plehve and Sergei,[2] and he knew intimately the characters I am interested in.) On this subject, I have a question for you: an acquaintance of mine, a young man from the Baltic States by the name of Hans von Eckardt,[3] would like to translate a small selection from the collection of memoirs of the great Russian Revolution (1904–7). Do you think that such a slim volume would find a publisher? How about in [the series] "Lutz's Collection of Memoirs"? The idea is *really* close to my heart because I happen to believe that we are now faced with a new type of man that we should become familiar with. I have even promised von Eckardt that I would write a preface to any such translation. Would you be willing to be our contact? If you yourself are interested in this problem, try to read at some time the other novel by Ropshin (*Als wär' es nie gewesen,* published by Rütten & Loening, Frankfurt a. M.), but again only as a *document* and not as a work of art.

My work progresses at a very slow pace.[4] Unfortunately, as a result of my work on *Aesthetics,* I have lost my ability to write concisely; and I am still in search of an appropriate narrative-essayistic style. But this is a problem better discussed in person than in writing. If one has to cover a lot of ground and one has the (unfortunate) tendency to trace every problem back to its roots, then it is absolutely necessary to arrive at the proper symphonic train of thought, which is quite different from a systematic-philosophical style of writing with its architectonic structure. If you are interested, I will send you a copy of the first chapter after it's completed. I have never felt so insecure about a work of mine! Would you in turn send me your new drama right away?[5] I should at least try to keep up with your artistic output.

After years of neglecting him, I have been reading a lot of Hebbel[6] again between breaks in my work. All in all, what a grand totality he is! Everything therein might well be problematic (but what is not in modern works of art?), but any second thoughts one might have seem so trivial next to the grandiosity of the whole.

I hope the matter of your divorce will soon be resolved.[7] When you wrote about the power of convention, you were thinking of the other parties involved, weren't you? In that case, you are certainly right. The power of structures seems to be increasing unabatedly, and for most people it represents the existing reality more accurately than does the really existent [itself]. But—and for me this is *the* ultimate lesson coming out of the war experience—we cannot permit that. We have to stress again that after all, we and our souls, are the only essentiality; and even all the eternal a priori objectifications of the soul are (to recall the beautiful metaphor of Ernst Bloch) nothing but paper money, of value only when redeemable in gold. It is true that the real power of the structures cannot be denied. But German thought since Hegel has been committing what amounts to a cardinal sin against the spirit *(Geist)*: it has administered a metaphysical sanctification to all power. Oh yes, the state is a power. Does it then follow that it has to be recognized as existing in the utopian sense of philosophy, that is, in the sense of true ethics acting at the level of essence? I don't believe so. And I hope to be able to protest vehemently against this view in the nonaesthetic parts of my book of Dostoevsky. The state (and all other structures emanating from it) are a power—but so are earthquakes and epidemics. Indeed, the latter are even harder to fight since we can do so only in a mechanical way. In our case, however, we have *ethical* means at our disposal. (I speak, naturally, both philosophically and morally *for myself* only. The practical-political aspect is too complex; we should discuss it in person.) I would really be interested to learn whether recent events, which after all have forced everyone to experience this problem, have made you think along these lines or given you the opposite orientation. There is practically no one who has remained the same.

My warmest greetings to Frau von Sch. and you.

Yours faithfully
G. v. Lukács,

1 See letter no. 132. Ernst informed Lukács that he has to come to Berlin to read the back papers.
2 See letter no. 132, n. 4.
3 Hans von Eckardt (1890–1957), born in Riga, studied philosophy in Moscow, Berlin, and Heidelberg, where he became a student of Alfred Weber. After having received his Dr.phil. in 1919, he stayed there and became professor and director of the Institute of Mass Communication at Heidelberg University in 1927. His works deal with sociology of culture and religion as well as political sociology. As his letters to Lukács demonstrate, he was an ardent admirer of Lukács's early works.
4 The planned Dostoevsky book, which was never completed.
5 Ernst's "Teutonic play," *Preussengeist* (The Prussian Spirit), was at that time staged in Weimar and Eisenach but never found a publisher. The play was about the necessity of sacrifice for the state, elevated to an exalted mystical "categorical imperative"; it marked the beginning of the estrangement between Ernst and Lukács.
6 Friedrich Hebbel (1813–1863), German playwright. Lukács considered him the founder of the modern tragic drama who possessed a tragic *Weltanschauung*. Lukács and his friends staged his *Maria Magdalena* (1844) at the Thalia Theater with great success. Hebbel's *Judith* provided the quotation for Lukács as illustration for his ethical considerations in joining the CP. In the drama, violence is justified from an ethical-religious point of view.
7 Lukács alludes to the acrimonious divorce proceedings between Paul Ernst and Lilli, his second wife.

134. TO PAUL ERNST

Budapest
May 4, 1915

Dear Herr Doctor,

Many thanks for your letter and the manuscripts. I am extremely happy about being able to see you again. I hope it will be possible, that is, I don't have to go to war. (There are new call-ups for the *Landsturm.* The first time I was found unfit for active duty, but what happens now is anybody's guess.)

As soon as we get together we have to try to reconcile our views on the state (and other constructs of the objective spirit). If you say the state is part of the self, that is correct. If you say that it is part of the soul, that is incorrect. Whatever we enter into a relationship with is part of our self (even the subject-matter of mathematics), but this self which "creates" those objects (in the sense that they are synthesized by reason) and thereby remains indissolubly connected to them is an *abstract,* a methodological concept; thus, while the created objects have a share in the self, the relationship is purely a methodological one, valid only in the immanent realm of the methodological sphere. The spuriousness consists of the self declared to be our soul. And since giving the subject the status of something substantial also renders the corresponding objects substantial, the "structures" become both real and metaphysical. But it's the *soul* alone that can possess a metaphysical reality. This is not solipsism. The problem is to find the pathways leading from soul to soul. Everything else has an instrumental quality and serves as means to that end. I believe that many conflicts would disappear if we'd arrived at the absolute priority of this realm over its derivatives (e.g., rights and duties emanating from an ethically internalized institution), in order not to make life absolutely devoid of conflicts but to make sure that conflicts emerge only in situations in which the soul finds itself at a crossroad. I certainly don't deny that there are people whose soul, at least in part, is ready and willing to enter into a relationship to the objective spirit and its structures *(Gebilde)*. I only protest against those who consider this relationship to be the norm and claim that everyone should associate the destiny of his soul with it. (For this reason, I consider the practice of general conscription to be the vilest slavery that has ever existed.) That is why I don't see in Ropshin[1]—considered as a document, not as a work of art—a symptom of a disease but rather a new manifestation of an old conflict between the first ethic (duties towards social structures) and the second (imperatives of the soul). The order of priorities always includes characteristic dialectical complications when the soul is not directed toward itself but toward humanity, as is the case with the politician and the revolutionary. Here the soul must be sacrificed in order to save the soul. One must become a cruel *Realpolitiker* out of a mystical ethic and has to violate the absolute commandment: "Thou shalt not kill," which is clearly *not* an obligation toward the structures. In essence, this is a very ancient problem expressed most pointedly perhaps by Hebbel's Judit: "and if God had placed sin between me and the act ordered for me to do, who am I to be able to escape it?"[2] Only the situation is new and the people are different.

You can gather from all this that I am not ideally receptive to your new dramas[3] (and since it is quite difficult to get rid of such *weltanschauliche* preconceptions, you must take all this into account when considering my impressions). The tragedy[4] nevertheless has made a great impression on me. Its construction is excellent and although it doesn't surpass *Brunhild,* in my opinion, I still think that you created something beautiful. It seems to me that in this play you have returned to your Demetrios-Canossa period[5] and that you have now succeeded in artistically creating something that you had aimed at before but had left fragmentary and problematic. Katte[6] is surely not only one of your finest heroes, in his simplicity and marvelous virility, he is also one of the finest characters in the history of German drama; in addition, he is an eminently Germanic hero. This character alone should ensure the great impact of your play. The king is also excellently portrayed. On the other hand, I find the figure of the Crown Prince[7] less effective. It seems to me—this being my only and maybe not so serious objection—that he is drawn too much from the perspectives of the other two and is in consequence overshadowed by them, since he is not their equal in their respective spheres of life. In my opinion, this has damaged the balance of the play and brings into question the noble intentions of the tragedy (namely, justice). In their eyes, the Crown Prince is simply an immature youth who still has to grow up and become a man. In that regard, the drama reminds me of the Prince of Homburg[8] except that your Crown Prince lacks his romantic and fascinating charm. (Rightly so, by the way, since this would not fit the economy of your drama.) But I do think that there is more to the theme than that. It seems that the Great "Fritz" became in time the greatest King Prussia ever had, precisely because he had to make the greatest sacrifice in order to become a *Prussian*. For him, the Prussian sense of duty that can satisfy and ennoble the weaklings and inspire them to great deeds was but an enormous renunciation—a renunciation of a more meaningful, more essential, and more humane life. It was a necessary renunciation; in order to *really* become a King, it had to be done. Only when the greater inner wealth of the Crown Prince is recognized and the end reveals itself as the supreme sacrifice (Katte gives his life, the King intends to sacrifice the father, the Crown Prince sacrifices his humanness), will the tragedy present a complete and rounded picture and make clear why Katte gives his life for the Crown Prince, which otherwise appears more a dynastic-legitimistic action than a purely humane act. I'd be very interested to learn whether you too perceive this interpretation of the conflict as being part of the immanent conflict. The same deficiency in tragic justice can be found in the episodic figure of the Queen. She is a superfluous character—justified only as a counterweight to Fräulein von Winterstein (that is, the Katte-Crown

Prince constellation on a much smaller scale); and she is drawn with a certain degree of contempt and meanness, in my opinion. In addition, I find the violent diatribes against England out of place in a tragedy; after all, it is not unworthiness and virtue that should engage in combat but two tragic, equal forces.

As to your other drama, *Weltende,* I have but a few formal objections to offer; the ideal content is—emotionally speaking—alien to me. I have the feeling that your metaphysics and your historical presentation does not add up to a perfect whole. Precisely because man's attitude toward the world and God's relation to it are so deep and beautiful and because the inner conversion of Germany and its elevation to be the bearer of the world spirit are so deeply felt, it is not permissible that in a life and death struggle (in your drama only, of course, regardless of what's going on in reality) its adversary be baseness personified (which would turn the world-historical struggle into mere moralizing); a worthy opponent can only be the world spirit *(Weltgeist)* of yesteryear. They [the British] may at the end *become* vile out of sheer desperation in the face of their approaching downfall (and this is already a technical-artistic problem that couldn't be judged *in abstracto,* only on the basis of a completed work); they may not, however, *be* basically vile if it is thought to be worthwhile (philosophically and artistically) to wage a war against them in order to occupy their place in the world. The God of this play cannot possibly believe that with a German victory the age of decency has replaced that of vileness. (I must emphasize: I am speaking of your play only. It is no concern of mine what the English in reality are. If anybody today would write a poetic work of hate in grand style à la Kleist,[9] I would have no artistic objections and wouldn't miss the presence of justice which the immanent logic of your drama demands.)

The flaw that I perceive in your play is not your fault but that of our age. I think, such allegories are possible only at times when conceptuality is not only a living force but also has a long tradition behind it. Then and only then can the personified concepts in the allegories have a *decorative life of their own* and offer the possibility of manifest variability in giving form to the allegory. (I am thinking here mainly of Dante's *Il Paradiso* but also of certain mystery plays.) This is what we lack today. And this is why your characters can *only* talk and why as decorative elements they are so much alike; they can only make manifest the acts of getting up and falling down (which if repeated becomes slightly comical). This makes the whole thing appear monotonous. Please do not misunderstand me! Far be it from me to expect organic sensuality creating liveliness in an allegorical play. But precisely for this reason, I *have* to demand variety and liveliness as a *decorative element,* which I don't find here. I believe that you have conducted an experiment which today nobody can successfully attempt.

Give my very best to Frau v. Schorn.

Greetings,
Yours,
G. v. Lukács

1 Ropshin or Boris Savinkov. See letters no. 132, n. 4. and no. 133.
2 See letter no. 133, n. 6.
3 *Preussengeist* and *Weltwende.* In his letter of April 28, 1915, Ernst informs Lukács that his new works illustrate how the war has left its imprints both on his thinking and artistic output.
4 *Preussengeist.*
5 Reference is to Ernst's early works, written between 1902 and 1906.
6 One of the main characters in *Preussengeist.*
7 The Crown Prince of the drama became Frederick the Great (1740–1786), champion of enlightened absolutism who made Prussia a great European power. He was also called "The Philosopher King". In his old age, his nickname was "der Alte Fritz". Hence Lukács's reference.
8 Lukács alludes to a drama, *Prinz von Homburg,* by Heinrich von Kleist (1777–1811), Prussian officer, poet and playwright. Among his works, *The Marquise of O,* and *The Broken Vessel.*
9 Reference is to Kleist's novelette, "Michael Kohlhaas," a short story of revenge and self-destruction.

135. TO FRANZ BLEI

Heidelberg
July 21, 1915

Dear Herr Doctor,

May I ask you a favor, that is, your mediation in the following matter: the enclosed dialogue[1] was published two years ago in the *Neue Blätter* at Hellerau and the issue in question has been unavailable for quite a while. Time and again I receive requests (especially now, from young people and students, who are out in the trenches) for copies of the dialogue. I should therefore like to ask you whether, in your opinion, it could be considered for republication in the Series *Der jüngste Tag?* And if not, do you have any other suggestion to make? My only concern is that it be by a respectable publisher, in soft cover (and at the first possible date).

Cordially,
Dr. Georg von Lukacs

[1] "Von der Armut am Geiste" (On Poverty of Spirit). See letter no. 81, n. 2.

136. TO PAUL ERNST

Heidelberg
August 2, 1915

Dear Herr Doctor,

Forgive me for being so late in answering your letter. Day after day I have kept hoping to receive the manuscript of Herr von Eckardt,[1] who was to translate the book on the Russian Revolution; but he was drafted (and sent to the front in the meantime), and the prospect for getting it is almost nil now. Well, another project to be shelved!

I hope we shall have the opportunity to talk in person about everything else. I read your article in the *Voss.[ische] Zeitung;*[2] in this case, one can speak of an eventual understanding but not of being convinced. I think I can understand your position and comprehend the motivating forces behind it; but I can also see its inherent dangers. (I promised to write an article on "The German Intellectuals and the War"[3] for the *Archiv;* if I ever come to it, you'll have a thorough grasp of my own position, unless, of course, we meet and discuss it in person.) Is your plan to come to Heidelberg still viable? I do hope so!

September will be for me "the month of destiny." I was called in for service again in August (the second time since the beginning of the war) and have been put on the reserve list for two more months; but it will be decided on September 20th whether or not the Moloch of militarism will swallow me up. (My friend, Prof. Emil Lask of Heidelberg University, fell on the front in May.) These short-range terms are very damaging to (the progress of) my work. I have already given up my Dostoevsky book; it has become too big a project. Out of it emerged a large-scale essay, called "The

Aesthetics of the Novel."[4] I'd be interested to hear what you think of it? Should I send it to you? And where to? I'll use the respite until the next call up (and possible service) to complete my old fragment on the "aesthetics of the nontragic drama."[5]

I am now going to Budapest for two weeks. My address there is still the old one: IV. Városligeti Fasor 20/a.

Kind regards to Frau von Sch.[orn].

Cordially yours,
G. v. Lukács

[1] See letter no. 33, n. 3.
[2] "Nationalcharakter und Staat" (The National Character and the State), in *Vossische Zeitung* (May 27, 1915).
[3] The article remained a fragment and was published in German in the Lukács issue of *Text+Kritik*, ed. by Frank Benseler, nos. 39/40 (October 1973), pp. 65–69. It has not been translated into English.
[4] *The Theory of the Novel.*
[5] See letter no. 96, n. 3.

137. TO MAX WEBER

Budapest
[Mid-December] 1915

Dear Herr Professor,

My heartfelt thanks for your letter and the reprint.[1] I am very much counting on your sending me all future reprints as your work progresses. What I have read so far made the same deep impression on me as did your presentation at your lecture in Heidelberg; moreover, I do not think that your concern about style is justified.

I am really looking forward to the publication of all of these essays collected in a book[2] and can hardly wait to be able to read them as a coherent whole.

I was anticipating your distaste for my "Aesthetic of the Novel".[3] I am very anxious to learn, however, whether the subsequent elaboration managed to put you in a more conciliatory mood, in other words, whether it was able to induce you to make your peace with the introduction.[4] For I cannot help believing that the work contains much that should appeal to you. I also realize that the essay as it stands[5] cannot effect a total reconciliation, that is, it cannot make evident the inevitability of such an introduction. For you see, the very much needed balance to the metaphysical beginning of the study shall be forthcoming only toward the end of the Dostoevsky book, in the form of a new, consciously felt and articulated metaphysics that emanates from literary and historical analyses, which, in turn, presuppose an aesthetic treatment of D's works—to be provided on the analytical level of Part Two.[6] For this reason, the work, taken out of its actual context, is assigned a dissonance that cannot be dissolved (and that, in my opinion, is rather of a formal structural nature than objectively based upon the contents). Were it not for my military service or for the fact that the end of the war is nowhere in sight, I would accept the consequences, give up the idea of publishing this fragment, and wait until the whole Dostoevsky book[7] is finished. But in this situation, in which there is no telling when I can return to any substantial work and whether (maybe years from now) I would return right away to this same project and not take up the *Aesthetics*[8] instead, I find it difficult even to contemplate waiting any longer. And as far as I am concerned, a complete revision is out of the question. Therefore, I am eager to have your impression as soon as you finish reading the piece.

How are things in Heidelberg? Are there any plans for filling the vacancy in philosophy?[9] If so, with whom? At the present time, I am stationed at the Office of the Military Censorship in Budapest. I have managed to do a little reading again lately and hope to be able to do more in the future as things settle down.

Please give my warmest regards to your wife. With best wishes and deep gratitude,

Yours,
Dr. Georg von Lukács

[1] Reference is to a series of studies, published as single articles under the title *Die Wirtschaftsethik der Weltreligionen* (The Economic Ethics of World Religions). Written around 1913, the first of these essays was published in the *Archiv für Sozialwissenschaft und Socialpolitik* (1916), 41(1): 1–87. Lukács obviously received a reprint.

[2] Published posthumously under the title *Gesammelte Aufsätze zur Religions soziologie.*

[3] Reference is to the "essay" entitled *Die Theorie des Romans.*

[4] Reference is to part 1, chapter 1, entitled "Integrated Civilisations," in *The Theory of the Novel*, pp. 29–40.

[5] Parts 1 and 2 of *The Theory of the Novel*. For data on its genesis, see "Preface", in ibid, p. 11.

[6] "Attempt at a Typology of the Novel Form," in *The Theory of the Novel.*

[7] See letter no. 132.

[8] See letter no. 126, n. 1.

[9] The vacancy was created by the death of Wilhelm Windelband, the Neo-Kantian philosopher.

138. FROM MAX WEBER

Heidelberg
December 23, 1915

Dear Herr Doctor,

You will find enclosed Dessoir's answer, which I have just received.[1] Shall I send him your manuscript now? And what is your reaction to his suggestions? The *technical* details (paragraphs for a better overview, for example) you can easily deal with, can't you? But how do you feel about the edits?

As I told you before, it is also my opinion that the first part is almost unintelligible to anyone but those who *know you* intimately. For this reason, I can understand D's demands.

All the best for Christmas and many thanks for your kind letter.

Yours faithfully,
Max Weber

[1] Dessoir's letter to Max Weber is extant. Max Dessoir (1867–1947), professor at the University in Berlin, editor of the *Zeitschrift für Ästhetik und Allgemeine Kunstwissenschaft,* returned the MS to Weber with the remark that only part 2 would appeal to the journal's readers. He expressed his willingness to compromise to the extent that part 1 would begin at p. 29. Weber must have been persuasive because Dessoir changed his mind. The study in question, "Die Theorie des Romans," was published in the *Zeitschrift,* no. 3–4, in 1916. It was published in bookform in 1920 (Berlin: Cassirer).

139. TO MAX WEBER

Budapest
December 30, 1915

Dear Herr Professor,

D.'s[1] letter did not come as a surprise; I have never had any illusions about his capabilities. Were it just that what he wrote represented his personal opinion, I would simply tell him in basic Hungarian that he can ". . . . his grandmother". Unfortunately, this was the only possibility for getting the manuscript published, which has become for me a matter of great urgency since, because of my military service, it seems to me rather unlikely that I could finish my book any time soon. (The whole affair would leave me cold had I seen any chances for that!) But I cannot agree to dropping the whole introductory part for objective reasons: first, the treatment—be it only by way of suggestion—of the Greek world and the Middle Ages is indispensable for the historico-philosophical comprehension of present-day reality; second, the difference between the epic and the dramatic art has to be discussed in order to make explicit the aesthetic-formal meaning of such concepts as "life and essence," "interiority," or "external reality"; third, it is absolutely necessary to allude to the structure of the epic forms because neither the typology nor the selection of the second part could otherwise be justified (e.g., the exclusion of such significant works as Constant's *Adolphe, Elective Affinities*[2] and others); fourth, the treatment of the difference between the closed-organic universe and the conventional, transcendental-inner world is an absolute prerequisite for the depiction of the conditioning of the novel form. And, finally, if the introductory part were to be excluded, could the end of the first part (re the "demonic") be understood or, for that matter, the analysis of the concept of time (in part two, re *Education sentimentale*)? Or how could one make clear the problematic of *Wilhelm Meister* without previous references to the problematic "nature" versus "the world of convention?" After having reflected on this interdependence, I cannot imagine your not seeing the objective necessity of the introduction (be it good or bad in itself). I have no objection to any of the lesser corrections. With regard to dropping the introductory part, may I suggest that you take up the matter once again with D.—provided, of course, that you agree with me—and propose to bring out the thing as it stands. Should that prove to be impossible, what do you think of dividing the study into two and offering the first part (I'd leave it up to your best judgment where to divide) to *Logos*[3] and giving the second to D.? I am absolutely convinced that my readers—of whom there aren't going to be too many—have to have the introduction in order to be able to comprehend the final part; thus, I cannot make any further compromise than to subject them to a little bit of extra work and have them put together the study from two different journals.

I would welcome your definitive opinion in the matter.

Also, is there anything definite you can tell about the forthcoming appointment to Windelband's chair?[4] Herr von Eckardt[5] recently wrote to me—based on information conveyed by your brother[6]—that both Rickert and Simmel are in the running.[7] Is this correct? If so, may I offer the following suggestion? Considering my present circumstances, namely the fact that due to the prolonged state of affairs it is inconceivable that I would be free from military service before the end of the war, and the impossibility of concentrated work on a profound study (such as the *Aesthetics*), the chances of my *Habilitation*—for which the subjective preconditions were finally at hand—have become remote. It would mean a great deal to me to have this situation resolved in some way, if possible during the war. What I have in mind is this: could Simmel (or Rickert, if that be the case) take care of my *Habilitation* on the basis of the completed chapters of the *Aesthetics?* I could put together by the summer semester two smaller studies in order to have something for the Colloquium and the Lecture;[8] a short leave in the fall would enable me to put on the finishing touches. But to do this I would definitely need to get the go-ahead from the faculty or a binding commitment on the part of either Simmel or Rickert. (Only on the basis of such a pledge would a leave be granted.)

As you must remember, the first two chapters add up to a relatively finished work. One could call it "An Approach to Aesthetics" or "Prolegomena to Aesthetics" or something like that if the gentlemen [Simmel or Rickert] would not find it comfortable to submit to the faculty for discussion an "unfinished" work (its completion hindered by the war and my military service, in these times certainly not a trivial excuse). Mrs. Gothein[9] has a copy of my manuscript and you can obtain it from her if need be. It would mean a lot to me if I could have your views on the matter.

There is not much to report about me that is of interest. Although I manage to get in a little work here and there, one adjusts to the changed psychological and physical conditions only with difficulty, and the situation doesn't make concentration easier. I'd be greatly interested to hear about the progress of the second part of your "World Religions".[10] Has it come out in the meantime?

Please give my warmest regards to your wife. Once again, with sincere regards,

Yours faithfully,
Georg von Lukács

[1] Dessoir. See letter no. 138, n. 1.
[2] Novel by J. W. von Goethe.
[3] German philosophical journal.
[4] See letter no. 137, n. 9.

[5] See letter no. 133, n. 3.
[6] Alfred Weber, professor of sociology at Heidelberg University.
[7] Heinrich Rickert, the Neo-Kantian philosopher, was chosen to fill Windelband's chair.
[8] Lukács's proposal, together with his "Curriculum Vitae" and the final negative decision of the faculty, was reprinted in German in *Text+Kritik*, no. 39/40 (October 1973). See Appendix, pp. 285 ff.
[9] Mrs. Marie-Luise Gothein, née Schröter (1863–1931), author of the then widely read book, *Die Geschichte der Gartenkunst* (1914). Wife of Eberhard Gothein, professor at Heidelberg University. See letter no. 104, n. 2.
[10] See letter no. 137, n. 2.

140. TO MAX WEBER

Budapest
January 17, 1916

Dear Herr Professor,

Thank you so much for your letter. I hope you'll be successful in persuading D. [Dessoir]. I will gladly take care of the minor changes (titles, paragraphs, etc.) so that this ill-fated work of mine[1] will come to a good end after all. I well understand that you have some misgivings about the particular mode of my writing but, as you know, I am unable to share them. I often reproach myself that within my chosen form I am producing uneven work (the theory of the novel has very different levels of intensity and concentration) and that it just has to be read twice. The question of whether or not it pays to do so has nothing to do with the question of form. Everything that is any good has to be read at least twice; if my writings were bad or empty, why go to the trouble of discussing them at all. But this is not a matter to be dealt with through the mail.

I am grateful for your information concerning the situation in Heidelberg.[2] Even without assurance, I would never for a minute have had any doubts as to your taking great interest in my affairs. I count it among my proudest possessions in objective achievements that my case, *as such,* has become important to you. All I wanted was to have a clear picture—as an obligation to myself, so to speak, which I often neglected in the past. Had I given it any *serious* consideration, it surely would have been a relatively easy matter to get habilitated with your brother[3] (e.g., in sociology); and the Rickert issue would now be more manageable, in the form of subsequent *Habilitation.* What I feared was merely that—out of indolence—I would miss out on a chance that *is definitely there.* It was the farthest thing from my mind to ask *you* to force the matter. Besides, I had not only Rickert but also Simmel in mind; as I hear from Herr von Eckardt,[4] Simmel is supposed to go to Heidelberg. Is that correct? All I want now is your *advice:* would it make sense for me to start preparing the exam themes and the try-out lecture right away (since it is out of the question that in my present situation I could continue working on the *Aesthetics*) so that *I'd* be all finished and done with by the time this confounded war comes to an end? Furthermore, do you see the slightest possibility that R.[ickert] or S.[immel] (in R.'s case, *after* we get acquainted personally) would accept what has already been done of the *Aesthetics* in lieu of a *Habilitationsschrift* and not insist on completion? (To complete it would mean another one-and-half-years of toil—time that could be substantially shortened by my lecturing in aesthetics following my *Habilitation.*)

Give my warm regards to your wife. It has nothing to do with disinterest that she didn't hear from me; partly it is because of the abnormal and inadequate kind of life I have to bear and partly because I am so starved for work that I try to use every free minute to get things done. In addition, my friends' personal problems have made great demands on my time.

Once again, many heartfelt thanks for everything (especially for the *Wirtschaftsethik;*[5] please, remember me at the time of the next installments). With the kindest regards

From your grateful
G. von Lukács

[1] *The Theory of the Novel.* See letter no. 138, n. 1.
[2] Weber presumably reported both on the appointment of Heinrich Rickert as the successor of Windelband and on Lukács's chances for a *Habilitation* and subsequent *Privatdozentur.*
[3] Alfred Weber, professor of sociology at Heidelberg University.
[4] See letter no. 133, n. 3.
[5] "Wirtschaftsethik der Weltreligionen." See letter no. 137.

141. TO KARL JASPERS

Budapest
May 3, 1916

Dear Dr. Jaspers,

My heartfelt thanks for your kind letter. If one can speak of one's peace of mind in this kind of situation, I was relieved to hear that besides the medical treatment based on correct and clear diagnostic evaluation, my wife also received other kinds of help.

I am truly and deeply grateful that you have been able to see the human side of the situation.

What you have to say about the totality of the situation makes good sense. If it is your opinion that Br.[uno] St.[einbach][1] cannot be released from the Sanatorium, it is a reality with which my wife must contend and recognize as unchangeable, whatever her innermost feelings are.

With regard to my wife's way of life, I have the following advice (knowing well, of course, that the distance and the accompanying ignorance of everyday concrete facts don't allow me to form a competent opinion) and request, firstly and foremostly (I'll write the Lederers[2] to that effect and I beg you to tell them the same) *not ever to try to persuade my wife to do something* that is disagreeable to her just because of me, to be considerate of me. She has to be able to act as if I didn't exist. (I may be overly anxious and exaggerating but please excuse my emphatic request.)

My impression is that my wife doesn't want and cannot give up the idea of living with B.[runo] St.[einbach] (and in my opinion, subjectively, she is absolutely correct in insisting on that), at least not until the time she can be of help to him, even if that is not the case objectively, but at least existing in the consciousness of B. S.

And so I am of the opinion—again emphasizing my incompetence—that we have to make this difficult mission as easy as possible for her. What allays my greatest anxieties is the fact that you share this opinion; at least, that was my impression. A complete or near complete break with Br. St. is imaginable only if his condition became—objectively and subjectively—hopeless. I am aware of the fact that living with him aggravates my wife's state of mind and I also well know that she *shouldn't* sacrifice herself; it is my sentiment, though, that we cannot stand between a human being and his destiny, that we do not have the right to do so.

(I am also afraid, of course, that if she felt she hadn't done everything possible, she could harm herself out of self-recrimination.) In case you haven't considered this possibility, please keep it in mind while discussing the issue with her.

May I ask you to let me know from time to time what's happening? And if it is possible—about the state of her health? I would also like to know whether you think that I should visit for a few days during my vacation?

With heartfelt thanks and in friendship,

As ever,
György Lukács

[1] Bruno Steinbach (1898–?), Austrian by birth, studied piano, moved in with Lukács and his wife while still in Heidelberg. Worked in the 1920s and early 30s at Radio Munich and kept in contact with Paul Ernst. According to Ernst's letter, he and Yelena still lived together in Miesbach, Bavaria, in 1922 and were harrassed by the *Fremdenpolizei* on account of their "strange" (Bohemian) appearance and behavior.

[2] Emil Lederer and Emmy Seidler-Lederer of Heidelberg. See letter no. 99.

142. TO KARL JASPERS

Budapest
June 23, 1916

Dear Herr Dr. Jaspers,

I thank you from the bottom of my heart for everything you have done for us—and for the letter. I understand your thinking that you haven't succeeded but the only efforts that were unsuccessful were those which could never be dealt with successfully. What was humanly possible was done, and I can only wonder with the dreadful scare still in my bones what would have happened if you hadn't been standing by Yelena and still helping her.

Of course, the best solution would be for Bruno to stay at the sanatorium and for Yelena to live in the small village of Neckargemünde, where I should join her (on my way to Heidelberg). This is a question which Yelena alone can decide. At the very moment that Bruno doesn't have to stay in the sanatorium, there is no legal measure to stop their moving to Heidelberg; and as far as Yelena is concerned, we can take it as a fact. The only thing that remains for us to do is to help her and try to ease her situation. But you see things the same way I do!

As far as I am concerned, I was glad to hear that you don't think it impossible for them to live together. It seems that it has become a necessity for her—and neither my sentiments nor my *Weltanschauung* would permit me to stand in the way of something that is somebody's destiny.

The only problem remaining beside the medical one (i.e., Bruno's reaction to me and its psychological consequences) is the question of my working conditions, which is entirely a practical one; let's hope that we'll be able to solve it.

It is extremely difficult for me to write about personal matters. Only this much: it's not Yelena's fate that has an accidental character, but rather Bruno's; I am thinking of his illness. For me, the relationship between Yelena and Bruno has been from the very beginning a matter of destiny, essential and necessary (on both their accounts); I have regarded it as a fact, as something belonging to my life. Bruno's illness is an accident, from the ethical, human, emotional, and life-course standpoint. I repeat, I can understand Yelena's refusal to accept an accidental occurrence and for not leaving Bruno to his fate—at least until it doesn't become impossible to stay with him. I cannot know whether or not we are facing a hopeless battle. I think so. This is no reason, though, to give up. And I can well understand that after Yelena's life has been so inexorably entwined with Bruno's she cannot be ready and willing to leave him to his fate if there is even just a slight chance that he'd develop differently. At this moment, the situation seems so hopeless, but I accept its existence as a fact—as a foundation stone on which my life is being built.

You would've understood all that even without being told. There is not much more one can add in a letter. Once more, please accept my thanks (and please let me always know the news). Until we meet again—in about five to six weeks I guess.

My heartfelt greetings,

As ever yours,
György Lukács

143. FROM MAX WEBER

Heidelberg
[August 14] 1916

Dear Friend,

To complement our conversation yesterday:

1. If you *change* your mind, that is, *decide* for *immediate Habilitation* and for *"sociology,"* I will try to help you along. You should then *tell* my brother[1] the following: "I had raised certain practical objections and recommended that you approach Rickert in any case." Nothing else. This remark will *not deter* him from taking you on, provided he *wanted* you to go ahead and habilitate yourself as a "sociologist," especially if you tell him that I am also ready and willing to help you work it another way.[2]

2. As to the *consequences:* any objection raised by Dr. Ruge or anybody else around him would not compel Rickert—*regardless of his intention*—to speak up against your lecturing in philosophy with a *Habilitation* as a political economist.[3] *You are not assured by any means* that such objections would not be raised by some of the *Privatdozents* around Rickert.

3. It is *questionable* that it would be *as* easy to get a subsequent *venia* in philosophy as you assume it would. In that case too, an *Ordinarius cannot* simply ignore the objections raised by others. In spite of all that, if you still *want* it done that way, it has to be that way. But I would bless the day that you would *free* yourself of the specter of the idea that it has to be now, as soon as possible, and absolutely the quickest way. The way you envision it (particularly *via Frau* Gothein)[4] does not quite come up to your stature and would prove to be an "emergency entry" only.

3. [sic!] The most direct road leads to *the* man whose field encompasses your *true* interest. Nothing prevents you from *telling* him openly that you were *vacillating* between whether you'd get your *Habilitation* as a *Dozent* of "meaning" *(Sinn)* or of (the empirical) "Being" *(Sein)* of the spirit (in the latter case also, as a "sociologist"); but *should you have a choice, you'd prefer the former.* Thus you'd be putting your cards on the table and yet it would not even block the other road for you.

I happen to know that R.[ickert] *wants* to get acquainted with you. It would be helpful if you could *force* yourself to go grazing on a sheep meadow in order to quiet your nerves and then get familiar again within a few weeks with the work you left [Aesthetics].

It seems to me as if you've shied away from R., as if you felt yourself being examined and scrutinized by him in his capacity as an *Ordinarius.* But he should have the opportunity to get to know your intellectual ability and there should be enough time, in my opinion, for him to do this. R. is not at all "petty minded" as you will see.

4. [sic!] I will have to be honest with you and tell you what a *very* good friend of yours—*Lask,* as a matter of fact—said of you: "he is a born essayist and will not stick with systematic (professional) work; he *should* not, therefore, habilitate." Needless to say, the essayist is not a whit *less* than a professional, systematic scholar—perhaps, just the opposite! But he has *no* place at a university and would not do much good for the institution nor, *what is more important,* for himself.

On the basis of what you read for us from the brilliant introductory chapters of your *Aesthetics,* I sharply disagreed with this opinion. And because your sudden turn to Dostoevsky seemed to *lend support* to that (Lask's) opinion, I *hated* that work and still hate it. *Basically,* I am of the same opinion. If it is really unbearably painful and inhibiting for you to complete a systematic work and let everything else go in the meantime, then, with a heavy heart, I have to advise you to forget about the *Habilitation.* Not because you don't "deserve" it, but because in the deepest sense it is not to your advantage and ultimately does not do the students any good either. In that case, your vocation is something else. But you will do as *you* deem right.

In warm friendship

Yours,
Max Weber

1 Alfred Weber, professor of sociology at Heidelberg.
2 In case Lukács decided to get habilitated in philosophy.
3 At that time, sociology and political economy were used interchangeably.
4 Partly by writing a review of Marie-Luise Gothein's book, *Geschichte der Gartenkunst* (History of Landscape Architecture) in *Archiv für Sozialwissenschaft und Sozialpolitik* (1915), partly by using Frau Gothein's extensive social contacts and influence.

144. FROM MAX WEBER

Charlottenburg
[August 23, 1916]

Dear Friend,

Many thanks! I just received your letter *today* due to a postal error. I'll be back in Heidelberg on September 3rd—or 4th—and hope to see you then.

1. *Lask*. It is true, indeed, that he said *both* things. He expressed his most urgent wish that you habilitate as in the *de facto* interest of the university. But he confessed to me at a later point that he started having second thoughts about your having the (intellectual) disposition to *stick with* the "professional" work, that is, to complete a systematic work. He wished to secure your intellectual prowess for the service of the university; but your particular essayistic *inclinations* made him wonder whether he is doing the right thing for *you,* and, *indirectly,* for the university, by suggesting and helping you to get into an (academic) "straight jacket." He kept deliberating with himself *whether* and *how* he should tell you about his doubts. *I* was the one who talked him out of it because I thought his doubts were without foundation. But you have known him well: how he turned everything over and over in his mind and when confronted, his doubts became even stronger and more subtle. One thing you can be sure of, namely, that you had in him an absolutely faithful friend. But when I pointed out to him the magnificence (and the true "craftsmanship") of the *second* chapter of your work,[1] he countered that with: "Yes, but how do we know whether he'll really undertake the rewriting of the *first* one and whether he'll arrive at a conclusion or will write at least a partial conclusion?" That was the last of our conversation about it. Thus, you are now *unjust* to him. I agree that he should have kept you informed about his doubts. That he didn't was surely due to his peculiar shyness and feelings of uncertainty.

I want you to become one of my colleagues as much as I have wanted anything. The question is: how to go about it. Be assured that *Rickert* won't regard you as just another "applicant" but as a *mind (Geist)* that interests him very much.

In friendship, as ever,

Yours,
Max Weber

[1] Previously referred to as *Aesthetics*, the work in question is the *Heidelberger Philosophie der Kunst, 1912–1914*, found in Lukács's estate and published posthumously (Darmstadt–Neuwied: Luchterhand Verlag, 1974). The second chapter is entitled, "Phänomenologische Skizze des schöpferischen und receptiven Verhaltens," pp. 43–150.

145. FROM KÁROLY (KARL) MANNHEIM

Budapest I.
Verbőczy Str. 11
September 6, 1916

My dear Friend,

Your note has helped me to see clearly during my days of vegetating (which take me further and further away from what I would like to hold on to) what I have lost and sends the pain of self-realization shooting through me.

You did me a good turn when you realized that it was not sympathy or consolation I needed, but rather a sharpening and deepening of confrontation. Today, I still only have a vague idea of what happened, but I believe that at the end of our sinking friendship I will know what today remains only a vague notion.

You were right to tell me that you can see even from afar what has happened to me. You have done me a favor, especially now when I have the increasingly inexorable feeling that those around me don't understand me at all, and consequently I suffer all the more from the destructive force of this blindness, because the only one who *saw* has looked away from me.

I am very thankful for your invitation sent through Edith;[1] I *would also like very much* to be with you but objective and personal reasons make it difficult to decide about going to Heidelberg. But I may be able to write you for sure within two or three weeks.

Permit me to shake your hand warmly and in true friendship,

Károly Mannheim

P.S. Special thanks for the address that you wired; in the meantime the matter has been settled favorably to my intense relief.

[1] Edith Hajós, wife of Béla Balázs.

146. FROM KARL JASPERS

Heidelberg
October 20, 1916

Dear von Lukács,

Both my wife and I thank you warmly for your study.[1] It was my intention to send along with my thanks my initial reaction to your work. By now I can see though that it will take a long time before I can comprehend and consequently form a firm opinion of it.

So far I have read chapters one to three of part one through honest efforts. I am unable to follow easily your line of thought with real comprehension because I am not familiar with your presuppositions—indeed, I don't even know what they are. Even the words I am familiar with, and with whose conceptual meaning I am at home (such as Life, essence, transcendental-logical, etc., etc.) I don't seem to recognize readily in the context of your work; so, for example, what you call the transcendental-logical topography (if I understand you correctly), remains alien to me. But—and I beg you to be content with this for the time being—I will keep on trying and hope that I'll have more luck with the second part.

Not sharing with you the same premises *(gleichsinnige Voraussetzungen)*, I run the risk of misinterpretation in my remarks. For example, concerning your typology of the Greek world, I cannot but immediately counter with the historical-empirical observation that I can already find the caesura in Homer's case (e.g., *οἷοι νῦν βροτοὶ ἐισνι* et al.);[2] essentially, what I perceive in your case is Platonism. In any case, it wouldn't make any sense to comment further—not until one has a firm grasp of the "idea".

There is only one thing—a purely technical one—which I can tell you safely: you would make it much easier for your readers in the future, if you presented to them a meaning of your basic concepts in a purely logical, so to speak, juristically precise form. The skeleton of austere thinking which suggests itself in your work would in that case promote the understanding of all the details for your readers. The complex conditions of "understanding" *(Verstehen)* should be included in the discussion. The situation is by no means as simple as it appears from my remarks.

Perhaps we will soon have the opportunity to discuss all this. Kind regards, also to your wife.

Yours very truly,
K. Jaspers

[1] *The Theory of the Novel*. See letter no. 138, n. 1.
[2] The quote is from *Ilias*, V., line 304.

147. FROM MARTIN BUBER

Heppenheim a.d. Bergstrasse
November 5, 1916

Dear Herr Doctor,

I have just learned that you live near me.[1] It would give me great pleasure to see you again, after all these years! Would you care to visit me at my home or would you prefer to meet in Heidelberg some time?

With warm regards,

Yours,
Buber

[1] Buber made his home in Heppenheim, a county seat in the state of Hessen, approx. 20 miles from Heidelberg, where Lukács was living at that time with his first wife, Yelena Grabenko.

148. FROM KÁROLY (KARL) MANNHEIM

Budapest I.
Verbőczy Str. 11
November 19, 1916

My dear Friend,

I hope you are not angry with me for writing so late even though I promised to let you know about my decision concerning the trip to Heidelberg. That I didn't come gave you the answer and now I should supply the reasons. At that time I thought that external, insurmountable obstacles stood in my way, but I owe it to our relationship to admit honestly that essentially an unforgivable inertia has held me back, and I have let external circumstances decide my fate.

I now see clearly that it was not so much my studies that suffered but rather that I missed out on many opportunities in our relationship—opportunities that I should have seized without hesitation. I must ask you for your continued interest in me which is important for me and which makes me so glad. I shall probably visit Heidelberg this coming summer but would like to get my doctoral degree first; that and my studies of logic and the history of philosophy take up most of my time.

I am alone a lot and I need to be for the time being, but I still cherish those Sunday afternoons[1] at Balázs's just as I did in the good old days.

You are greatly missed by the Sunday Circle—individually and collectively. We have been thinking about putting together a Yearbook[2] and want you to give some thought to it and decide sooner or later what you will publish in it.

I know more or less what has happened to you[3] and would like to hear that your work is progressing.

Many thanks for the reprint of *Die Theorie des Romans.*[4] Let me reciprocate with a review of mine (published in *Athenaeum*[5]) which is my first published work and is dedicated to you.

If you'd care to write to me either about this or anything else, you'd make me happy; if not, I shall wait patiently.

With warm greetings,
Karl Mannheim

[1] Reference is to the Sunday Circle, an informal gathering of like-minded Budapest intellectuals who met regularly at the home of Béla Balázs, starting 1915. It was patterned after the Weber's Sunday afternoon *jours* in Heidelberg. "Only people who are metaphysically inclined are invited," wrote Balázs in his diaries. Lukács selected the topics for discussion whenever he was in Budapest. Ethical problems, Kierkegaard, Dostoevsky, et al. were the focus of interest. Beside Balázs and Lukács, among its members were: Arnold Hauser, Karl Mannheim, Michael Polányi, Béla Fogarasi, Frigyes Antal, Emma Ritoók, Lajos Fülep, Géza Róheim, René Spitz, Anna Lesznai, and others. From out of this gathering grew the Free School of the Humanities in 1917.

[2] Project did not materialize.

[3] Mannheim may have been thinking of two important events in Lukács's life: first, his auxiliary military service (from 1915 to late 1916), from which his father's connections finally rescued him so that he could return to his work in Heidelberg, and second, the most-talked about aspect of Lukács's life around this time—his marriage, complete with a *ménage à trois,* which in Balázs's words was a "terrible and unmitigated hell".

[4] A German-language version of *The Theory of the Novel,* just published in the *Zeitschrift für Ästhetik und allgemeine Kunstwissenschaft* (1916), nos. 3–4.

[5] Review of Arthur Liebert's work, *Das Problem der Geltung,* in *Athenaeum* (Hungary), II, 3 (1916), pp. 489–93.

149. TO MARTIN BUBER

Heidelberg
Kepplerstrasse 28
December 16, 1916

(Postcard)

Dear Herr Doctor,

As agreed, I shall be arriving in Heppenheim on Monday afternoon, at 3 : 40 p.m.

Respectfully yours,
G. v. Lukács

150. FROM MAX WEBER

Heidelberg
[January 7, 1917]

Dear Friend,

A colleague from Leipzig notified me of his visit tomorrow (Monday) afternoon; I can't possibly say no. Would you have time Tuesday afternoon? I leave it up to you whether you come by tomorrow (Monday) morning, or in the morning hours the day after (Tuesday) or Wednesday *morning* (any time you wish, up to one o'clock), or even Wednesday *afternoon*. To make sure, please give me a telephone call. I am looking forward to the continuation of the continuation [sic!];[1] my interest is great.

Greetings in friendship,

Yours,
Max Weber

[1] Weber referred here to Lukács's lecture on aesthetics a few days before at a meeting of the sociological association in Heidelberg.

151. FROM ERNST TROELTSCH

Berlin
January 10, 1917

Dear Herr Doctor,

Finally, I had time to finish your "Roman"[1] during the Christmas holiday and now I can express my thanks. You must know yourself that it makes for a difficult reading because it is full of abstractions, and one has to provide the illustrations for most of them. Consequently, one often remains doubtful whether or not one subsumed or concluded correctly. Apart from that, I have gained a lot from the book.

I am in complete agreement with certain parts such as those dealing with antiquity or Christianity. In my opinion, however, you depict Christianity as a more problematic world than it really is; and you somewhat hastily assign to it a position of transcendentality *(Transzendentalität)*, pure and transparent merely by way of the subject's recognition, which not only assumes but knows every objectivity as a priority of the formation on the part of the subject. This, after all, represents only one philosophical standpoint in our modern world but certainly not its self-awareness, which is infinitely more varied and, I believe, often more substantial than that. For this reason, I am inclined to be less pessimistic about the epic giving way to the novel. However, I can well see the validity of your main points. But again, I can trace a lot of joyous story telling in a realistic vein; and also see little moral application. I am thinking of Scott, Dickens, and George Eliot. I would assume that your characterization applies to certain kind of novels only, in which case you do not so much mean the novel *per se* but rather the personality of the writer. Regardless, I will further reflect upon all this, and perhaps become more familiar with your thinking.

Your sincerely devoted,
Ernst Troeltsch

P.S. I assume you have received my "Augustin"[2] in the meantime.

[1] *Theorie des Romans* (The Theory of the Novel).
[2] "Augustin. Die christliche Antike und das Mittelalter," in the Appendix of *De civitate Dei* (Berlin, 1915).

152. TO GUSTAV RADBRUCH

Heidelberg
March 11, 1917

Dear Herr Professor,

I have put off answering your letter for an inexcusably long time, but I was hoping somehow that you would make it to Heidelberg so that we could discuss your article[1] in person. Then I had some writing chores to attend to, so I must beg your forgiveness for not writing sooner.

I found your article extremely interesting. To give you my impression of it is quite difficult because I am in almost complete agreement with most of what you say. Some of the ideas expressed in your treatise I myself once planned to take up in an essay, "The Intellectuals and the War,"[2] which I started working on in the summer of 1915. The draft[3] interrupted my work on it and the essay remains unfinished. There was one idea above all that I wanted to explore because of its utmost importance, namely, that the whole complex problem of "power" *(Macht)* constitutes a hypostasized methodological prerequisite to the science of political history. I have also found myself on familiar territory with you when you differentiate between the concepts of "meaning" *(Sinn)* and "significance" *(Bedeutung)*. Your interpretation of the question of "guilt" *(Schuld-Frage)* as well as your views on the symptomatic significance of the refusal of all the parties involved[4] to accept responsibility for this war (an interpretation, by the way, for which you laid the necessary groundwork with your excellent analysis of the connection between war and diplomacy) is a very important contribution. Therein lies the problem that befits this war alone.

I have just realized that I am not just making some random remarks but am beginning to write an essay: this in itself should tell you how much I liked your treatise. At this point, after a very thorough reading, I even find it hard to discover any points of disagreement. Should you manage to come to Heidelberg after all, we could still have a lively, hearty discussion about all this.

I am working away on my *Aesthetics*[5] and hope to be able to finish the first volume (approx. 900 pages) by summer. And that's all the news around here. Lederer[6] is presently in Berlin and Frau Lederer[7] is with her sister in Przemysl.

How are things with you? Let me hear from you occasionally. Warm greetings from Ljena and myself.

Yours,
G. v. Lukács

1 "Zur Philosophie des Krieges" (On the Philosophy of the Present War), in *Archiv für Sozialwissenschaft und Sozialpolitik,* 44 (1917–18). Highly critical of such war apologists as Scheler and Gomperz, Radbruch compared the war to the figure of the Golem, i.e., "a clay figure . . . which has mysteriously succeeded in acquiring a soul of its own, and which subsequently unfurls a life that is blind, stupid, and terrifying, yet, quite omnipotent". (Editor's trans.)

2 Correct title is "Die deutschen Intellektuellen und der Krieg" (The German Intellectuals and the War). See letter no. 136, n. 3.

3 His father's influence rescued Lukács from active duty. He worked in the Office of Military Censorship in Budapest.

4 Allusion to Germany, the Austro-Hungarian Monarchy, and the Allied Powers.

5 Only one chapter was published at that time in *Logos* under the title "Die Subjekt-Objekt-Beziehung in der Ästhetik" (Subject-Object Relations in Aesthetics) (1917).

6 Emil Lederer (1882–1939), German political economist, one of Germany's most prominent social scientists in the interwar period. Born in Pilsen into a Jewish middle-class family, studied economics in Vienna (with Hilferding and Bauer), Berlin, and Munich. He moved to Heidelberg, became editor of *Archiv für Sozialwissenschaft und Sozialpolitik*. From the mid-1920s he was a professor in Heidelberg and later in Berlin, replacing Werner Sombart. He fled Nazi Germany and became Dean of the University in Exile, in New York City. Among his works: *Grundzüge der ökonomischen Theorie* (1922) and *State of the Masses. The Threat of the Classless Society* (New York: Norton, 1940).

7 Emmy Lederer. See "Biographical Notes". The visit mentioned is to a sister who was stationed in Przemysl as a nurse; because of the many fierce battles raging in and around the city, it was sometimes referred to as the "Verdun of the East".

153. FROM EMMA RITOÓK

Budapest
March 17, 1917

Dear Gyuri,

Edith told me yesterday that I am allowed to write in Hungarian[1] and that you haven't been notified about the start-up of the "Free School of the Humanities" of which you are a participant. The increasing interest in matters of metaphysics seems to go hand in hand with increasing laziness, because at every Sunday gathering[2] somebody or other has volunteered to write to you and ask for your participation. The inaugural lectures were already given yesterday by Herbert and Fogarasi.[3] You in all likelihood know exactly what direction the School has taken; what it is based on, what it intends to disseminate and make available to those interested but, of course, not in any popularizing form. The other participants are: Fülep, Hauser, Lukács (!), Mannheim, Ritoók, Antal and Kodály.[4] We scheduled you for May because you mentioned in one of your letters that you will come to [Buda]Pest at that time. We count on your giving four lectures on ethics; please don't disappoint us. I especially would welcome your lectures on ethics because I have been thinking about some problems ever since you talked about them at last year's Sunday gatherings. I am more and more convinced that I can't avoid taking a stand against your views. I cannot do it in principle until I hear your lectures.

I have another favor to ask. I heard that your *Aesthetics* is in Budapest. Since I am laboring on the problem of form and Herbert mentioned your work on the subject, may I ask you to let me read your manuscript? I heard that Antal has it; I believe I need it more than he does. Besides, I would finish it fast and return it to him.

Please give me your answer to both of these questions as soon as possible—especially with regard to the lecture. You can also notify Herbert; he is the clearing house.

Until we meet,

Emma

[1] Reference is to the censorship, since Lukács was at that time in Heidelberg.
[2] The Sunday Circle. See letter no. 148, n. 1.
[3] Herbert is Béla Balázs. For Béla Fogarasi, see letter no. 102, n. 9.
[4] Reference is to Lajos Fülep, Arnold Hauser, Karl Mannheim, Frigyes (Frederick) Antal (1887–1954), Hungarian-Jewish art historian, studied under Wölfflin and Dvořák in Berlin and then in Vienna, where he received his Ph.D. in 1914. Left Hungary in 1919. He lived in Vienna and Berlin and finally settled in England in 1934. He was a member of the Sunday Circle and the Free School of the Humanities. Among his works: *Classicism and Romanticism* (1966). Zoltán Kodály (1882–1967), Hungarian composer, musicologist, originator of the "Kodály Method," and with Bartók renewer of folk music. Close friend of both Bartók and Béla Balázs. Among his best-known works: "Psalmus Hungaricus", "János Háry" and "The Dances of Galánta".

154. FROM MARTIN BUBER Heppenheim a.d. Bergstrasse
April 3, 1917

Dear Herr Doctor,

It is with pleasure that I comply with your wish and send along a copy of the new edition of my *Baalschem*[1] with the inscription of a saying so dear to me.

I plan to be in Heidelberg on Saturday afternoon, the seventh, and if the time suits you, I would like to come and see you for an hour or so.[2]

Your sincerely devoted,
Buber

[1] *Die Legende des Baalschem,* new revised edition of the 1908 publication. Both Buber and Lukács refer to the volume as either Baalschem or Baal-Schem. Rabbi Israel's name was Baal-Schem Tov (1700–1760).

[2] In November of the same year, Lukács left Heidelberg for good and again settled in Budapest.

155. TO PAUL ERNST Heidelberg
July (?), 1917

Dear Herr Doctor,

I read your letter with true concern. I still hope that this painful affair of the auxiliary service will be resolved agreeably. Surely you must have some connections who could successfully intervene. In our "barbaric" and "chaotic" Austro-Hungarian Monarchy, this could not have happened. Unless they were due to be sent to the front, the ten to twelve people who were doing important creative work would be spared the trouble. I am still hopeful that the question of service will be settled.

If possible I shall go to Lauenstein.[1] I don't know about the Webers.[2] They are visiting relatives somewhere in the Rhineland (I don't know exactly where) and won't be back in Heidelberg for a few weeks. Thus I won't be able to speak to them about the Nobel Prize[3] until later. What do you think, can one go to Lauenstein passively, I mean, without being obliged to give lectures or something like that? At present I am in a depression, a kind never experienced before; I am absolutely unable to work.[4]

It is very difficult to respond in writing to the rest of your letter. You must know that with all my heart I want you to receive the Nobel Prize. I also expect a great deal from what you are working on now, but on certain concrete questions we have parted ways. Your plan concerning Northern France is not only impractical but in my opinion—even if it were feasible—it is horrible. Excuse these harsh words but my feelings are aroused when *any group of people* is treated this way, especially if it is a great nation like France, whose culture—never so close to me as the German or the Russian—is an integral and sacrosanct part of ours regardless of what nation we belong to. Just as I protest in my soul against the aggressive plans of England and France, so do I protest any action of that sort on the German side. I wish for a peace based on the *status quo,* not because nothing else is possible but because that *alone* would give some meaning to the senselessness of the war and would put an end to its madness. The attitude of the German *Reichstag* and the *Reichskanzler*—as you correctly observe—is cowardly and deplorable: they have reservations about it but agree to it nevertheless, because this rape (of nations) has proved hopeless. They have no honest and clear intention either to conquer or to reach an agreement because they are beholden to and the messengers of the General Staff. (For me, the German civil government *en gros* resembles a sort of a war-time press headquarters.) However, we should discuss all this, not to reach an agreement, to be sure (that is beyond the rational and the possible), but for the sake of clarifying our own points of view.

Please, let me know about the outcome of your auxiliary service situation.

Kind regards to your wife.

Yours,
Georg von Lukács

[1] Lauenstein Castle on a bare peak in Thuringia. The Jena publisher and book-dealer, Eugen Diederichs, convened a diverse group of artists, scholars, et al., in the fall of 1917 to discuss cultural and political questions and to exchange "ideas about the meaning and the mission of the age". Max Weber was present, so was Paul Ernst, Werner Sombart, Toennies, Meinecke, and many of the younger generation (Ernst Toller, et al.). See Marianne Weber, *Max Weber* (New York: Wiley Interscience, 1975), pp. 596–602. Lukács did not attend.

[2] Max and Marianne Weber. There is mention in her book of a visit to Örlinghausen, where Weber "was surrounded by the children of the family."
[3] Ernst's letter is not extant. Presumably he expressed his hope that his friends would submit his name to the Nobel Committee.
[4] Most likely due to his marriage situation.

156. FROM HEINRICH RICKERT

Heidelberg
September 3, 1917

Dear Herr Doctor,

I have read your treatise[1] with lively interest, and I can't think of anything in the form of criticism that I have to add. It is quite another question whether your reflections will enlighten those who know almost nothing about Lask.

May I offer one rather insignificant correction? Insigificant, because it has nothing to do with Lask. On page 3, you make a reference to "Windelband's discovery of the specificity of historical conceptualization". For myself, I would refrain from any such statement because it was that very essence of the historical concept formation that Windelband overlooked in his deservedly famous speech; indeed, the problem has been concealed behind the screen of his contrasting law and *Gestalt*. Max Weber was therefore rather skeptical about such contrasts until Part Two of my *Grenzen*...[2] convinced him that there are such things as historical "concepts". In consequence, I'd replace "Windelband's" with the word "the" on page 3, line 13. Then everything would be satisfactory.

On the same page, way down, you write *"viel mehr"* as one word. This is confusing; namely, soon the expression *"vielmehr"* follows. I would omit the first *viel*.

With friendly greetings,
Yours,
Rickert

[1] "Emil Lask," in *Kant-Studien* (1917–18), pp. 349–170.
[2] *Die Grenzen der naturwissenschaftlichen Begriffsbildung*, 2 vols., published in 1898 and 1902 respectively.

157. TO PAUL ERNST

Heidelberg
September 5, 1917

Dear Herr Doctor,

Nothing has come from Lauenstein.[1] My plans are still in flux, especially with regard to the date of my departure. My wife will be going to a place near Munich for the winter and I'll wait here until everything has been arranged satisfactorily for her. As things stand now, I believe I'll still be here at the end of September. The only thing I know for certain is that I will settle in Budapest; it offers the only possibility for me to devote myself to work and to block out "Life". Even in Neustadt I would not be able to get away from it and I am completely worn out by all that contact with "reality".[2] Neustadt is out of question as a "place to work" not least because of the lack of electricity.

We will certainly meet before my trip to Budapest. I will inquire here about a boarding house.

As for politics, let's talk about it in person.

My warmest greetings (also to your wife).

Yours,
Georg von Lukács

P.S. Your labors on behalf of Balázs (and Dr. von Bubnoff)[3] are appreciated.

[1] Reference is to the planned conference at Lauenstein Castle. See letter no. 153, n. 1.

[2] Lukács alludes to this tortured relationship with Yelena and the *ménage à trois* they had in Heidelberg. See letters 141 and 142 to Karl Jaspers, who was Yelena's and Bruno Steinbach's psychiatrist.

[3] Nicolai von Bubnoff (1880–1962), Russian-born philosopher. He became a *Privatdozent* at Heidelberg in 1911. Lukács asked Ernst to place Bubnoff's MS on Nietzsche (*Nietzsches Kulturphilosophie und Umwertungslehre,* 1924).

158. TO THOMAS MANN

Budapest
February 18, 1918

Highly Esteemed Herr Mann,

Our mutual friend, Dr. Franz Baumgarten, has mentioned to me that you have expressed interest in my old (1909) essay on your *Royal Highness*.[1] Since I do not plan a German-language publication of my old Hungarian essays at any time in the near future, I do not possess a translation of any of them which I would consider stylistically adequate.

The enclosed translation[2] was prepared at my request by a lady friend who is also an admirer of your work. The translator aimed only at communicating the content of the essay; it was not at all done with the intention of publication and does not pretend to be stylistically perfect, which does not have to be pointed out to you.

I am extremely glad to have been able to do this small favor for you.

With my deepest respect,
Dr. Georg von Lukács

1 "Thomas Mann új regénye" (Thomas Mann's New Novel), originally published in *Nyugat*, November 1909. See "Royal Highness," in Georg Lukács, *Essays on Thomas Mann* (London: Merlin Press, 1964), pp. 135ff.

2 This German version was first published in the fifth ed. of *Thomas Mann* (Berlin/East: Aufbau Verlag, 1957), pp. 121ff.

159. TO PAUL ERNST

[Vienna?]
[?] 1918

Dear Herr Doctor,

I have to bother you again with a request. I would like to go to Germany in the fall and need a "residence permit" to do so. My friend, Dr. Staudinger,[1] whom you are acquainted with, spoke with the minister about this. It is necessary to submit an application, stating the purpose (scholarly work, etc.) of the stay, as well as several affidavits *(Gutachten)* from prominent Germans, to be enclosed with the application. Could you do this for me? What is needed are a few lines about the significance of my work for Germany, etc., etc. Please send it to me as soon as possible (Vienna, VIII, Landergasse 20).

The pessimistic tone of your letter made me sad. Unfortunately it is difficult if not impossible to deal with these questions in a letter: but I would like to talk to you. I would then tell you about the hope and confidence which has been growing in me, despite the many problems of my personal fate.

That it is so, has, of course, everything to do with one's philosophical point of view. And that could be explained only in a book or in a discussion. I am hopeful Germany will offer me the opportunity for both. And I do hope that our discussion will precede the completion of the book.

My heartfelt greetings to your wife.

Yours in continued friendship,
G. Lukács

[1] Hans Staudinger (1889–1980), economist and sociologist, student of Max and Alfred Weber in Heidelberg where he became a close friend of Lukács. A Social Democrat, he served as state secretary in the Prussian Ministry of Trade and Commerce (1919–27). Briefly imprisoned by the Nazis, he fled Germany in 1933 and joined the faculty of the University in Exile in 1934 where he later became the permanent Dean (1952–59). Author of *The Inner Nazi* (1981).

160. TO PAUL ERNST

Budapest
Gyopár Str. 2
April 5, 1919

Dear Herr Doctor,

Many thanks for your letter. Its contents have meanwhile become null and void in more than one sense.[1] To begin with, as a leading member of the then persecuted Communist Party, I lost my chances of ever attaining an academic post. Secondly, since the proclamation of the dictatorship of the proletariat a week ago, I have been the Commissar of Education.

For months now, I haven't done any work at all and probably shall not be able to take up my work for years to come. As a rule,

I am busy from dawn until late in the evening with affairs of the most diverse sort. After all the discussions we had had about politics, you should not be surprised that things worked out this way. But that I have landed here, that is, in such a high position!

More about all this when we meet again. I am hopeful that we will—in spite of everything.

Give my best regards to your wife and to all my friends in Germany.

Yours,
Lukács

1 Ernst presumably informed Lukács of the possibility of a lecturership through the mediation of Paul Natorp at Marburg. Although Lukács for years was desperately seeking such an opportunity, he could not follow up on this offer as he joined the Hungarian Communist Party in mid-December 1918.

161. FROM MAX WEBER

Munich
[March ?] 1920

Dear Friend,

I am glad to learn *finally* from an authentic source how things are with you for I hope not to miss out on a meeting with Dr. Manheim [sic!].[1] Until now, the *only* news I had received was a very desperate letter from your dear father, and there were no details except that you are still up to your neck in politics or at least in its consequences.

Most esteemed friend, *of course* we are separated by our political views! (I am absolutely convinced that these experiments *can* only have and will have the consequence of discrediting socialism for the coming 100 years.) Besides, if I have to be quite honest— regardless of an answer to *that* question—presumably there is a different answer to the other one, namely: was that *your* "calling" or what ever? Understandably, you claim sole right to decide about that. And still—whenever I think of *what* the present (since 1918) political goings-on cost us in terms of *unquestionably* valuable people, regardless of the "direction" of their choice, e.g., Schumpeter[2] and now you, without being able to see an end to all that, and, in my opinion, without achieving anything (after all, don't we all stand under the domination of alien powers?) then I cannot help feeling bitter about this senseless fate. I don't know whether or not you have received Paul Ernst's "offer"?[3] Here, in the *city* of Munich it is *extremely* unlikely that I would be able to secure a permit of residence for you; I know of no way. And *whatever* your plans may be, you should get away from that atmosphere in Vienna where everything simply goes around in circles. How about Italy or Germany—for I cannot imagine Paris being a possibility at this time. As far as Germany is concerned, the *passport* presents the main difficulty, and I don't see how I could help there. The *maximum* you could expect *here* is to obtain a permit of residence for 14 days—and even that seems to me a utopian idea at present. But let me know *how* one *can* be of help to you. (I did not sign the recent public "appeal"[4] because I had written earlier to the Ministry of Justice in Budapest on your behalf and noted there that I would *not* join any public action.) This affair should be settled in some way or other and you should be given back to the tasks that you set for yourself and that your talents have set for you, especially at a time when *everything* will be reactionary for decades to come.

Warm regards, also from my wife.

As ever,
Max Weber

[1] Weber must have meant Karl Mannheim.

[2] Reference is to Joseph Alois Schumpeter (1883–1950), Austrian-born political economist, who in 1932 emigrated to the United States. Author of *Capitalism, Socialism, and Democracy* (1942).

[3] In a letter of January 20, 1919, Lukács's father spoke of his "despair over the fate of [his] child" and asked for Paul Ernst's "help and counsel" based on his past admiration of Georg Lukács, "the writer, scholar, and scientist." The father also offered full financial backing of any initiative Ernst might undertake. Ernst obviously came up with an "offer" for Lukács because in a second letter, dated March 4, 1920, the older Lukács expressed his "innermost feelings of joy and gratefulness" for Ernst's invitation to Georg Lukács to stay with him and his family in Germany. He also asked Ernst not to reveal to his son that the invitation was extended at his request (and with his help). This is obviously the offer Weber refers to. For the whole correspondence between Ernst and the Lukács family see: *Paul Ernst und Georg Lukács: Dokumente einer Freundschaft* (Emsdetten/Westf.: Verlag Lechte, 1974), pp. 157–59.

[4] The public appeal "Zur Rettung von Georg Lukács" (Save Georg Lukács) appeared in the *Berliner Tageblatt,* November 12, 1919. The appeal was organized by Baumgarten and was in "defence of not Georg Lukács, the politician, but Georg Lukács, the man and thinker." It was signed by: Franz-Ferdinand Baumgarten, Richard Beer-Hofmann, Richard Dehmel, Paul Ernst, Bruno Frank, Maximilian Harden, Alfred Kerr, Heinrich Mann, Thomas

Mann, Emil Pretorius, and Karl Scheffler. According to Baumgarten, Ernst Troeltsch and Max Weber refused to sign, as did Stefan George, the poet, and Gerhart Hauptmann, the dramatist. Lukács's friend and Heidelberg colleague, Emil Lederer, had supposedly also planned to organize a "Heidelberg appeal", which did not come to pass. See ibid., pp. 153–57.

Weber died in June 1920 and Lukács's letter to his widow is a moving document about the human side of the "Weber—Lukács story." Lukács wrote: "The thought terrifies me that the distance. . .erected between us in the last years cannot be removed anymore. I've always found the fact of separation, the spatial as well as the divergence of views stupid, senseless and a mere empirical necessity. I knew that one could remove all what separates us with a few words, talking man to man. . .and now one can never speak those words anymore. It has always been among the few hopeful thoughts which nurtured my human existence that the day would come when I'll sit down and talk with Max Weber. The number of people whose judgment about the human condition in which we live—whether we do the right thing or not—is so small, that one almost gives up this *Gemeinschaft* and freezes into solitude."

APPENDIX

DOCUMENTATION OF LUKÁCS'S ATTEMPT AT *HABILITATION* AT THE UNIVERSITY OF HEIDELBERG* (1918)

To the Esteemed Faculty of Philosophy of the Rupprecht-Karl University of the Grand Duchy of Baden, at Heidelberg.

The undersigned, Dr. Georg von Lukács (Keppler Street 28, Heidelberg), hereby requests the Esteemed Faculty of Philosophy to grant him the *venia legendi* in philosophy on the basis of the enclosed supporting material.

May 25, 1918

Most respectfully,
Dr. Georg von Lukács

* The files pertaining to Lukács's attempt at *Habilitation* are housed at the University Archives, Heidelberg: "File no. III. 5a, 186: *Fakultätsakten Dekanat v. Domaszewski* 1918/19, fol. 223–53." For an account of the events surrounding Lukács's unsuccessful try for a German academic career see: Gerhard Sauder, "Von Formalitäten zur Politik: Georg Lukács's Heidelberger Habilitationsversuch," in *Zeitschrift für Literaturwissenschaft und Linguistik*, nos. 53/54 (1984), pp. 79–106. Prof. Sauder transcribed and reprinted nine documents from the folder.

CURRICULUM VITAE[1]

I was born in Budapest, on April 13, 1885, son of József von Lukács, *Hofrat* of the Hung.[arian] Cr.[own], Director of the Hungarian General Credit Bank; I am a Hungarian citizen, of Lutheran confession. At the completion of my secondary education at the Lutheran Gymnasium of Budapest, I received my maturity certificate *(Reifezeugnis)* in June 1902. I then embarked on a study of law and national economy at the University of Budapest and received a doctorate in law from the University of Kolozsvár[2] in October 1906. During my aforementioned studies, literature and art history as well as philosophy moved to the center of my interests. Thus, after briefly serving with the Royal Hungarian Ministry of Commerce, I decided to devote myself exclusively to the study of these areas and attended the universities of Budapest and Berlin. While none of the professors at the University of Budapest exerted any measurable influence on my development, I was inspired by and benefited in a decisive way from the lectures of Professors Dilthey and Simmel. The influence of Dilthey consisted mainly in the awakening of my interest in cultural-historical interconnections; I am greatly indebted to Simmel for demonstrating to me the possibility of a sociological approach to cultural objectifications. At the same time, I benefited greatly from the diverse methodological works of Max Weber. In November 1909, the University of Budapest conferred on me a doctoral degree in philosophy.

The beginnings of my literary activities preceded this latter phase of my studies. Some of my essays, collected in my book, *Die Seele und die Formen,* are the product of an earlier period, as is the first version of my *Entwicklungsgeschichte des modernen Dramas,* written in Hungarian, which received the prize of the Kisfaludy Society of Budapest in February 1908. The completely revised work was subsequently published by the Kisfaludy Society in 1912. Negotiations about a German-language edition—in Alfred Weber's "Sociology of Culture Series"—were interrupted by the outbreak of the war. So far, only chapter 2 (which together with chapter 1 comprised my doctoral dissertation at the University of Budapest) has appeared in print, in the *Archiv für Sozialwissenschaft und Sozialpolitik,* in the spring of 1914.

Following my doctoral exams, my interest increasingly turned toward purely philosophical problems, albeit without abandoning my awareness of particular problems of literature and the arts. In the fall of 1909 I moved to Berlin and lived there until the spring of 1911, a stay interrupted only by an occasional trip to Italy. During that time my philosophical studies focused on classical German philosophy, on Kant, Fichte, Schelling, and Hegel. The ever clearer comprehension of the concept of value *(Geltungsgedanke)* soon led me to modern German philosophy, above all to Windelband, Rickert, and Lask. In addition, the methodological stimulus of Husserl's writings had a great impact on me. From Berlin I moved to Florence, only to leave after one year in order to settle in Heidelberg permanently. My decision to move was motivated by my desire to meet and have personal contact with the men whose writings had so greatly influenced my development. I developed an especially close relationship with Emil Lask and have published a lengthy article in the *Kantstudien* in his memory. In the first years, my sojourn in Heidelberg was interrupted by trips to Holland and to Rome and more recently by my military service. I married Miss Helena Grabenko, daughter of Andrej Michailowitsch Grabenko, *semstvo* secretary of Cherson district, in Heidelberg in the spring of 1914.

This period saw the first draft and then the almost completed writing of a systematic philosophy of art. I have also written several works on ethics and on the theory of science *(Wissenschaftslehre),* most of which are yet to be published.

My published works are as follows:

1. *Die Seele und die Formen* [Soul and Form]. Essays. Berlin, 1911. The volume contains, among others, the essay "Metaphysics of Tragedy," which had also been published in *Logos,* II, 1911.
2. *Entwicklungsgeschichte des modernen Dramas* [History of the Development of Modern Drama]. Publication of the Kisfaludy Society, Budapest, 1912. German-language publication of Chapter 2, "Zur Soziologie des modernen Dramas" [Sociology of Modern Drama] in *Archiv für Sozialwissenschaft und Sozialpolitik,* 1914.

3. *Methologie [sic!] der Literaturgeschichte* [Methodology of the History of Literature], 1910, in Hungarian.
4. Reviews of substance in *Archiv für Sozialwissenschaft und Sozialpolitik* on methodological problems in the social sciences.
5. Small-scale works relating to problems of form in literature, published in diverse journals.
6. *Die Theorie des Romans* [Theory of the Novel]. Published in *Zeitschrift für Aesthetik und Allgemeine Kunstwissenschaft,* XI, 3–4, 1916. (This work represents the introductory chapter of a large-scale work.)
7. "Die Subjekt-Objekt Beziehung in der Aiesthetik [sic!]" [The Subject-Object Relation in Aesthetics]. In *Logos,* VII, 1 (1917–18). The article constitutes one chapter of my otherwise unpublished *Philosophy of Art.*
8. "Emil Lask: Ein Nachruf" (E. L. Obituary). In *Kantstudien,* XXII, 4 (1918).

Proposed Topics for the Colloquium:

1. Søren Kierkegaard's Critique of Hegel.
2. The Difference between the Concepts *"Gelten"* and *"Sollen"*.
3. Phenomenology and Transcendental Philosophy.

[1] Marked "Curriculum Vitae", "Schriftenverzeichnis" (Bibliography) and "Colloquiumsthemen" (Topics for Colloquium), dossier no. 224–27. First publication in *Text+Kritik,* no. 39/40, "Georg Lukács Issue" (1973), p. 5. See also in Sauder's account, pp. 98–100.

[2] At that time both the cultural and political center of Transylvania. After the Versailles Treaty gave the former Hungarian territory to Romania, it became known as Cluj-Napoca.

1 Leo Popper, Lukács's friend,
with his fiancée Beatrice de Waard
c. 1909–10 *(Lukács Archives)*

2 Lukács's father, József Lukács
(Lukács Archives)

3 Lukács's mother, née Adele Wertheimer
(Lukács Archives)

4 Irma Seidler,
the great love of the young Lukács *c.* 1908–10
(photo: Sándor Kohlmann, Lukács Archives)

5 Georg Lukács in 1911
(photo: Edith Hajós, Lukács Archives)

6 Hilda Bauer
(Lukács Archives)

7 Participants of the Sunday Circle:
from left to right, Károly Mannheim, Béla Fogarasi, Ernő Lorsy, József Nemes Lampérth, Elza Stephani, Anna Schlamadinger, Edith Hajós and Béla Balázs, *c*. 1915–16
(Petőfi Literary Museum)

8 Yelena Andreyevna Grabenko,
Lukács's first wife
(Lukács Archives)

9 Gertrud Bortstieber, Lukács's second wife before their marriage *(Lukács Archives)*

Georg Simmel

10 Portrait of Georg Simmel on a postcard, with his signature

11 Philosopher
Bernát Alexander
c. 1912
*(photo: Aladár Székely.
Association of
Hungarian Photographers)*

12 Karl Mannheim

13 Leo Popper, Károly Polányi and Mihály Polányi

14 Philosopher
Ernst Bloch
(Lukács Archives)

15 Heidelberg
philosopher
Emil Lask

16 Aesthete and critic Ferenc (Franz) Ferdinand Baumgarten *(photo: Bosholm, Strasbourg. Petőfi Literary Museum)*

17 German poet and playwright Paul Ernst *(Paul Ernst Archives)*

8 Lukács with representatives of the proletariat and the Red Guard in 1919 *(Film Archives of the Hungarian Film Institute)*

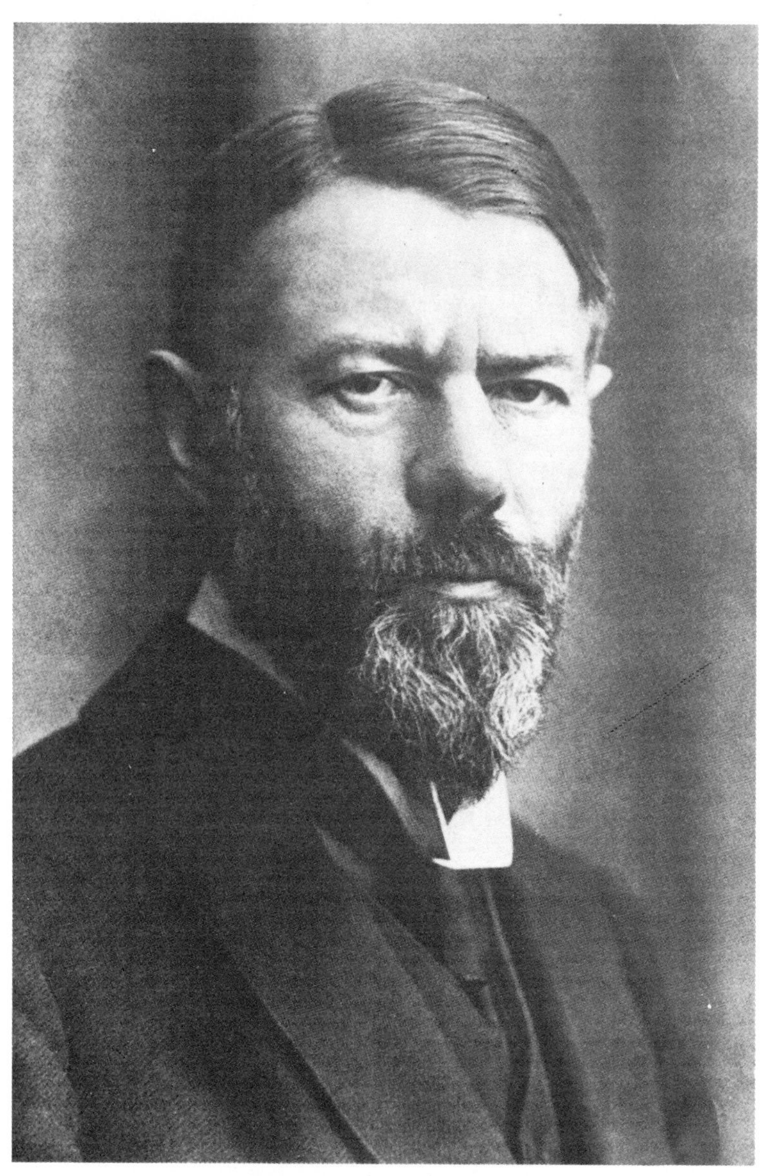

19 Portrait of Max Weber

FROM DEAN DOMASZEWSKI

Heidelberg
December 7, 1918

Esteemed Herr Doctor,

I am taking the liberty to inform you that under the present circumstances the Faculty of Philosophy is not in the position to admit a foreigner, especially a Hungarian citizen, to *Habilitation*.

While fully recognizing the worth of your scholarly achievements, I nevertheless have to ask you in the name of the Faculty to withdraw your application for a *Habilitation*.

Respectfully,
Prof. v. Domaszewski
Acting Dean

TO DEAN DOMASZEWSKI

Budapest, I.
Gyopár Str. 2
December 16, 1918

Esteemed Herr Professor:

Thank you for your friendly letter. I am hereby withdrawing my application without any misgivings, especially since in the meantime I have put myself at the disposal of the Hungarian government and have been so intensely involved in the work of several commissions that it would be hardly possible for me to travel to Heidelberg in any case. May I ask you to hand over to Prof. Gothein all the submitted material, books, manuscripts, and documents; he will save them for me. If per chance I am to be reimbursed for part of the fees paid, I should like to ask you to deposit the sum in my account at the South-German Discount Bank.

Please convey my sincere thanks to the Faculty of philosophy for their kindness in handling my case. I remain

Respectfully yours,
Dr. Georg von Lukács

BIOGRAPHICAL NOTES

ALEXANDER, BERNÁT (1850–1927), Hungarian philosopher and aesthetician. Professor of the history of philosophy at the University of Budapest. Father of the renowned psychoanalyst, Franz Alexander. From 1878, president of the Hungarian Philosophical Society, and editor of *Athenaeum*, the society's journal. Author of *Művészet. A művészet értékéről. A művészeti nevelésről* (Art. The Value of Art. Art Appreciation) (1910). Mentor of a whole generation of Hungarian humanists.

BALÁZS, BÉLA (Herbert Bauer) (1884–1949), poet, playwright, librettist, teacher, critic, novelist, a major theoretician of the cinema, revolutionary. Born Herbert Bauer in Szeged to a Hungarian-Jewish father and a German-Jewish mother, Jenny Levy, both teachers. Promoted to Dr. phil. at the University of Budapest in 1909, he met Lukács the same year and they became intimate friends for a decade. Reworked folktales into plays, wrote the librettos for Bartók's *Bluebeard's Castle* (1911) and *The Wooden Prince* (1916). Initiator of the Sunday Circle, and lecturer at the Free School of the Humanities in 1917–18. Participated in the Commune of 1919, and fled to Vienna after its overthrow. Emigrated to Moscow in the 1930s and returned to Hungary after 1945. Among his works: *Der Geist des Films* (1930) and *Der sichtbare Mensch oder die Kultur des Films* (1924).

BÁNÓCZI, LÁSZLÓ (1880–1945), studied law, later became legal counselor at one of the administrative organs of the unions. Member of the Social Democratic Party. One of the con-founders and president of the Thalia Society, the revolutionary theater at Budapest from 1904 to 1908.

BAUMGARTEN, FERENC (FRANZ) FERDINAND (1880–1927), Hungarian aesthete and literary critic. Born into a Jewish upper-class family of Budapest, he studied at the universities of Budapest, Strasbourg, and Heidelberg. From 1909 he settled in Germany and lived in Munich and Berlin. Based on his wide contacts in German intellectual circles, he promoted Lukács's work vigorously. Established the Baumgarten Prize in his native land for young Hungarian poets and writers (1923–49). Author of *Das Werk Conrad Ferdinand Meyers* (1917).

BENDEMANN, MARGARETE VON, née SUSMAN (1874–1966), German-Jewish essayist and literary critic, friend of George and Gertrud Simmel, Ernst Bloch, and several members of the Stefan George Circle. Emigrated to Switzerland. Author of several volumes on feminist themes, modern poetry, and Simmel.

BENEDEK, MARCELL (1885–1969), Hungarian literary historian, critic, and translator. Childhood friend of Lukács, cofounded with him the Thalia Society in 1904. Studied at the University of Budapest and from 1912 taught Hungarian and German literature at a Budapest gymnasium. During the 1919 Hungarian Republic of Councils, he became a university lecturer but was removed after the collapse of the Commune. Worked as a free-lance critic and writer. From 1945 professor of literature at the universities of Kolozsvár (Cluj-Napoca, Romania) and Budapest, respectively. Author of the autobiography, *Naplómat olvasom* (Reading My Diary), 1965.

BERTAUX, FELIX (1881–1948), French scholar of modern German literature. Translated and helped to popularize the work of Lukács, Thomas Mann, and other German writers in France. Coeditor of the journal *L'Effort Libre*.

BLEI, FRANZ (1871–1942), Austrian writer, literary critic, and translator. Lived in Munich and Berlin and later emigrated to the United States. Founder and editor of several journals (*Hyperion, Philobiblion*, et al.).

BLOCH, ERNST (1885–1977), German-Jewish writer and philosopher. While in Berlin, his philosophical mentor was Georg Simmel (1910–11). Bloch was instrumental in introducing Lukács to Simmel. Until 1918, he was a close friend of Lukács, moved to Heidelberg with him, and through Lukács became a member of the so-called Max Weber-Circle. He became a pacifist and a non-party Marxist during World War I and moved to Switzerland. Emigrated to the United States in 1938 but returned to Europe in 1949 and accepted a professorship at the University of Leipzig. He fled East Germany after the erection of the Berlin Wall in 1961 and was offered a university chair at Tübingen, where he died. Among his works are: *Geist der Utopie* (1918), in the tradition of Jewish apocalyptic literature combined with socialism; *Thomas Münzer als Theologie der Revolution* (1921); and his three-volume magnum opus, *Das Prinzip Hoffnung* (1954, 1955, 1959).

BORTSTIEBER, GERTRUD (1882–1963), second wife of Lukács, friend of his sister, Mária, she was a frequent visitor at the Lukács home and knew Lukács since 1902. Studied mathematics and physics at the universities of Vienna and Budapest; in 1908 married Imre Jánossy, a mathematician, who died young. She had two sons, Lajos Jánossy, later a prominent nuclear physicist, and Ferenc Jánossy, professor of economics in Budapest, who is the executor of Lukács's literary estate. Fled Hungary in 1919 with her children and settled with Lukács in Vienna, where they were married in 1920. They had one daughter, Anna, who lives in Budapest. During their years in exile in Vienna, Berlin, and Moscow, she was the intellectual partner and source of inspiration for Lukács, who admittedly contemplated suicide after her death and felt that he could not go on working without her constructive critical presence. *History and Class Consciousness* (1923) and the *Aesthetic* (1965) are dedicated to her.

BUBER, MARTIN (1878–1965), mystic, aesthete, utopian socialist, philosopher of religion. Vienna-born, raised and educated in Lemberg, then part of the Austro-Hungarian Monarchy. Studied at the universities of Vienna (with Alois Riegl), Leipzig, Zurich, and Berlin (under Dilthey and Simmel), and received his Ph. D. from the University of Vienna in 1904. Since 1919, teacher at the newly founded *Jüdisches Lehrhaus* in Frankfurt am Main and Guest Professor of Theology and Jewish Ethics at the University of Frankfurt from 1923. Resigned in 1933, but stayed on in Germany until 1938, when he emigrated to Palestine. Became Professor at the Hebrew University in Jerusalem. Among his many works are *Ekstatische Konfessionen* (1909), *Ich und Du* (I and Thou), published in 1923, *Paths in Utopia* (1958), *On Judaism*, ed. Nahum N. Glatzer (1972), and *The Tales of Rabbi Nachman* (1970). He was the renewer of Hasidism.

ERNST, PAUL (1866–1933), German writer, poet, and dramatist. Best known representative of the so-called neo-classical style. Wrote several dramas in the grand tradition of the "tragédie classique" on medieval and Teutonic themes *(Canossa, Brunhild, The Prussian Spirit),* all of which were about absolute moral values. His aesthetic and literary works show his romantic-anti-capitalistic sentiments, his sorrow at the passing of community values and the mechanization of modern life. Had much in common with Lukács besides a preference for the tradition of classicism. Ideological differences during and after World War I led to their estrangement. Their correspondence from 1910 to 1926 was fully preserved and published in German in 1974 *(Paul Ernst und Georg Lukács: Dokumente einer Freundschaft).*

FEJÉR, LIPÓT (1880–1958), mathematician. Born and educated in Budapest, received his Ph. D. in 1902 and became professor of mathematics at the University of Budapest (from 1911 until his death). Teacher of generations of Hungarian mathematicians including John von Neumann and Georg Pólya.

FERENCZI, SÁRI (1887–1952), Hungarian writer and literary historian. Studied at the University of Budapest, edited a collection of Transylvanian ballads (1912). Wrote several novels (*A vörös daru,* 1919). Moved to Berlin in the 1920s and ceased publishing.

FÜLEP, LAJOS (1885–1970), art historian, philosopher. Collaborated with Lukács on several projects, such as the journal, *A szellem* (1911). Travelled widely in Italy and France; was appointed professor of art history during the 1919 Hungarian Republic of Councils but was removed after its collapse. Remained in Hungary, and lived in the Southern part in "inner emigration". His main work, *Magyar művészet* (Hungarian Art) was published in 1923.

GRABENKO, YELENA (OR JELENA) ANDREYEVNA (1889–?), "daughter of Andrej Michailowitsch Grabenko, *semstvo* secretary [civil servant] of Cherson," according to Lukács's curriculum vitae of 1918. She studied to be a painter, joined the Socialist Revolutionary (SR) Party, took part in the 1905 Revolution, and later fled to Paris and then to Heidelberg, where she met Lukács. Lukács reconstructed his reasons for marriage as follows: "Situation in Heidelberg: the existence of a 'free floating intellectual' with adequate financial means. Necessity of marriage because of the war: J. G. is Russian, her only protection: Hungarian citizenship. Her love affair [with that musician] is imminent. The three of us living together. Inner separation amidst physical proximity. Real solution: friendly parting but only after the war." (From a transcript of Lukács's reminiscences at the Lukács-Archives, Budapest; translated by the editors.)

HEGEDÜS, GYULA (1870–1931), Hungarian actor. From 1906 taught at the Academy of Performing Arts and after 1907 at the Music Academy of Budapest. Author of several plays.

JASPERS, KARL (1883–1969), German philosopher, an early representant of existential philosophy. Studied medicine and became a well-known psychiatrist before World War I. Taught at Heidelberg University and was a member of the so-called *Max Weber-Kreis,* where he met Lukács. After 1948, professor at the University of Basel. Author of *Allgemeine Psychopathologie* (1913) and *Vernunft in Existenz* (1935).

JÁSZI, (OSCAR) OSZKÁR (1875–1957), publicist, sociologist, political scientist and bourgeois-radical politician, was a leading spokesman for the radical intelligentsia at the turn of the century. Chairman of the National Bourgeois

Radical Party from 1914; member of the 1918 democratic republican government of Count Mihály Károlyi. Emigrated in 1919 and became editor of the *Bécsi Magyar Újság* (Viennese Hungarian News). Settled in the United States in 1925 and became professor of political science at Oberlin College. His *Dissolution of the Habsburg Monarchy* (1929) is the standard work on the nationality problem of the Austro-Hungarian Empire.

LASK, EMIL (1875–1915), German-Jewish philosopher. Born in Wadovic near Cracow, studied under Windelband, became professor of philosophy at Heidelberg University in 1910. Represented—along with Windelband and Rickert—the Badener or Southwest German School of Neo-Kantian philosophy. Close friend of the Webers and Lukács. Volunteered for service and fell on the Galician front on May 26, 1915. The Webers called his death a "senseless sacrifice". Lukács's obituary appeared in the *Kant-Studien*, (1918). Main works: *Die Logik der Philosophie und die Kategorienlehre* (1911) and *Die Lehre vom Urteil* (1912).

LEDERER-SEIDLER, EMMY (1885–1933), sister of Irma Seidler, married to Emil Lederer, professor at Heidelberg University and later at the New School for Social Research in New York City. Her articles appeared in the *Archiv für Sozialwissenschaft und Sozialpolitik*. Co-author of *Japan, Europa* (1929). Well-known hostess in Heidelberg. Committed suicide (like her sister) before their impending emigration.

LIGETI, PÁL (1885–1941), Hungarian painter, architect and writer, schoolmate of Lukács. Author of *Der Weg aus dem Chaos* (1931) and other works in Hungarian.

LUKÁCS (LŐWINGER), JÓZSEF VON (1857–1928), father of Lukács. Son of a small artisan in Southern Hungary, talented, hard-working, and self-educated (spoke several languages and was a connoisseur of the arts and literature), he was named Director of the Anglo-Austrian Bank in Budapest at the age of twenty-five. Raised to nobility in 1899 as "szegedi von Lukács". Married Adele Wertheimer of Vienna and they had four children, János (1884–1944), György, Mária (1887–1980), and Pál (1889–1892). Director of the General Credit Bank from 1906. Respected as a generous patron of young artists, writers, and musicians (e.g., Béla Bartók). Removed from his post by the Horthy regime on account of his son's political involvement. Regardless of their ideological differences, he remained an affectionate parent; sacrificed a good portion of his fortune to facilitate in September 1919 his son's escape to Vienna.

LUKÁCS, MRS., née ADELE WERTHEIMER (1860–1917), mother of Lukács. Vienna-born, moved to Budapest at her marriage but never mastered the Hungarian language. Lukács often spoke of his strained relation to her.

LUKÁCS, MÁRIA (MICI) (1887–1980), sister of Lukács, studied music with David Popper and Béla Bartók. Married to Richard Lessner, later to Otto Popper. Lived in England with her second husband. Died in Austria.

MANN, THOMAS (1875–1955), most likely the greatest twentieth-century German man of letters. Mann and Lukács maintained a life-long respect and admiration for each other along with a certain degree of distance, especially on the part of Mann. They met in January 1922 in a hotel room in Vienna where Lukács lived in exile. Mann's impressions were incorporated into his fictional character, Leo Naphta, of *The Magic Mountain*.

MANNHEIM, (KARL) KÁROLY (1893–1947), born and educated in Budapest, known as the founder of the sociology of knowledge. Chose Lukács as his intellectual mentor, but their close relationship came to an abrupt end in 1916 for unknown reasons. Attended the so-called Sunday Circle, and was, with Lukács, one of the founding members of the Free School of Humanities (1917–1918). Left Hungary in 1919, took his *Habilitation* under Alfred Weber in Heidelberg; taught epistemology and sociology at the universities of Heidelberg and Frankfurt (Main). Emigrated to England in 1933 and held teaching positions at the London School of Economics and at the University of London (from 1941 until his death). Among his works: *Ideology and Utopia* (1926); *Man and Society in the Age of Reconstruction* (1940), and the pathbreaking essay, "Conservative Thoughts".

OSVÁT, ERNŐ (1877–1929), Hungarian literary critic, writer, and journalist. Founder of several journals *(Figyelő, Magyar Géniusz)* for the promotion of modern poetry and Hungarian culture. Influential editor of *Nyugat* (from 1908 until his death). Committed suicide following the death of his only daughter. Author of posthumous *Osvát öszszes írásai* (1945).

POLÁNYI, (KARL) KÁROLY (1886–1964), economic historian. Born in Vienna, raised and educated in Budapest. Studied law and philosophy there. One of the founders of the Galileo Circle, a club of radical and socialist students. Editor of the journal *Szabadgondolat*. After 1918, moved to Vienna, then to England, and, finally, to the United States in 1940. Became resident scholar at Bennington College, where he wrote his famous treatise, *The Great Transformation* (1944); from 1947 to 1953, visiting professor at Columbia University.

POPPER, LEO (1886–1911), born in Budapest, son of David Popper, the world-famous cellist. Studied painting, sculpture, and music. Contracted T. B. at an early age and spent much of his short life in sanatoriums in Austria and Switzerland. His essays on aesthetic problems and his art criticism impressed his contemporaries and influenced the early work of Lukács. Popper wrote in German and also translated some of Lukács's essays into German. He published in *Die Fackel* (of Karl Kraus) and in *Die Neue Rundschau*. A slim volume of his collected essays was published in Hungary in 1983.

RADBRUCH, GUSTAV (1879–1949), German legal scholar, professor at the universities of Königsberg, Kiel, and Heidelberg, well-known Social Democrat; belonged to the small circle of scholars who opposed the war, among them Ernst Bloch, Karl Jaspers, Lukács, and Emil Lederer. With his wife Linda, he often attended the Sunday gatherings (Max Weber Circle) at the house of Max and Marianne Weber.

RÉVÉSZ, GÉZA (1878–1955), psychologist. Born in Hungary, studied philosophy and psychology at the universities of Berlin, Munich, and Göttingen. Habilitated in Budapest in experimental psychology. In 1918–19 became the first professor of experimental psychology at the University of Budapest. After 1919 Director of the Institute of Psychology in Amsterdam. Among his numerous works are *Zur Grundlegung der Tonpsychologie* (1912), and *A tehetség korai felismerése* (1918), which appeared in German as *Das frühzeitige Auftreten der Begabung und ihre Erkennung* (1921).

RICKERT, HEINRICH, Jr. (1863–1936), German Neo-Kantian philosopher, belonged—along with Windelband and Lask—to the Baden School. Taught at the universities of Freiburg (1894–1915) and Heidelberg from 1916. Among his works: *Kultur und Naturwissenschaften* (1899) and *Philosophie des Lebens* (1920).

RITOÓK, EMMA (1868–1945), Hungarian philosopher and writer, a friend of Ernst Bloch, Lukács, and Balázs (who first met her in a Simmel Seminar in Berlin, around 1906). Member of the Sunday Circle. Later supported the Horthy regime and denounced her former friends and associates in a book entitled *A szellem kalandorai* (Adventurers of the Spirit, Budapest, 1922).

SALOMON, ALBERT (1891–1966), German sociologist. Studied with Simmel in Berlin and Max Weber and Emil Lask in Heidelberg. Taught political sociology at the universities of Cologne and Berlin. Emigrated to the United States and became professor of sociology at the New School for Social Research in New York City. Editor of the journal, *Die Gesellschaft* (1928–31). Author of *German Sociology* (1945) and other works in German.

SALOMON, GOTTFRIED (1896–1964), German sociologist. Was a student of Simmel and Franz Oppenheimer. Emigrated first to France and in 1941 to America. Professor of Sociology at the New School for Social Research and after 1959 at the Johann Wolfgang Goethe University at Frankfurt am Main. Author of several books in German.

SEIDLER, IRMA (1882–1911), born into a well-to-do Hungarian-Jewish family of Budapest; among her cousins were Karl Polányi and Ervin Szabó, Syndicalist-Marxist, one of Lukács's intellectual mentors in Marxism. Her brother, Ernő Seidler, was a co-founder of the Hungarian Communist Party in 1918, only to perish in the Stalinist purges. Lukács met her on December 18, 1907, when she was studying to be a painter. Between May 28 and June 11 of 1908, they travelled together in Italy in the company of their mutual friend, Leo Popper, a promising art historian. Irma then went to Nagybánya (now Baia Mare, Romania), a famous art colony and maintained a heavy correspondence with Lukács, who finally refused to commit himself. Married Károly Réthy a fellow-painter, but the marriage did not work out. After an unhappy affair with Béla Balázs, one of Lukács' friends, she committed suicide on the evening of May 18, 1911, by jumping into the Danube. This tragic incident engendered Lukács's sole literary work "Von der Armut am Geiste" (On Poverty of Spirit), published in *Neue Blätter* (1912). Lukács dedicated his *Soul and Form* to her memory.

SIMMEL, GEORG (1858–1918), German philosopher and sociologist. Professor at the universities of Berlin and Strasbourg. One of the main representatives of *Lebensphilosophie*. Author of *Philosophy of Money* (1900) and more than a dozen volumes on problems of philosophy and sociology. Many young Hungarians such as Lukács, Balázs, Ritoók, and Baumgarten belonged to his "Private Seminar" in Berlin, prior to World War I. One of the main influences on the young Lukács, who acknowledged that his "*History of the Development of Modern Drama* is truly a Simmelian work."

SOMLÓ, (FELIX) BÓDOG (1873–1920), Hungarian-Jewish legal scholar and sociologist. Studied in Kolozsvár (now Cluj-Napoca, Romania), Leipzig, and Heidelberg. Professor at Kolozsvár University (1898–1918) and at the University of Budapest (1918–19). Editor of *Huszadik Század* (Twentieth Century). In 1901 he founded the Society for Social Sciences. Committed suicide in 1920. Author of *Gründung einer besch* eibenden Soziologie* (1909) and *Juristische Grundlehre* (1917).

TROELTSCH, ERNST (1865–1923), German philosopher of religion and history. Professor at the universities of Heidelberg (1894–1914) and Berlin (1914–1918). Author of *The Social Teachings of Christian Churches and Groups* and other works.

WAARD, BEATRICE de (1888–1962), Dutch-born bride of Leo Popper. Studied music and painting. Moved to Paris after Popper's death.

WEBER, ALFRED (1868–1958), German sociologist, brother of Max Weber. Professor at Heidelberg University. Author of *Kulturgeschichte als Kultursoziologie* (1935) and other works.

WEBER, MAX (1864–1920), German sociologist. Studied law, economics, history, and philosophy at the universities of Heidelberg and Berlin. Married Marianne Schnitger (1870–1954), who edited his work after his death and wrote a biography of him. Held professorships at the universities of Freiburg and Heidelberg. In 1897, a nervous breakdown disrupted his academic career. Handed in his resignation in 1903 and did not take up teaching again until 1918, when he accepted a position in Vienna. Moved to Munich permanently in the spring of 1919, where he succumbed to pneumonia on June 14, 1920. Directed the *Archiv für Sozialwissenschaft und Sozialpolitik* from 1904 on and became editor of the *Grundriss der Sozialökonomik* in 1909. Despite his absence from academia, he remained at the center of a circle of scholars. The Webers instituted a Sunday afternoon open house (Weber Circle) and Lukács regularly attended from 1912 to 1917. Author of many seminal works, among others: *Economy and Society*, 3 vols., *The Protestant Ethic and the Spirit of Capitalism*, and *The Sociology of Religion*.

ZIEGLER, LEOPOLD (1881–1958), German philosopher, student of Eduard von Hartmann and author of the study *Das Weltbild Eduard von Hartmanns* (1910). His other works dealt with problems of a religious-metaphysical nature.

LIST OF LETTERS

1.	From	Marcell Benedek (in Hungarian)	August 20, 1902
2.		László Bánóczi (in Hungarian)	August 5, 1906
3.		Gertrud Bortstieber (in Hungarian)	September 7, 1906
4.		László Bánóczi (in Hungarian)	November 26, 1906
5.		Irma Seidler (in Hungarian)	December 31, 1907
6.		Pál Ligeti (in Hungarian)	January 4, 1908
7.	To	Ernő Osvát (in Hungarian)	January 20, 1908
8.	From	Bernát Alexander (in Hungarian)	January 21, 1908
9.		Lipót Fejér (in Hungarian)	February [8], 1908
10.		Károly (Karl) Polányi (in Hungarian)	February 8, 1908
11.		Gyula Hegedüs (in Hungarian)	April 7, 1908
12.		Irma Seidler (in Hungarian)	July 3, 1908
13.		Leo Popper (in Hungarian)	July 7, 1908
14.	To	Ernő Osvát (in Hungarian)	July 10, 1908
15.	From	Károly (Karl) Polányi (in Hungarian)	July 21, 1908
16.		Irma Seidler (in Hungarian)	August 5, 1908
17.		Irma Seidler (in Hungarian)	September 20, 1908
18.	To	Ernő Osvát (in Hungarian)	September 28, 1908

19.	From	Irma Seidler (in Hungarian)	October 25, 1908
20.		Irma Seidler (in Hungarian)	November 2, 1908
21.	To	Irma Seidler (in Hungarian)	November ?, 1908
22.	From	Leo Popper (in Hungarian)	November 23, 1908
23.		Károly (Karl) Polányi (in Hungarian)	December 9, 1908
24.		Károly (Karl) Polányi (in Hungarian)	December 18, 1908
25.		Leo Popper (in Hungarian)	January 6, 1909
26.	To	Sári Ferenczi (in Hungarian)	January ?, 1909
27.		Bódog (Felix) Somló (in Hungarian)	February 14, 1909
28.	To	Leo Popper (in Hungarian)	mid-April 1909
29.	From	Leo Popper (in Hungarian)	April 19, 1909
30.	To	Leo Popper (in Hungarian)	April 25, 1909
31.		Leo Popper (in Hungarian)	May 22, 1909
32.	From	Ferenc (Franz) Ferdinand Baumgarten (in German)	May 27, 1909
33.		Leo Popper (in Hungarian)	June 7, 1909
34.		Ferenc (Franz) Ferdinand Baumgarten (in German)	June 9, 1909
35.	To	Leo Popper (in Hungarian)	mid-June 1909
36.		Leo Popper (in Hungarian)	mid-July 1909
37.	From	Georg Simmel (in German)	July 22, 1909

38. To	Leo Popper (in Hungarian)	July 25, 1909
39. From	József von Lukács (in Hungarian)	August 23, 1909
40.	Oszkár (Oscar) Jászi (in Hungarian)	August 26, 1909
41. To	Leo Popper (in Hungarian)	October 26, 1909
42.	Leo Popper (in Hungarian)	October 27, 1909
43.	Paul Ernst (in German)	March 10, 1910
44.	Irma Seidler (Réthy) (in Hungarian)	March 23, 1910
45. From	Irma Seidler (Réthy) (in Hungarian)	March 24, 1910
46.	Ernst Bloch (in German)	April 22, 1910
47. To	Lajos Fülep (in Hungarian)	May 24, 1910
48.	Leo Popper (in Hungarian)	May 28, 1910
49.	Leo Popper (in Hungarian)	June 8, 1910
50.	Leo Popper (in Hungarian)	June 15, 1910
51. From	Mrs. József von Lukács (in German)	June 23, 1910
52.	Károly (Karl) Mannheim (in Hungarian)	July 3, 1910
53.	Bernát Alexander (in Hungarian)	August 23, 1910
54. To	Leo Popper (in Hungarian)	early October 1910
55. From	Leo Popper (in Hungarian)	October 7, 1910
56. To	Leo Popper (in Hungarian)	October 25, 1910
57.	Leo Popper (in Hungarian)	December 10, 1910
58.	Leo Popper (in Hungarian)	December 20, 1910
59.	Lajos Fülep (in Hungarian)	December 21, 1910

No.		Correspondent	Date
60.		Beatrice de Waard (Bé) (in German)	December 22, 1910
61.	From	Franz Blei (in German)	December 26, 1910
62.	To	Franz Blei (in German)	December ?, 1910
63.		Leo Popper (in Hungarian)	February 11, 1911
64.		Martin Buber (in German)	February 13, 1911
65.		Martin Buber (in German)	February 20, 1911
66.	From	Martin Buber (in German)	February 21, 1911
67.	To	Paul Ernst (in German)	March ?, 1911
68.	From	Károly (Karl) Mannheim (in Hungarian)	March 13, 1911
69.	To	Leo Popper (in Hungarian)	March 19, 1911
70.	From	Irma Seidler (Réthy) (in Hungarian)	April 16, 1911
71.	To	Irma Seidler (Réthy) (in Hungarian)	April 18, 1911
72.		Martin Buber (in German)	April 20, 1911
73.	From	Martin Buber (in German)	April 22, 1911
74.	To	Martin Buber (in German)	April 24, 1911
75.	From	Bernát Alexander (in Hungarian)	May 4, 1911
76.	To	Leo Popper (in Hungarian)	May 19, 1911
77.	From	Leo Popper (in Hungarian)	May 24, 1911
78.	To	Leo Popper (in Hungarian)	May 26, 1911
79.	From	Leo Popper (in Hungarian)	June 26, 1911
80.	To	Paul Ernst (in German)	July?, 1911
81.		Leo Popper (in Hungarian)	August 7, 1911

82.		Leopold Ziegler (in German)	August 10, 1911
83.	To	Leo Popper (in Hungarian)	August 27, 1911
84.		Paul Ernst (in German)	[September ?], 1911
85.		Paul Ernst (in German)	[October ?], 1911
86.		Martin Buber (in German)	[November ?], 1911
87.		Paul Ernst (in German)	[November ?], 1911
88.	From	József von Lukács (in Hungarian)	November 17, 1911
89.		Martin Buber (in German)	December 3, 1911
90.	To	Franz Blei (in German)	[December 10], 1911
91.	From	Bernát Alexander (in Hungarian)	December 11, 1911
92.	To	Martin Buber (in German)	December 20, 1911
93.		Leopold Ziegler (in German)	January 1, 1912
94.	From	Károly (Karl) Mannheim (in Hungarian)	January 5, 1912
95.		Margarete von Bendemann (in German)	January 25, 1912
96.		Károly (Karl) Polányi (in Hungarian)	January 27, 1912
97.	To	Paul Ernst (in German)	February 15, 1912
98.	From	Károly (Karl) Mannheim (in Hungarian)	March 3, 1912
99.		Emmy Lederer-Seidler (in Hungarian)	May 17, 1912
100.		Georg Simmel (in German)	May 25, 1912
101.		Emil Lask (in German)	June 11, 1912
102.		Bernát Alexander (in Hungarian)	June 24, 1912
103.		Ferenc (Franz) Ferdinand Baumgarten (in German)	July 8, 1912
104.		Max Weber (in German)	July 22, 1912

105.		Ernst Troeltsch (in German)	August 1, 1912
106.	To	Margarete von Bendemann (in German)	September 25, 1912
107.	From	Alfred Weber (in German)	November 8, 1912
108.		Georg Simmel (in German)	[?], 1912
109.		Max Weber (in German)	January 28, 1913
110.		Max Weber (in German)	January 29, 1913
111.	From	Félix Bertaux (in French)	January 31, 1913
112.		Béla Balázs (in Hungarian)	[January], 1913
113.	To	Félix Bertaux (in German)	[March], 1913
114.	From	Max Weber (in German)	March 6, 1913
115.		Max Weber (in German)	March 10, 1913
116.		Max Weber (in German)	March 22, 1913
117.	To	Lajos Fülep (in Hungarian)	[early May], 1913
118.	From	Géza Révész (in Hungarian)	May 24, 1913
119.	From	Albert Salomon (in German)	May 27, 1913
120.	To	Paul Ernst (in German)	[early June], 1913
121.	From	Max Weber (in German)	October 3, 1913
122.		Yelena Andreyevna Grabenko (in French)	October 15, 1913
123.		Yelena Andreyevna Grabenko (in French)	October 29, 1913
124.		Max Weber (in German)	November 6, 1913
125.		Max Weber (in German)	November 7, 1913
126.		József von Lukács (in Hungarian)	May 25, 1914
127.		Mária (Mici) von Lukács (in Hungarian)	[June ?], 1914
128.		Gottfried Salomon (in German)	July 3, 1914
129.		Károly (Karl) Mannheim (in Hungarian)	July 25, 1914
130.		Károly (Karl) Mannheim (in Hungarian)	November 14, 1914

131.		Béla Balázs (in Hungarian)	February 28, 1915
132.	To	Paul Ernst (in German)	[March ?], 1915
133.		Paul Ernst (in German)	April 14, 1915
134.		Paul Ernst (in German)	May 4, 1915
135.		Franz Blei (in German)	July 21, 1915
136.		Paul Ernst (in German)	August 2, 1915
137.		Max Weber (in German)	[mid-December], 1915
138.	From	Max Weber (in German)	December 23, 1915
139.	To	Max Weber (in German)	December 30, 1915
140.		Max Weber (in German)	January 17, 1916
141.		Karl Jaspers (in German)	May 3, 1916
142.		Karl Jaspers (in German)	June 23, 1916
143.	From	Max Weber (in German)	[August 14], 1916
144.		Max Weber (in German)	[August 23], 1916
145.		Károly (Karl) Mannheim (in Hungarian)	September 6, 1916
146.		Karl Jaspers (in German)	October 20, 1916
147.		Martin Buber (in German)	November 5, 1916
148.		Károly (Karl) Mannheim (in Hungarian)	November 19, 1916
149.	To	Martin Buber (in German)	December 16, 1916
150.	From	Max Weber (in German)	[January 7], 1917
151.		Ernst Troeltsch (in German)	January 10, 1917
152.	To	Gustav Radbruch (in German)	March 11, 1917
153.	From	Emma Ritoók (in Hungarian)	March 17, 1917
154.		Martin Buber (in German)	April 3, 1917
155.	To	Paul Ernst (in German)	[July ?], 1917
156.	From	Heinrich Rickert (in German)	September 3, 1917
157.	To	Paul Ernst (in German)	September 5, 1917
158.		Thomas Mann (in German)	February 18, 1918
159.		Paul Ernst (in German)	[?], 1918
160.		Paul Ernst (in German)	April 5, 1919
161.	From	Max Weber (in German)	[March ?], 1920

reason (although the difference appears the same, formally speaking) that everything that is *only a metaphor* in art (after all, all art is closed) is in the case of *literature a fundamental difference of forms;* the difference between the form of drama and the (primitive epos) epic. Because of its spatial nature, art at one point or another has to be finite; the possibility of its continuation is but a metaphor. In the case of the epic form to which I referred, it is not a metaphor but partly an historical and partly a formal truth. Let's go from here to my main argument: the objection you raised here (re: metaphysics) can be applied to all of my writings as well—especially to the first chapter of my book.[6] What is, after all, my aesthetics based on? On the assumption that all genuine and profound need for expression finds its own typical way—its scheme, if you will—which is the form. (By now, I've arrived at the innermost roots of the problem: the content of our self cannot be communicated; a scheme of the art work alone is capable of communicating a reflection of the contents to the receiver. The conscious application of this insight is the artistic form; just think of the Oedipus example I have in the first chapter of my book.)[7]

I concede only this much: that it was premature of me to try to work out a theory of the epic form, and that it is too artificial and inconsequently presented in my "Sterne." It may be so—it is indeed probable. But I regard my approach as basically correct, and I think—at least for now—that I am on the right track. I think it is necessary for my development and the idea happens to be mine (which doesn't mean that it would not be a deep and great feeling to work it out together with you). Besides, although I had sensed the problem of "organicity" and "unity", I have become fully conscious of it through your theory of the *Allteig* (universal substance).[8]

In a word, if you send the article, send the detailed critique along. [. . .] After you have read all the essays for the planned collection, tell me whether or not I should go ahead with the publishing. Only if it appears to make a unified, strong, rich, and good volume will I consider its publication; because it is not that important, nor am I in any big hurry to have something published.

One more thing: I was very vehement in my counterargumentation. If you wonder why, it is because I wanted to make my stand loud and clear. I know that I'll have to reflect on it for a while. Will keep you informed.

INDEX

Another thing: I have been greatly helped by your letter; I am thankful and glad to have read it. With warm embrace, yours,

Gyuri

[1] Reference is to Leo Popper's letter of October 25, 1909, containing a sharp criticism of Lukács's "Sterne" essay, followed by a telegram of Popper asking Lukács to destroy the letter unread. Presumably, Lukács sent a telegram to Popper stating that since the letter came first, he had already read the letter.

[2] See "Richness, Chaos, and Form: A Dialogue Concerning Lawrence Sterne," in *Soul and Form*, pp. 124ff.

[3] See "Biographical Notes".

[4] Popper wrote, among others: "I don't like this article... not well executed, formally speaking. ...It is excellent in terms of psychology... but there is an arbitrariness in connecting it up with eroticism," etc., etc.

[5] Popper's "A Dialogue on Art," written in German in 1906, begins as follows: "As you know, there are two different art forms: closed and open, the former being the realization of [illegible]... the finite and the infinite." Lukács incorporated some of it in his Sterne essay. See *Soul and Form*, p. 144.

[6] First published in Hungarian in *Esszék és Kritikák*, pp. 5ff. *Dramabook*:

[7] The German edition of the *Dramabook*, entitled *Entwicklungsgeschichte des modernen Dramas* (Darmstadt-Neuwied: Luchterhand, 1981), see p. 29. Lukács states, among other things: "Die Totalität und den Reichtum des Lebens kann das Drama nur rein formal ausdrücken."

[8] See Letter no. 29, n. 12.

42. TO LEO POPPER

Budapest
October 27, 1909

My sweet good son,

Since yesterday I have done nothing but think about your letter. (Your second letter has also arrived in the meantime.) Well, I again reread the Sterne essay and now I am going to tell you what I have to say: I sensed too that something was wrong with the "eroticism" if it was meant to be the same as I had understood it to be at the very beginning of the project when we discussed it. As you know, the essay wasn't finished in Lucerne, and I continued to work on it in [Buda]Pest—making numerous minor changes along the way with regard to the conception of the whole. Your objection is correct as far as it goes, but what is there is not the same as what was intended (it is a different question whether it has come off...). I feel stronger than ever that this essay is a satire, complementing Beer-Hofmann and George,[1] do you understand? My remark should be taken symbolically; remember, you wrote upon receiving the

certain things, especially if you'd heard it from others instead of me. In that case, my motives might be even more misunderstood than this way. I owe it to myself, dear Madame, to write you today just as I owed it to myself to dedicate the work to you.

You probably don't need and hardly expect thanks, nor my gratefulness of love, so this letter is written because I need the assurance that I was finally able to tell you how it was. What I couldn't tell there (in the book) I tell you now: those few months when I had the good luck to have known you and been close to you were so significant for me, it was so intense and gave me so much that I can say with every certainty that without this experience I would never have become what I am today—at least, I'd be a poorer and lesser man. At that time, I believed that it meant the same thing for you too; today I know better. I see clearly that I was not more than an accidental constellation, a rather pleasant preoccupation in the final interlude of the play.

You came up to Budapest, not yet healthy enough to work; and there were other things missing in your life—which you obviously now have—and you were bent on making the best of a rather unpleasant transitional period in your life. There was I, in a crowd of insufferably smart or insufferably stupid people, and you found me to be cleverer, more entertaining, refined, and—certainly more cultured; and I didn't bore you with my talk until—until talks turned to more meaningful things. The fact that those talks with you became the ultimate content of my life; and from which I derived undreamed-of pleasure and riches is my luck, good or bad. This fact doesn't put you under any obligation; I am obliged, though, to thank you with deepest gratitude and love for everything you have done for me, what you meant to me and what you made of me.

There is another thing, dear Madame, for which I have to express my thanks and I do it today. Until I was lucky enough to get to know you, I was convinced (although retaining a degree of hope for the opposite and not daring to draw the final conclusion) that my mode of existence would inevitably exclude me from all human community and make it impossible to ever become the meaning of someone's life. In one of your weaker moments, you declared that I was mistaken; since I had never been so close to anybody before, I succumbed to believing you. The facts showed me otherwise; now I not only know, but hold on to the belief that what I first thought was true, and it is all right with me. (I don't mean that it [illegible], I cannot accept the fact that I offered a makeshift metaphysics. I state only what I know for sure (even if it sometimes is expressed obscurely because I still don't know everything about it). For example, you don't find a word about how individual elements of the two great opposites relate to each other because I myself don't know yet.

[illegible] you see now why I talk too much. It is that I consider the matter important, and I *have to* make you see that I am right and [illegible] at most a meeting of minds in this matter; and also because every word you utter is of importance to me. But you know that.

I have [illegible] moved me to tears; [illegible] if that would be possible, it brought you even closer to me. For this reason, I am afraid of one thing: since I think I now perceive the center of things differently, does it mean that a distance has come between us? Will I be somewhat diminished in your eyes? Give me your assurance, please (although I think that our bond is strong enough, but I am certain only of my feelings toward you and not of yours toward me; thus, I am a little scared). I embrace you with great [illegible]

Gyuri

P.S. Give my regards to Bé.

1 Two essays from *Soul and Form*.
2 See letter no. 29.
3 In *Soul and Form*, p. 151.
4 Ibid., p. 150.
5 Ibid., p. 12.
6 Ibid., p. 144.
7 In the German edition, *Entwicklungsgeschichte . . .*, p. 29.
8 *Wednesday*, Budapest paper. Excerpt from the *Dramabook*. "A dráma formája" ([illegible] 1906).
9 See letter no. 3, n. 1.
10 Lukács soon dropped the plan.
11 Schlegel developed his concept of Romanticism "as progressive universal poetry" in his work, *Athenäum Fragments*. He stated that "romantic poetry is still in the making; indeed, the fact that it is forever becoming and can never be completed constitutes its very essence. It is infinite because it is free and it holds as an absolute law that the caprice of the poet is supreme. . . ."
12 In *Soul and Form*, p. 149.
13 "[Irony] is best able to hover between what is portrayed and what has to be presented, to float on the wings of poetic reflection free from all real and ideal interest, raising this reflection again and again to a higher power, and multiplying it as in one endless series of mirrors."
14 "Ethics or—since we're speaking of art—form . . . is an ideal outside the self," in *Soul and Form*, p. 149.

be a surer bet, both intellectually and financially. My answer is not a vague promise; by the time the journal is realized, I might contribute more.

As far as my publications are concerned, I wish I could send you a copy of my book,[3] but I don't have one left. If you want to read it, the Vedres[4] family would surely lend you theirs. I am expecting the reprints of my latest treatise any day[5] and will send you one as soon as I get them. Have you seen the journal, *Renaissance?*[6] It is not quite good yet, but it has more decency and respect for scholarship than the *Nyugat*. For the present and for my meager accomplishments it is my chosen outlet. Would you care to send them some of your papers (until the real journal comes along, that is)? Judging from the attitude of its staff, your contribution would respectfully be accepted.

Sincere regards,
Yours,
György Lukács

[1] See letter no. 4, n. 2.
[2] Plan of founding a "house journal" on philosophy and culture, which later became *A Szellem* (Spirit).
[3] *A lélek és a formák* (Soul and Form).
[4] Márk Vedres (1870–1961), leading Hungarian sculptor, member of the activist avant-garde group *Nyolcak* (The Eight). Through his wife, Mária Polacsek, he was related to the Polányis, Irma Seidler, and Ervin Szabó.
[5] Reference is made to the essay, *"Megjegyzések az irodalomtörténet elméletéhez"* (Notes on the Theory of the History of Literature), published in the *Alexander-Emlékkönyv* (Alexander-*Festschrift* on the occasion of his sixtieth birthday), Budapest: Franklin, 1910, pp. 388–421.
[6] *Renaissance,* the cultural revue, was launched in 1910. For a short while, Lukács and his friend, Béla Balázs, took over the editorship but abandoned the journal by October 1910. It folded at the end of the same year.

48. TO LEO POPPER

Berlin
May 28, 1910

My dear son, Leo,

How times are changing! I don't write letters anymore either! Although I think of writing daily and have had many things in mind, nothing comes of it, which is not a bad sign in itself. It is not a loss for you because you never needed it (you understand what I mean by that), and it is especially good for me. It means that the senti-

ıld be so but only that once it has to be so I better be aware .) For this, I again have to thank you and I am doing it here now. I think you'll misunderstand me—as is inevitable. Today ı glad that you can't ever comprehend my state of mind. Why ıld understanding be so important anyway? I obviously cannot ain the whole thing to you in a few words (so that you won't irony where there is none and value judgment which is not nt!). There are people who understand and cannot live; and there are the others who can live but cannot understand. The kind can never reach the other even though he understands; second kind can never grasp the essence but it doesn't matter. feeling of love or hate, the liking of somebody or the possib- of learning to like somebody exists, but the concept of under- ıding does not.

'ou, dear Madame, won't understand what I meant; and because vently wish you to be happy, I am glad that you won't. I told you his because I felt it imperative to let you know about it. It may vey to you the extent of my unchanged sympathy, my gratitude my respect for what is the essence of your strength. I also want ımphasize that I don't expect any degree of appreciation of my ermost feelings. I wrote this for my own sake; you are not in d of anything coming from me. With a special intensity of feel- , I wish you every happiness and good tidings.

Your respectful friend,
Dr. György Lukács

e letter no. 20.
ıe Hungarian edition of the essay collection, *A lélek és a formák. Kisérletek* oul and Form. Experiments). with the dedication "To Those From hom Received" (Budapest: Franklin Társulat, 1910).
› Leo Popper.

FROM IRMA SEIDLER (RÉTHY)

Budapest
March 24, 1910

ar Gyuri,

My heartfelt thanks for the book. There was never the slightest ıger of misunderstanding on my part—even without your ac- npanying comments.

My sincere regards,
Irma Seidler R.[éthy]